The City of New York

DEPARTMENT OF CONSUMER AFFAIRS
80 LAFAYETTE STREET, NEW YORK, NEW YORK 10013
Telephone: 566-

Bruce C. Ratner, Commissioner

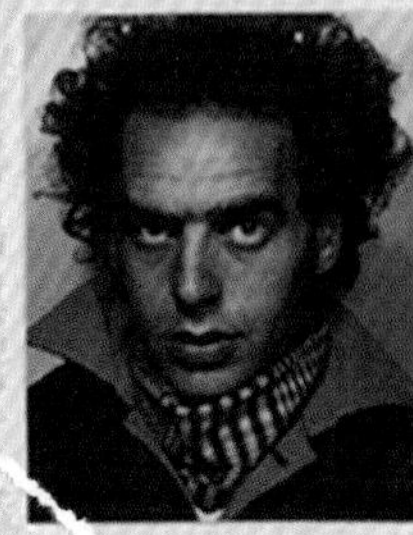

Michael Bielicky
243 East 13th Street #15
New York, N.Y. 10003

Date: November 12, 1980

Re: Horse Drawn Cab Driver
776215

By order of the Commissioner this is to certify that a license has been approved and is in effect for the above business or individual

Very truly yours,

Karen Miller

Karen Miller, Director
License Issuance Division

KM/cc

NOT VALID AFTER THIRTY (30) DAYS
OR WITHOUT SEAL

SEAL

Michael Bielicky
Perpetuum Mobile

Edited by Peter Weibel
and Zdeněk Sklenář

ZKM | Center for Art and Media Karlsruhe, Germany
Galerie Zdeněk Sklenář, Prague, Czech Republic
DCV – Dr. Cantz'sche Verlagsgesellschaft, Berlin, Germany

zkm karlsruhe Galerie Zdeněk Sklenář DCV

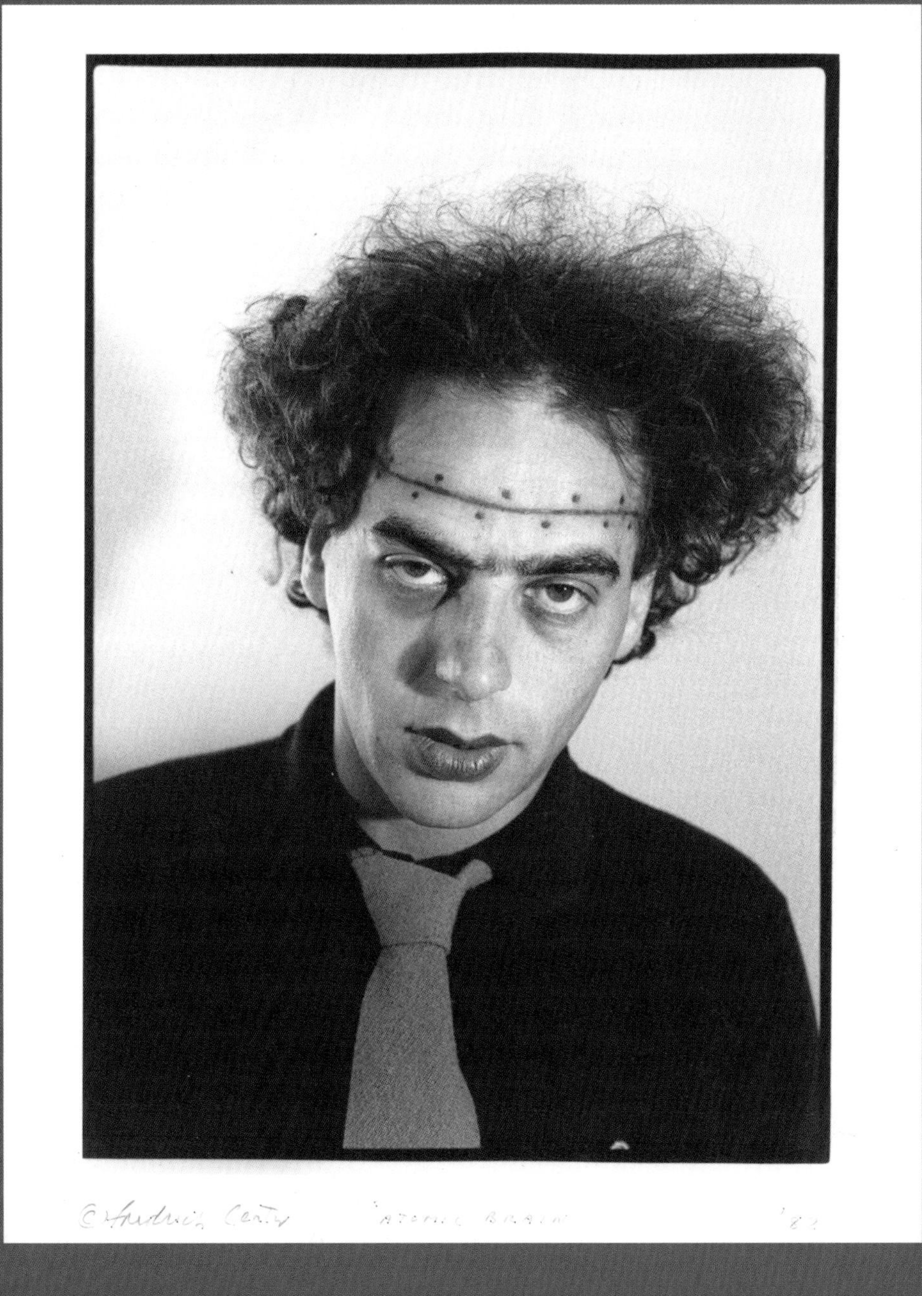
'ATOMIC BRAIN'

Foreword and Afterword

This book is a rollercoaster ride through four decades of my creative and personal life. In this open, Talmud-like universe, you can start at any point. You can experience it forward and backward: each user can and ought to have their individual path.

From around 2005, practically all projects were created in collaboration with Kamila B. Richter, who made our projects and our lives so magical.

This book and the exhibition *Perpetuum Mobile* at the ZKM | Center for Art and Media Karlsruhe could only have come about through the commitment, support, and sympathy shown to me by many creative and idealistic friends and colleagues. I am grateful especially to Peter Weibel, with whom I have been collaborating for more than thirty years and who always believed in my potential by supporting me and showing my work around the globe.

Nam June Paik, my professor (whose assistant I would later become), helped me to see the world in a global-technological, nonlinear way. I was lucky to be in a dialogue with Vilém Flusser, Peter Sloterdijk, Woody and Steina Vasulka, and many others for many years. With Peter Weibel and Peter Sloterdijk, I have experienced intensive and enlightening "Karlsruher Gespräche" (Karlsruhe evening conversations) for nearly twenty years.

Thank you, Fred Cantor, a dear friend from my New York days and beyond, for your amazing photographic inspirations.

A big thanks also goes to the authors in this book, who have contributed wonderful texts – Bettina Korintenberg, Peter Weibel, Peter Sloterdijk, Siegfried Zielinski, Mel Alexenberg, Jorge A. Fernándes Torres, Norman M. Klein, and Paul Kenig – as well as testimonials (Maxim Biller, Georg Dietz, David Galloway, Elena Lappin, and Nikolas Maak, among others).

Thank you, Alex Wenger, André Bernhardt, Andreas Siefert, Andres Jungwickel, Ariel Sindermann, Axel Heide, Bernd Lintermann, Daniel Heiss, Dirk Reinbold, Gideon May, Kimin Han, Lukas Böhm, Lukas Feller, Nikolaus Völzow, Pantos, Paul Kenig, Wilhelm Brodt, and Xicht for your support in realizing and programming our projects. Without you, our work would have been less data driven, less immersive, less interactive, less mixed reality, and certainly less inspiring.

A special thanks goes as well to the gallerist Zdeněk Sklenář from Prague as a second editor of this book. He and the other creators of this publication – Paul Kenig, Jens Lutz, and Sascha Fronczek – I thank from the bottom of my heart for this wonderful book, which is the Noah's Ark of my life.

I invite all readers to accompany me on this hopefully entertaining and tireless journey through four decades of media art, through the works, the events, and the incomparable atmosphere and spirit of optimism that we wanted to make tangible through this book.

Michael Bielicky

Table of Contents

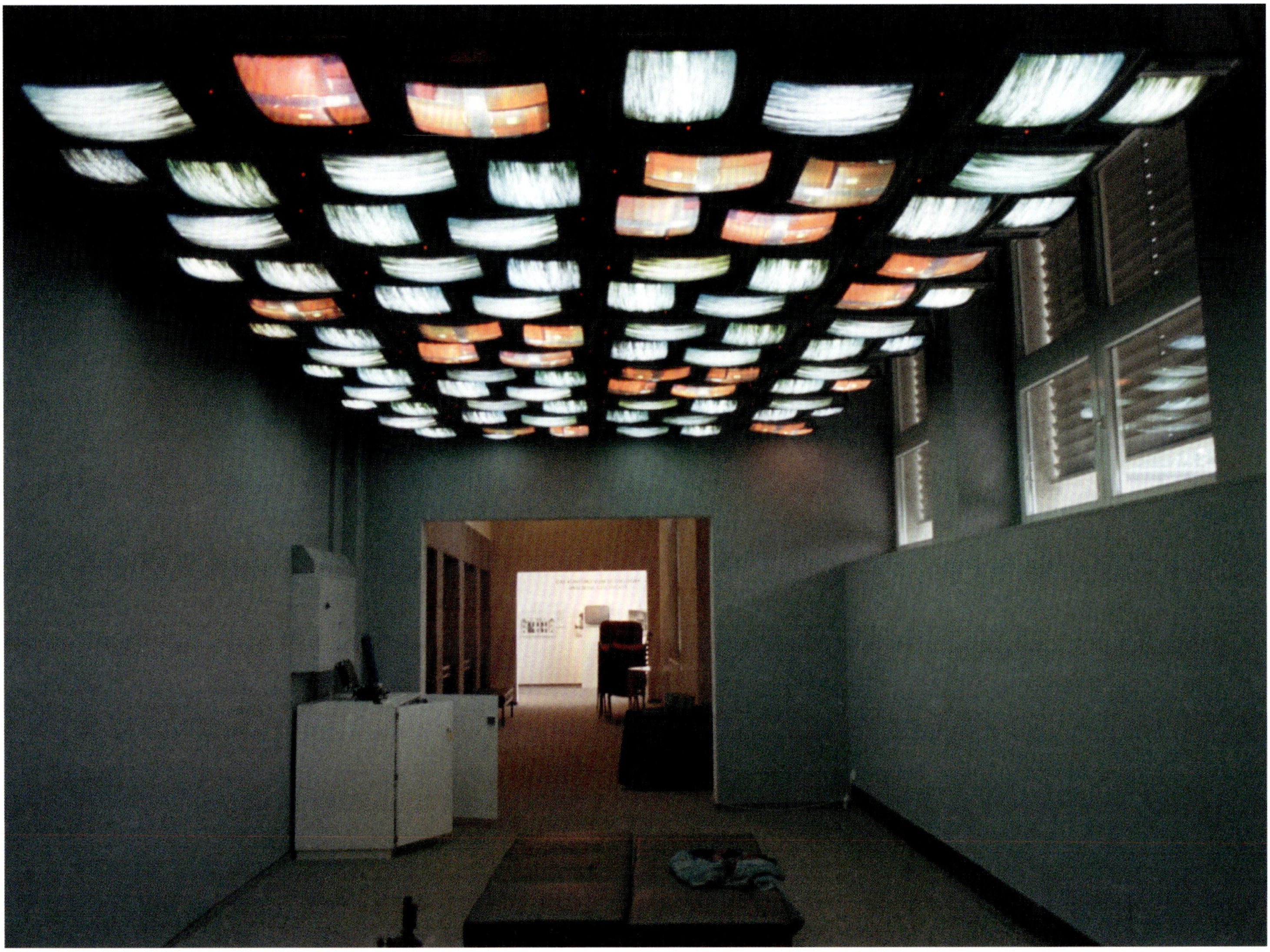

Nam June Paik, *Fish Flies on Sky*, 1983-85/1995, multi-monitor installation. Installation view, Kunstpalast, Düsseldorf, 1996.

Perpetuum Mobile: Fish Flies on Sky

Bettina Korintenberg

Fish Flies on Sky (1983–1985) by Nam June Paik and *Perpetuum Mobile* (1986) by Michael Bielicky, both revealing a unique fusion in 1986. Engaged by the process, we fall almost in thrall to the experience[1]: lying under the TV environment of video art doyen Nam June Paik and gazing up at the monitor sky, one is captivated by the constant stream of images in *Perpetuum Mobile*. This environment is pervaded by a tension that has characterized Michael Bielicky's works to this day and has its roots in his teacher Paik's practice as much as in his own background, Jewish culture: an idiosyncratic combination of technology and spirituality, combined with a fundamentally critical and ironic attitude as well as a constant meditation on the limits of reality and virtuality; all set in motion, and in the context of a media ecology that is transforming itself through technological progress, always being worked out afresh.

Düsseldorf – New York – Düsseldorf: Epicenters of Experimental Art

Having grown up in the 1950s and 1960s in post-Stalinist Prague, Michael Bielicky's 1969 emigration to Germany – moreover to Düsseldorf, the then capital of experimental art – constituted a radical change in his life as a fifteen-year-old. He plunged straight into the bohemian life of the late 1960s, with its rejection of convention and bourgeois tradition, going with the spirit of the time with long hair and the typical flower-embroidered, sheepskin jacket. He promptly made contact with the Jewish Community and began to deal explicitly with his Jewish origins and culture – an expression that could only have met with difficulty before in the environment in Czechoslovakia characterized by anti-Semitism.

During the 1960s, Düsseldorf had evolved into a pulsating center of contemporary art, with an enthusiasm for experimentation that attracted artists from around the world. Karl Ruhrberg, the founding director of the Düsseldorf Kunsthalle, went so far as to call it "Paris on the Rhine," and defined the city as the artistic metropolis of the late twentieth century.[2] Even in the early days, this unconventional art world exerted a strong attraction on Bielicky.

In 1967, the Creamcheese opened, a *Gesamtkunstwerk*, offering a bar, stage, music club, and artists' pub. It was developed by Günther Uecker in collaboration with media artist Ferdinand Kriwet and filmmaker Lutz Mommartz; Bielicky was a frequent guest. He regularly encountered the protagonists of the era there: Joseph Beuys, Otto Piene, Heinz Mack, Günther Uecker, Gerhard Richter, Daniel Spoerri, and many others. The name, Creamcheese was derived from the fictional character, Suzy Creamcheese, with whom the U.S. composer and musician, Frank Zappa conducted an imaginary dialogue in the song by his band, The Mothers of Invention, titled *The Return of the Son of Monster Magnet* (1966). The interior was designed as an experimental confluence of light, sound, visual effects, and music. As inspiration, Uecker drew on experiences from his 1964/1965 residence in New York City, where discotheques had developed into multimedia spaces of complete sensual experience in the progressive post-war scene, such as the legendary, The Dome. One entered the Creamcheese down a long corridor, passed by a tapestry by Ferdinand Kriwet and Uecker's *Elektrischer Garten* [Electric Garden] (1966), and ended up in a dark antechamber facing a wall of shelves stacked with 24 television sets in rows. Here, one could follow the action taking place in the room that backed on: a sort of discotheque with lighting and projection systems, where theater plays, concerts, performances, and fashion shows were performed. Such legendary bands as Kraftwerk and Can played there; Joseph Beuys, the artist duo Peter Weibel / Valie Export, and many others performed their art shows here. Behind a twenty-meter-long bar designed by Heinz Mack, Blinky Palermo, and Katharina Sieverding poured the drinks.[3]

The *Creamcheese-Manifest* [Creamcheese Manifesto] demanded the autonomy of self-determination for the space, while also emphasizing the relevance of contemporary media by stating: "Present-day art requires present-day information carriers. [...] Contemporary art uses contemporary media productively."[4] Various defining topics and themes, such as shadow and light, kinetics, and a merging of art and media technology – which, still coming from the ZERO group, were then blended at the Creamcheese into a rather provocative Fluxus attitude – play an important role in Bielicky's artistic stance. The influence of "Information Carriers of the Present" on society was a theme that would run through all the artist's works. Bielicky's works always evolve from an intense dialogue with the specific current developments in media technology, reflecting their influence in a critically ironic way on the perception and actions of the individual and society. The spirit of the progressive Düsseldorf art scene was strongly influenced by Nam June Paik, who "smuggled in such, at first glance, disparate phenomena as anarchy and technology."[5] Early on, the trio Beuys, Paik, and George Maciunas opened the Düsseldorf art world to the Fluxus movement, which was distinguished by a radically provocative stance, unrestricted experimentation, examination of media and inter-media issues, collective thinking and action reaching beyond the boundaries of individual disciplines, as well as by the aim to open up art to society, through collectivity and participation. These aspects are still palpable today in Michael Bielicky's artistic explorations.

And it was in the Düsseldorf Kunsthalle that Michael Bielicky saw his first video installation, *Duchampiana: Nude Descending a Staircase* (1976)[6] by Shigeko Kubota, Nam June Paik's partner. Bielicky's enduring enthusiasm for this installation is an omen of his artistic path ahead, in which the medium video would play a key role and Nam June Paik would become his most important mentor.

Yet before actually pursuing art, Michael Bielicky took a different turn, taking up medical studies in Düsseldorf. Three years later, realizing he was off his path, he quit his studies and went to New York City. The vibrant city full of new impressions lured him behind a photographic camera, through whose lens he followed the inhabitants of the urban space. An absurd coincidence one day made his acquaintance with the photographer Fredrich Cantor: Bielicky was out walking with a female companion who likewise lived at Westbeth – one of the first artists housing complexes, converted by Richard Meier and located since 1970 in the former Bell Laboratories building. Standing at a traffic light, Fredrich Cantor asked the lady with Bielicky if she was Eve. That actually happened to be her name, and the ensuing conversation led to a friendship between the two men. Cantor would become an important source of inspiration to Bielicky, he admired Cantor's work and found significant orientation in its aesthetics. Back in Germany, Bielicky continued his preoccupation with photography, working both as an assistant to fashion photographer Dieter Eikelpoth and for *Monochrom*, a magazine focused on the Düsseldorf lifestyle and the art and cultural scene.[7] Bielicky's photographic output from this period consists largely of portraits showing

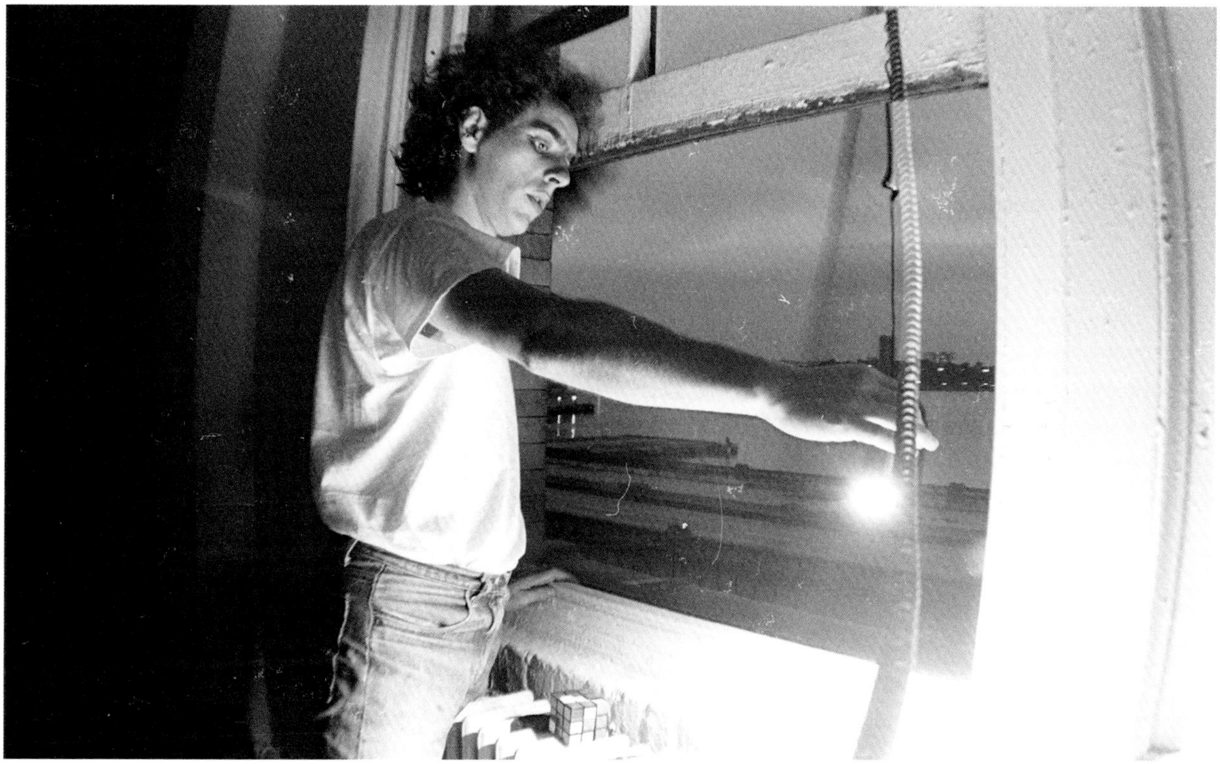

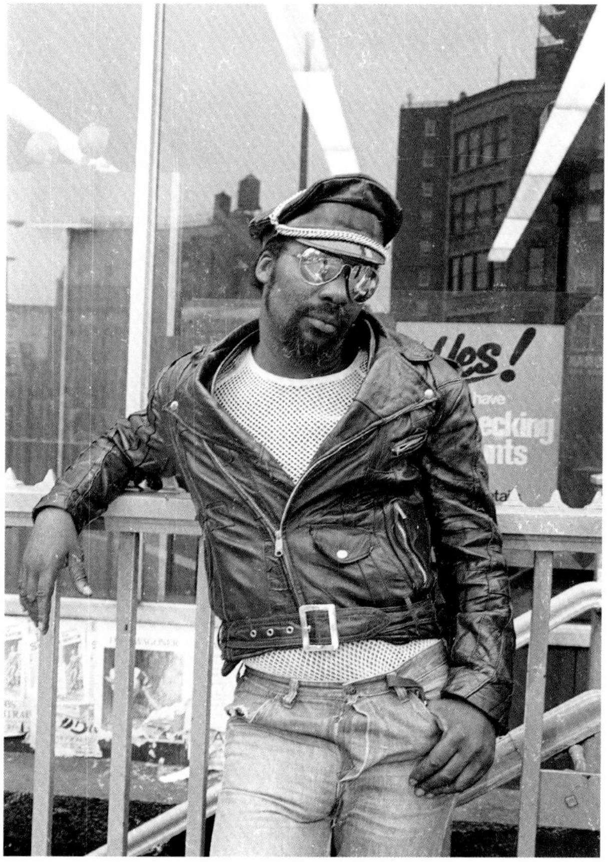

Photographs for *Zukunft issue*, *Monochrom Extra,*
1985, analog black-and-white photographs.

striking characters or friends and family members in bizarre situations and perspectives. Using a flash technique borrowed from Cantor, he lends the captured figures an often-ghostly distant look, as if they belonged to another reality. The photographic works created during this period result in Michael Bielicky's 1984 admission to Bernd Becher's photography class at the Düsseldorf Art Academy, studying together with Thomas Struth, Andreas Gursky, and Thomas Ruff. But soon after he transferred into Nam June Paik's class, which led to one of the most important decisions for his artistic oeuvre – his orientation toward the medium video, not in any categorically absolute way, but with an approach like that of his teacher Paik himself: an interdisciplinary practice, ever seeking challenge and dialog.

Paik's class gathered young artists from around the world with such diverse core disciplines and interests as painting, sculpture, video, and performance, which fostered an unconventional, open and, above all, keenly experimental atmosphere. It was Paik's free spirit, along with his limit-transcending understanding of art, urging one to leave one's own medium, to personally become active and creative, that led Bielicky to discover his mentor in Paik.[8] "Paik used video technology extensively; yet all the while exploring its limits, critically questioning and ironizing it. Similarly, the 'students of Paik' see technology only as a contemporary means for answering contemporary questions,"[9]: a credo Bielicky adopted as well in his recurring examination of technological change and the essence of technology, and of its social, philosophical, and political implications.

Düsseldorf had a pioneering role in video art in the early 1980s – more than any other place in Germany, its Art Academy invested the greatest interest in the medium of video[10]; and in Nam June Paik, it had recruited the medium's most famous representative as an instructor, creating the first professorship for video art in all of Germany.[11] A productive center for the then nascent media art arose through the interplay of the openness and progressiveness of the Rhenish art scene at that time. With his switch to the medium of video, Michael Bielicky suddenly found himself at the heart of this lively setting – presenting his works at the Videonale in Bonn from its 1984 inception on; as well as at the 1988 launch of the VideoFilmFest section[12] of the Berlin International Film Festival; or in the Japanese edition of *Infermental 8*.[13]

The works from the 1980s are mainly shorter videos, for which Bielicky experimented by mixing two video signals via time base corrector, permitting error and misuse, chance and improvisation, as was likewise practiced by Paik. *Perpetuum Mobile* stood out because it was shown on Paik's own video installation *Fish Flies on Sky*, which allowed the video images to dance on the 88 monitors in the sky. In *Perpetuum Mobile II* (1990) we find an early indication of an approach that would find later expression in Bielicky's data-driven narratives – in the overabundance of animated people, kaleidoscopically abstracted and shown as patterns requiring re-attribution with information content – initial elements that would reappear, from 2004 on, in the pictogram language created by the artist duo Michael Bielicky and Kamila B. Richter. The incisive video piece *Fat Corner*, developed from 1986 to 1987 in collaboration with Ricardo Peredo, expresses the ambivalence of the figure Joseph Beuys, hovering between a radical art position under the Fluxus banner and an absurd personality cult, while also taking a critically ironic look at the Academy of Fine Arts in Düsseldorf as a whole. Quite in the spirit of Beuys and the beginnings of the German video art movement – which, within the Fluxus context, produced an "anti gesture, a playful, often destructive, sometimes only ironic defamiliarization of objects, values, traditions, yet always an irritation"[14] – the monitor is tipped on its side: viewers are going to either become personally active and shift the monitor into a horizontal position, as they are prompted to do in an ironic gesture of reverence toward Beuys; or remain in an uncomfortable posture, with head tilted. They can either become active or adapt themselves to absurd structures – a pointed conceptual decision that matches the *zeitgeist*.

The Deep Time[15] of Media

In Michael Bielicky's artistic production, we find a convergence of several lines of influence: of his childhood in 1960s Prague, defined by an avant-garde film and media culture; of Czechia's overall media-historical significance; and of Jewish spirituality and cultural history.[16] Bielicky himself describes the fantastical and avant-garde films of Czech film director Karel Zeman, combining reality and virtuality, as an enduring source of inspiration. The immersive experiences of his childhood, encountered at the amusement park on the Výstaviště Praha exhibition ground – *The Battle of Lipany* (1897–1898), a 360-degree panoramic painting with 3D effects by Czech painter Luděk Marold; and the Russian *Kinopanorama*, which let him feel the influence of the virtual realm on reality – left an equally deep impression.[17] These are prime examples of a highly innovative scene, eager to experiment and, above all, technophile, which radically questioned and expanded the traditional concept of cinema with such interactive cinema formats as *Kinoautomat* and *laterna magika*[18], as well as by means of advanced animation technology, while pre-thinking key developments of our media ecology today. The artist's fascination was roused, both with film and its transposition into other media, and with the blurring of reality and virtuality – central thematic complexes he would later continuously examine.

Closely tied up with this inclination for experimentation and innovation with media is the role played by the Czechia, especially Prague, in the media-historical "deep time," which is, in turn, inseparable from Jewish Kabbalistic traditions. A key figure here is Rabbi Loew (Judah Loew ben Bezal'el), a well-known Jewish scholar and mystic in sixteenth century Prague. He was an extraordinary practitioner of the teachings of Kabbalah and alchemy, and

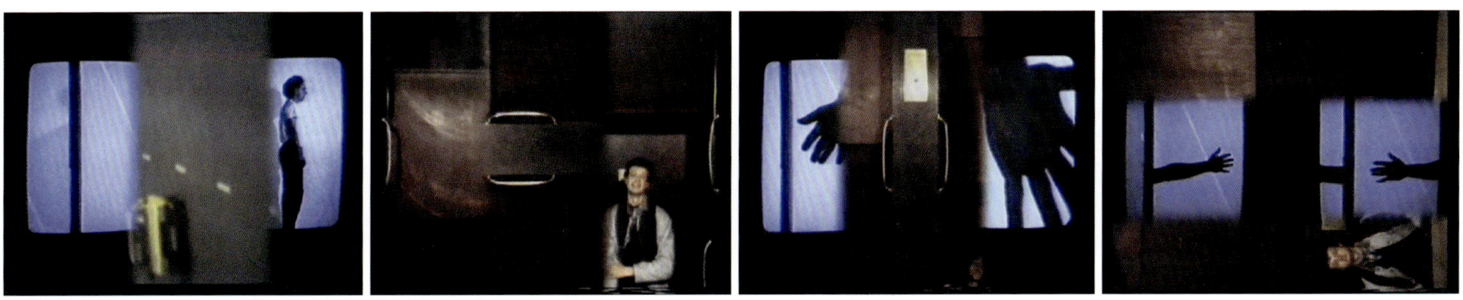

Perpetuum Mobile, 1986, single-channel video. Screenshots.

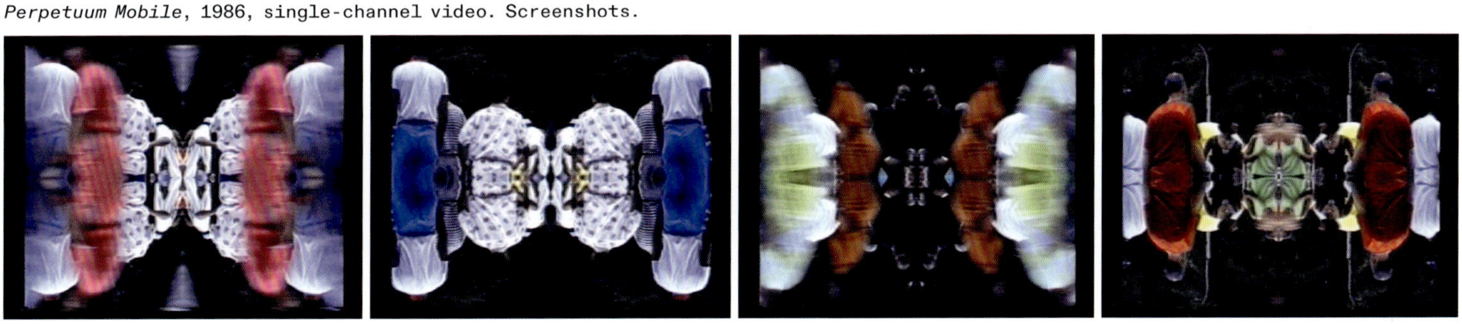

Perpetuum Mobile II, 1990, single-channel video. Screenshots.

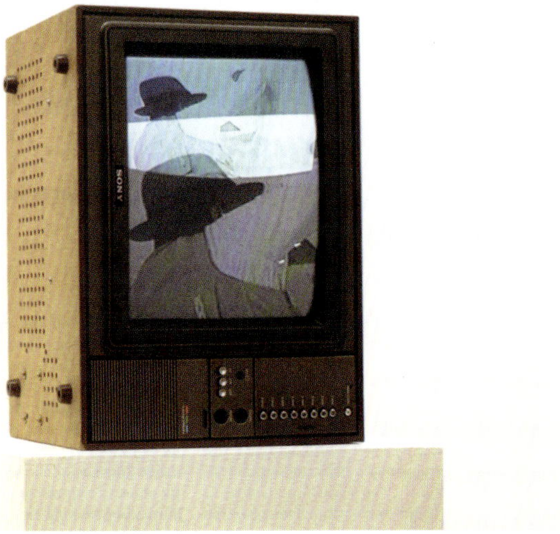

Fat Corner, with Ricardo Peredo, 1987, single-channel video. Video installation.

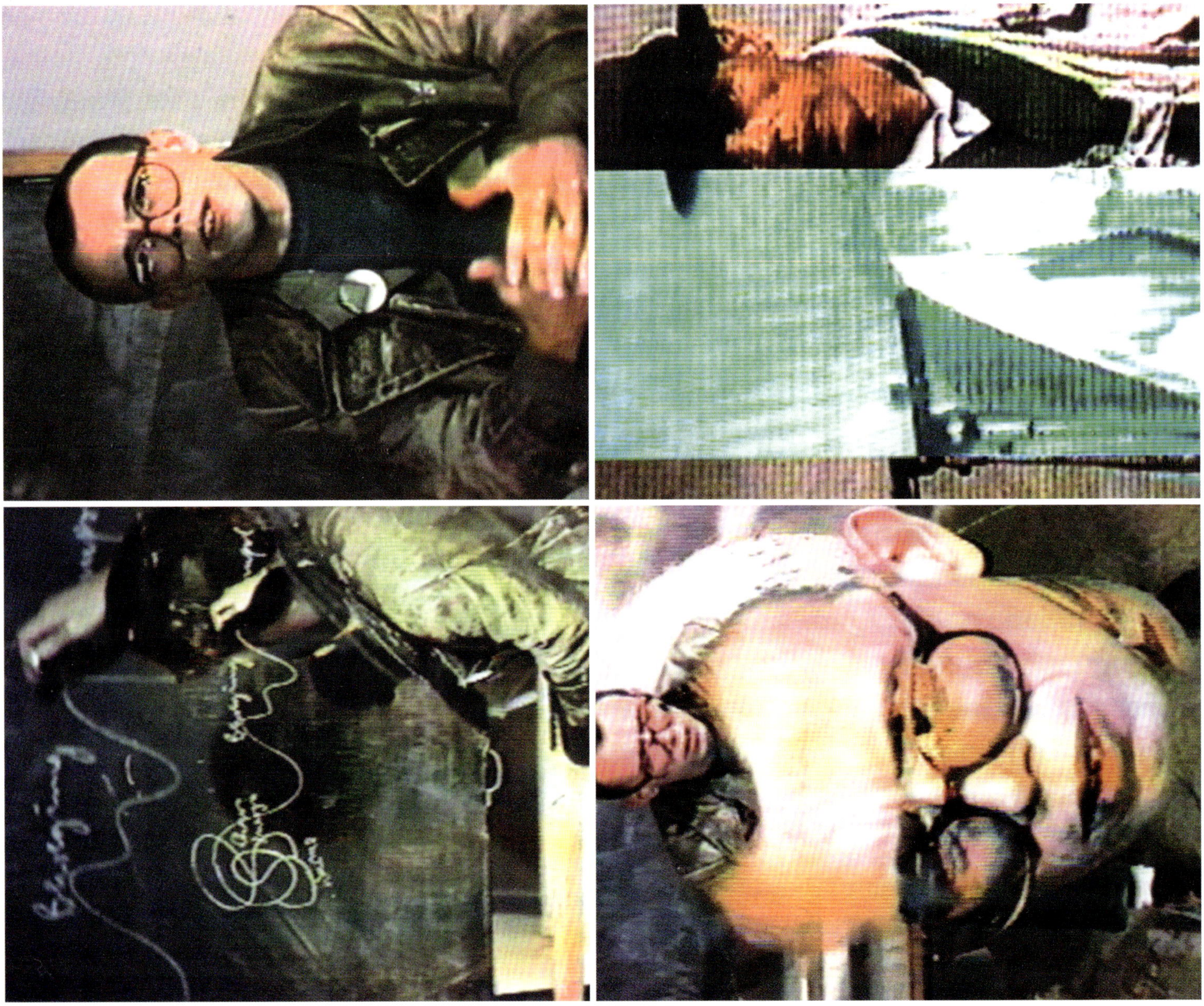

Fat Corner, with Ricardo Peredo, 1987. Screenshots.

as a visionary of visual media technology and cybernetics and the creator of the Golem of Prague, Loew is an important figure of historical reference to Michael Bielicky. Legend has it that, under the rule of Rudolf II, Rabbi Loew formed clay into a golem (the Hebrew word for unformed matter), which he brought to life by inserting a piece of paper bearing the mystical name of God into his mouth. The golem can be interpreted as a sort of predecessor of the robot and, thus, also of the computer – an analogy that, in 1965, led the Jewish religious historian Gershom Scholem to call the supercomputer at the Weizmann Institute of Science, in Rehovot (Israel), "Golem of Rehovot."[19] Another milestone in the history of the robot was Karel Čapek's play *R.U.R. (Rossum's Universal Robots)*, written in 1920 and premiered in 1921. Here, the Czech writer renders a dark vision of a future in which the "robots" – a sort of artificial, automatized human produced by the company R.U.R. and equipped with astonishing intelligence – cheaply, and with no rights, performed their labor. Čapek clearly based the conception of his robot on Rabbi Loew's golem figure. Derived from the Czech word *robota* [compulsory, or forced labor], the term "robot" spread from the drama into everyday language. The word was actually coined by Karel's brother Josef, a painter, graphic artist, and writer who often illustrated his brother's literary works. Bielicky's fascination with 1920s avant-garde art is evidenced in his extensive collection of literary works of the period, with a focus on the joint works of the Čapek brothers, but also those of Karel Teige, which is characterized by a reduced, iconic title design-based on a fusion of Cubism and folk art, and which later inspired the development of his iconic pictogram language for the data-driven narratives.

With both of his video works, *Golem Is Alive* (1988) and *Next Year in Jerusalem (Homage to Rabbi Loew)* (1988) Bielicky directly references the media-historical context of Prague and Jewish spirituality. Together they interlink the Kabbalistic creation tradition and the critical reflection of media. While the telematic installation *This Year in Jerusalem* (2006) pursues this critical reflection on media history, its statement extends even further, replacing religious, mythical experience with technical wish fulfillment. *Exodus*, the virtual teleperformance Bielicky produced for *The Wired World* at the 1995 Ars Electronica, also posits an analogy between a religious event – the exodus of the Israelites from Egypt into the freedom of the Promised Land – and a historic technological moment: the development of the internet and, thus, the departure from physical into virtual space.

Media Archetypes

At the end of his studies, with the creation of his first video sculpture, *Menorah/Inventory* (1989), Bielicky found his own personal mode of expression for reflecting on religion and technology, reality and virtuality, as well as history and the present, that would become a characteristic of all his video sculptures to come. Although he has selected an old Jewish symbol, the seven-branched menorah, here he is subjecting religion in the media age to partially ironic reflection, as the flames are technologically generated and able to be controlled by humans. Instead of the seven candles, the light from which represents the presence of God, the candelabrum is crowned by seven monitors. Flickering on the screens are digital flames, which are being sent to the antennas by a hidden transmitter. Technology has supplanted religion.[20] *Menorah/Inventory* drew international attention and was bought within the year by Heinrich Klotz, founding director of ZKM | Karlsruhe, with a second version commissioned by Daniel Libeskind for the Jewish Museum Berlin.

The other video sculptures in this cycle also deal with archetypes of information transmission and knowledge processing: *Sefiroth Tree* (1990) refers to the diagram composed of ten spheres, or *sephiroth*, representing the Tree of Life in Jewish tradition. *The Inner Observer* (1992) reinterprets the seven-branched candelabrum as a hanging sculpture. *The Name* (1990) deals with the form of the spiral, which in a variety of contexts functions as an information carrier: DNA is encoded in a double spiral, electronic information is recorded in spiral form on video and audio tapes; in Judaism the Torah is a scroll whose knowledge unfolds through the process of unrolling and display. This idea was expressed by the artist Mel Alexenberg in the catalogue for *LightsOROT* [21], the exhibition he produced with Otto Piene, in 1988 in collaboration between MIT's Center for Advanced Visual Studies and the Yeshiva University Museum in New York. For Bielicky, this catalogue would become an inexhaustible source of inspiration for his own work. The video sculpture conveys the idea of a spiral being an information carrier as a half-mystical, half-technological experience: The monitors, in which the information manifests itself in the image of a flame, receive their signal from the black-reflecting ball, which functions undetected as a transmitter.

Media Art Pioneers

Many of Bielicky's artistic works were produced in connection with major centers and personalities within the emerging media art sphere: significant junctures being the Ars Electronica during the years of Peter Weibel's curatorship in 1992, 1994, and 1995; ZKM | Karlsruhe; as well as encounters and lifelong friendships with such central figures of media philosophy and art as Mel Alexenberg, Vilém Flusser, Norman M. Klein, Peter Sloterdijk, Woody Vasulka, Peter Weibel, and Siegfried Zielinski.

The Ars Electronica in Linz is one of the most important forums for digital art in German-speaking areas. From its very launch in 1979, it became a key platform for artists operating at the interface of art, technology, and society. Bielicky made his video sculpture *The Inner Observer* – a meditation

Karel Čapek, *R.U.R. (Rossum's Universal Robots)*, 1920. A play in three acts. Book cover.

on the essence of light as a source of knowledge within the context of Jewish faith and the development of technology – for the Ars Electronica group exhibition *Endo and Nano. The World from Within* (1992). Two years later, as his contribution to the Ars Electronica's *Intelligent Ambience*, Bielicky developed his teleperformance *Intelligent Mailman* (1994), a very early artistic application of GPS – a technology developed by the military – in which he reflected the rising replacement of analog practices with digital substitutes and critically addressed the advent of comprehensive surveillance systems. Another year later, he extended his idea of teleperformance: out of Ars Electronica *Mythos Information – Welcome to the Wired World* (1995) – which was proleptically concerned with the digital age just before the triumphal entrance of the internet – came *Exodus*, wherein the artist again transposed military GPS technology to the artistic sphere. Bielicky spent four days following the trail of the biblical Exodus through the Israeli Negev Desert, equipped with a portable GPS device, a modem, and a mobile phone. The GPS data were transmitted through the internet to Linz, where visitors could follow the artist's progress live, via graphic 3D projection. Three times daily through live hook-up, he reported to the audience about his journey.

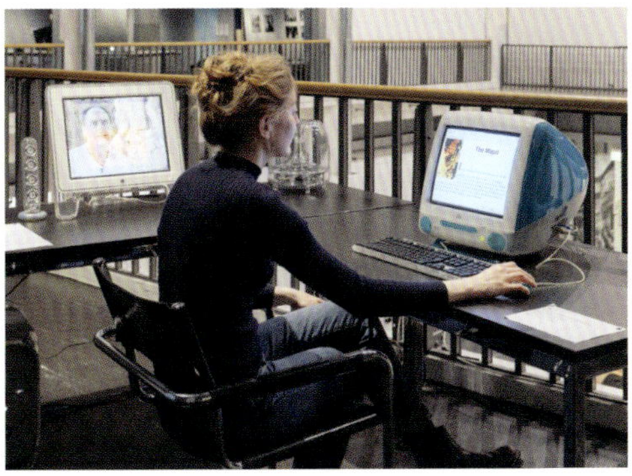

Exodus, 1995, teleperformance. Documentation by Israeli television. Installation view, ZKM | Karlsruhe, 2019.

Two key projects were carried out in collaboration with the ZKM | Karlsruhe Institute for Visual Media. The interactive environment *Delvaux's Dream* (1998–99) plays with the dream of being able to enter a painting. This project required the development of a virtual model of a painting and a tracking system with a piece of special software. The visitors' movements were then tracked by a blue box set-up and transferred to the 3D model of a painting by Belgian painter Paul Delvaux (1897–1994). The fusion of real and virtual worlds could be viewed simultaneously via video projection in the ZKM Atrium. The event of entering the painting was indeed visible to others, whereas the actual experience remained obscured from those within the installation, since they were moving about in an abstract blue background world – unlike in later virtual reality situations. The result was a sort of observed immersion. For a showcase pavilion in Germany's "Motor City" of Wolfsburg in 2000, at which the Czech automobile manufacturer *Škoda* is represented, Bielicky, in collaboration with Bernd Lintermann of ZKM | Institute for Visual Media (today ZKM | Hertz-Lab) and then guest artist Torsten Belschner, developed the interactive environment *Room with a View*. Visitors would enter a dome-shaped interactive encyclopedia, displaying a structure that resembled Wikipedia, founded a year later. In a 360-degree dome-based projection, with a diameter of twelve meters and a height of nine meters, users could explore both the present and history of Czech culture in virtual worlds. A touchpad gave access to seven environments dedicated to the topics of literature, art, and architecture, offering an immersive experience of new perspectives and interconnections between them.

Alongside the technological innovations Bielicky was developing in these progressive and vibrant spheres, the media philosopher Vilém Flusser became an important intellectual dialog partner for Bielicky, with whom he also shared a Jewish cultural background. After meeting at the European Media Art Festival (EMAF) in 1988, the two men stayed in touch, and in 1991 Bielicky accepted Flusser's invitation to visit him and his wife Edith in Robion in Provence. The outcome of this stay was an impressive media-historical document, the video *Flussers Fluss* (1991–94). The work invites viewers to enter a dialog situation with Flusser, accompanying him on a walk through a Mediterranean landscape; as they listen to his incisive and, to this day, topical observations on the correlation between communication

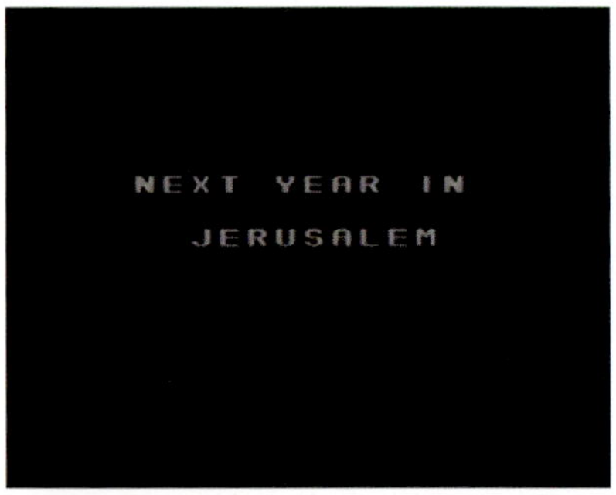

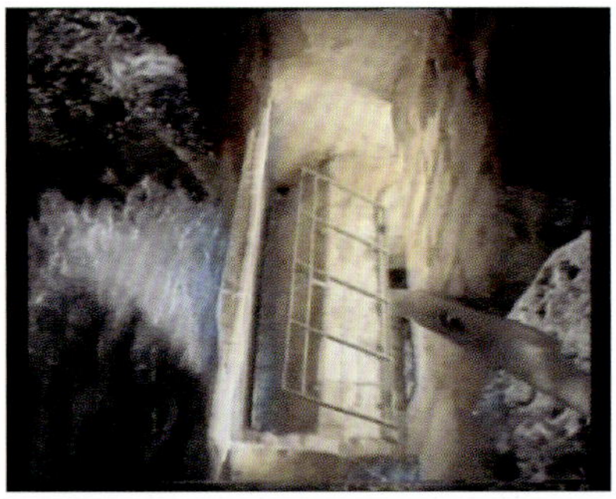
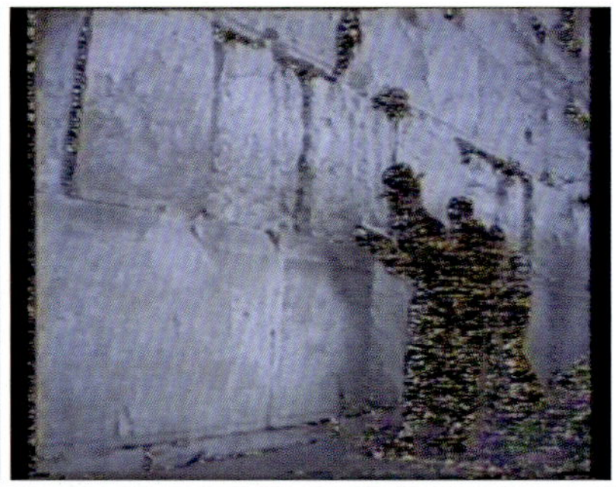

Next Year in Jerusalem (Homage to Rabbi Loew), 1988, single-channel video. Screenshots.

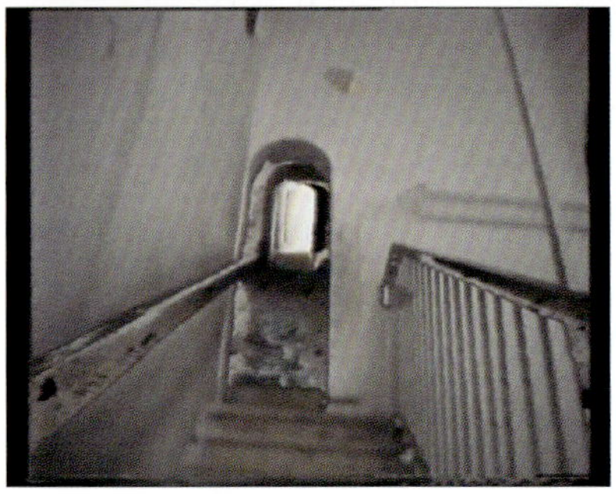
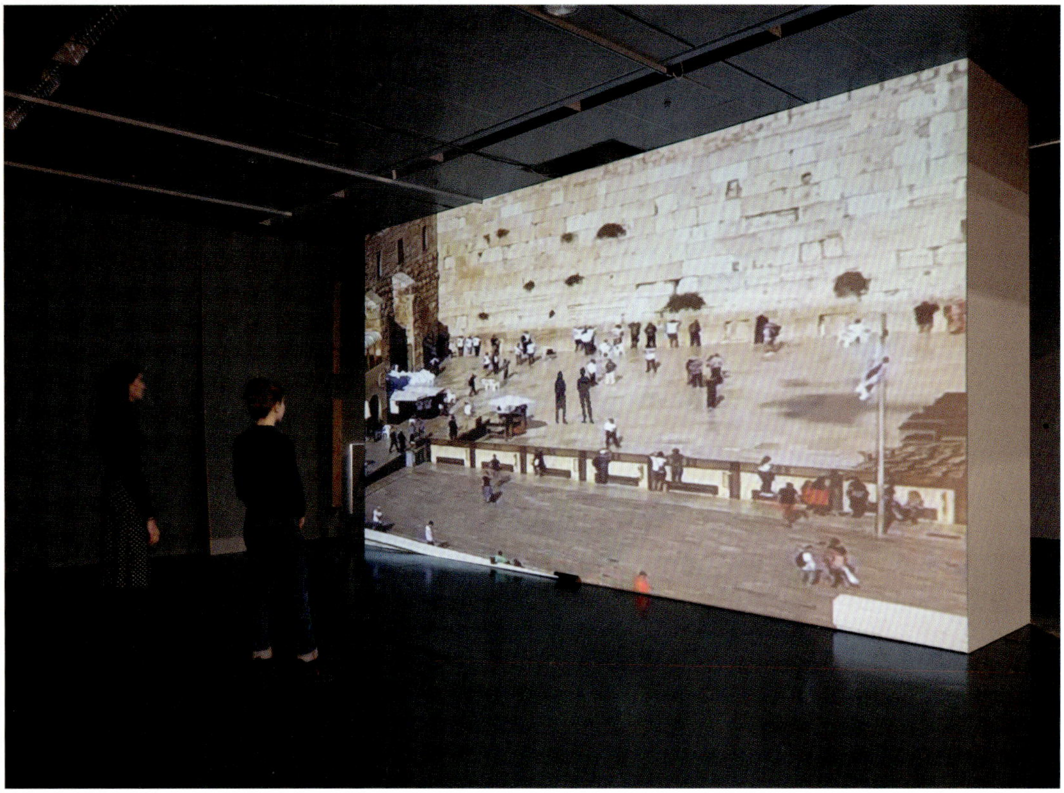

This Year in Jerusalem, 2019, real-time telematic installation. Installation view, ZKM | Karlsruhe, 2019.

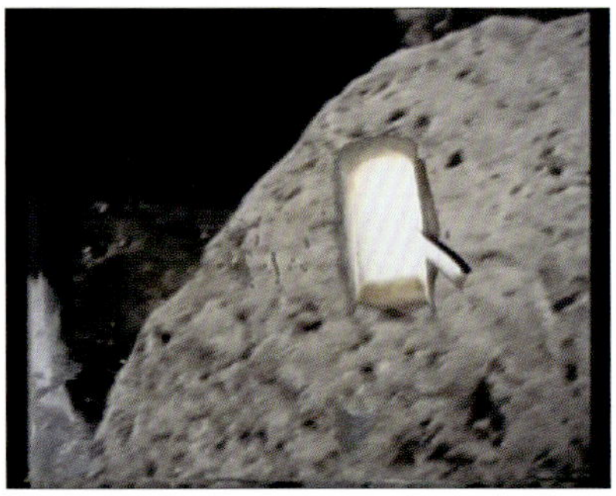
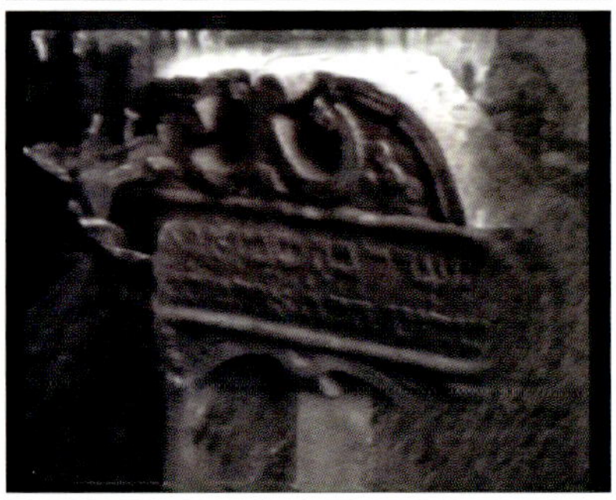
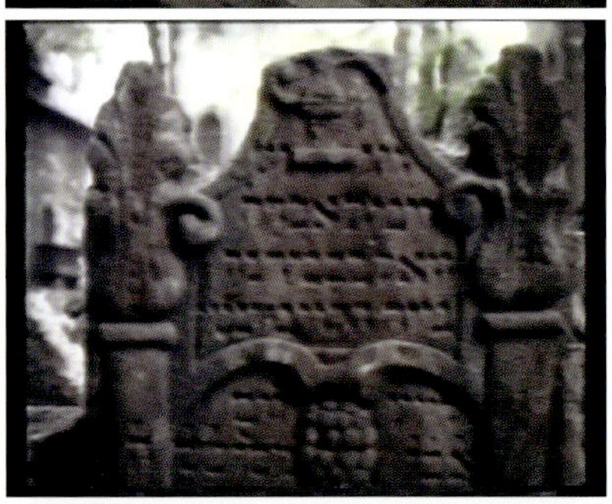
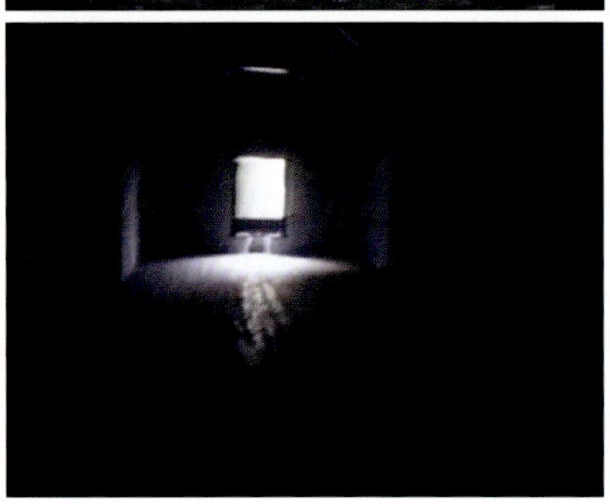
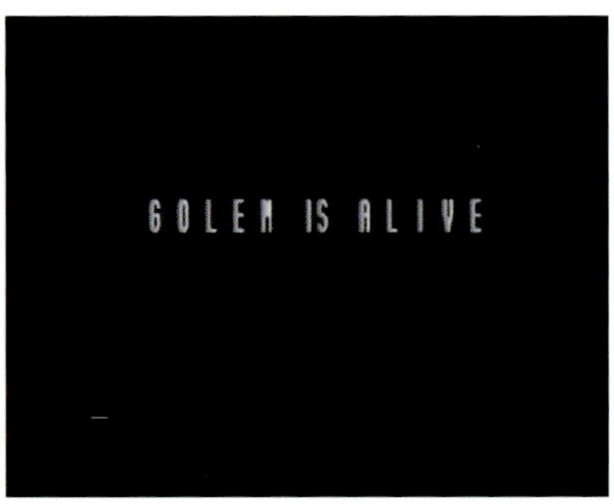

Golem Is Alive, 1988, single-channel video. Screenshots.

structures and telematics, and society and power in the context of European history.

Media Ecologies and Data-driven Narratives

2004 marks the beginning of a new chapter in Bielicky's artistic endeavors: the collaboration with his partner Kamila B. Richter. Together they created space-shaping Web art works based on a dynamic pictogram language, coining the term "data-driven narratives," and integrating real-time data from such sources as Twitter and Google News. The conception of these works was informed by Bielicky's on-going examination of the new narrative principles of our media ecology. *Falling Stars* (2004) marked the beginning of the duo's artistic collaboration, including a series of projections in public space. For the Prague-Berlin Festival, they used a generator to project ironically charged icons of popular media stars onto the Berliner Volksbühne theater building. The series *Falling Life* (2005–07) and *Falling Times* (2006–09), moreover, integrate real-time information from the internet: This content, reduced to headlines and keywords, is translated into a simple, universally comprehensible pictogram language to illuminate the cityscapes of Barcelona, São Paulo, and Karlsruhe. Users can participate in online versions of the work

Room with a View, 2000, immersive interactive installation with 360 degree dome projection. Installation view, ŠKODA Pavilion, Autostadt, Wolfsburg, 2000.

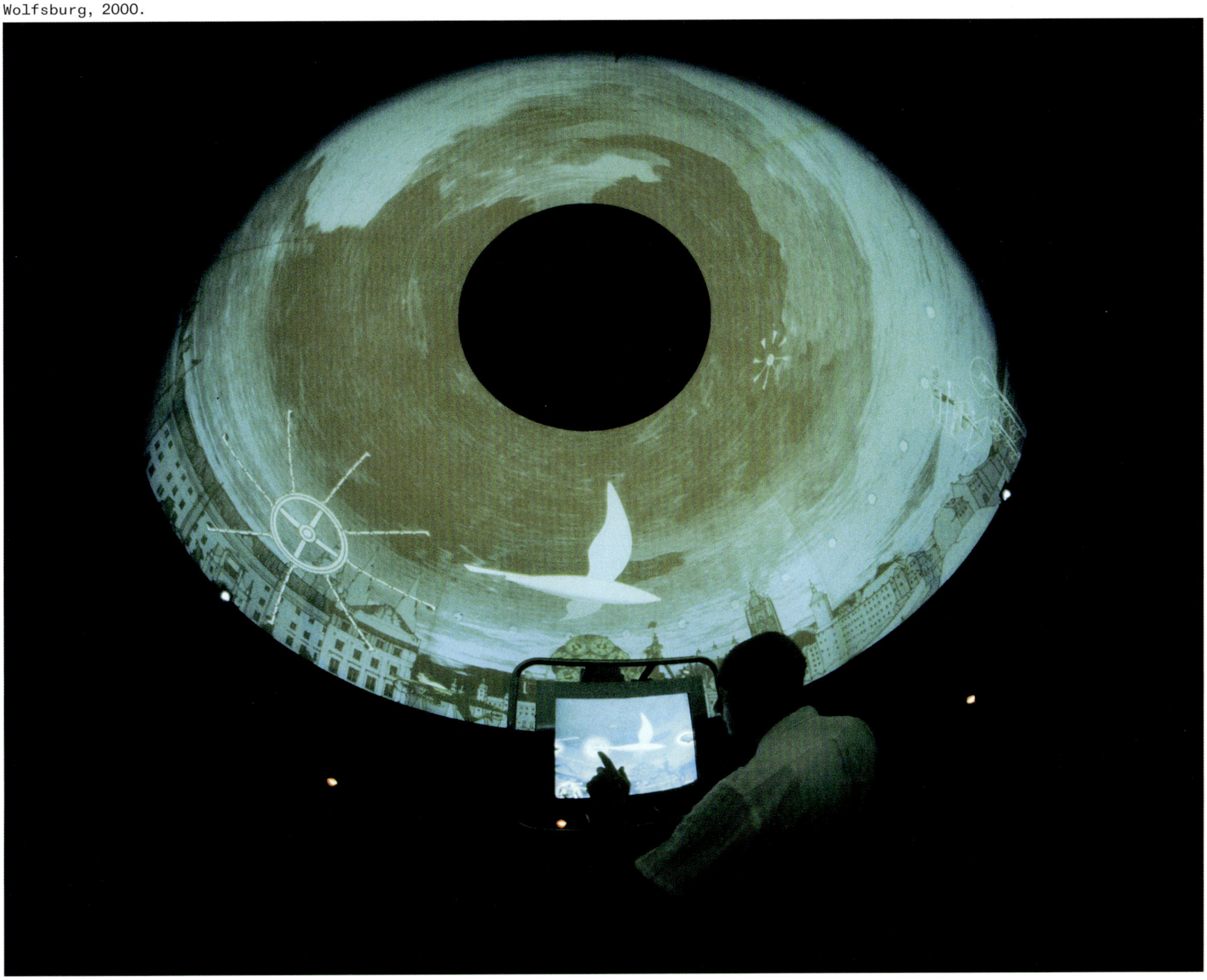

and assign meanings to the icons. The pictograms, thus, become an arbitrary pattern – a reference to the triviality of contemporary media reporting, which often prioritizes spectacle and decoration over information content.

Viewed from the outside, the *Data Labyrinth* (2016) initially appears to be a material-immaterial object, an architecture of light. Once visitors enter through it, though, they lose themselves in a data space that is being generated in real time from Twitter messages, as they are translated into a poetic world of words and letters moving around and through them. The digital-data world reveals itself through a simple interface: profane webs from the world of everyday use form the basis of a sophisticated projection, creating an analog equivalent of virtual Web structures. As a hybrid of both the analog and digital world, the work raises the tangible sense that the human being, due to the presence of their own body, can never entirely leave the analog world; and that they are surrounded by a digital sphere, perceivable only in fragments. The installation *Columbus 2.0* for the Third Sevilla Biennale, *YOUniverse* (2008/09), curated by Peter Weibel, takes our daily, exponentially growing flood of information literally, staging the consumers, on the one hand, as agents of action, actively using a steering wheel to move themselves through a giant "Sea of Data"[22] of real time information; while, on the other hand, this sea bears a life of its own and an energy that threatens to overwhelm us human beings. A complex and key work in this series of data-driven narratives is *Garden of Error and Decay* (2010–19) – a Web installation for the Fourth Moscow Biennale, *Rewriting Worlds* (2011), curated by Peter Weibel, at the which the duo proceeded to show around the world in a number of site-specific variations. Comic-like pictograms slowly move across the image. They emerge as dark testimony to the catastrophes of our times: terrorist attacks, environmental disasters, political scandals, fraud, betrayal, and death. The pictograms – real-time visualizations of text messages posted on Twitter – create the sort of open, nonlinear narrative structure characteristic of our algorithmically defined media environment. Visitors can seemingly control the narrative: when they use the joystick to fire a shot, this either eliminates or amplifies an image of disaster. Whereas, in actual fact, the result of these actions depends on the rise or fall of stock prices, already predetermining it. The installation critically underscores the opacity of our data-controlled environment that makes us puppets of power structures operating in the background.

Evolving over time, Bielicky's media hybrids have a singular way of bringing together the analog and the digital world. There is a spectral quality about them, something uncanny that simultaneously touches and confounds us. This kind of permanent irritation continuously challenges the viewer. The works initiate a questioning and enquiry of one's own being and the social context in which we live, with a focus on the media ecology that to a large extent determines our lives in individual and social structures. The artist, thus, creates an opportunity for critical examination of the nature of technology, of its material and immaterial significance, as well as of its influence on our perception and our actions.

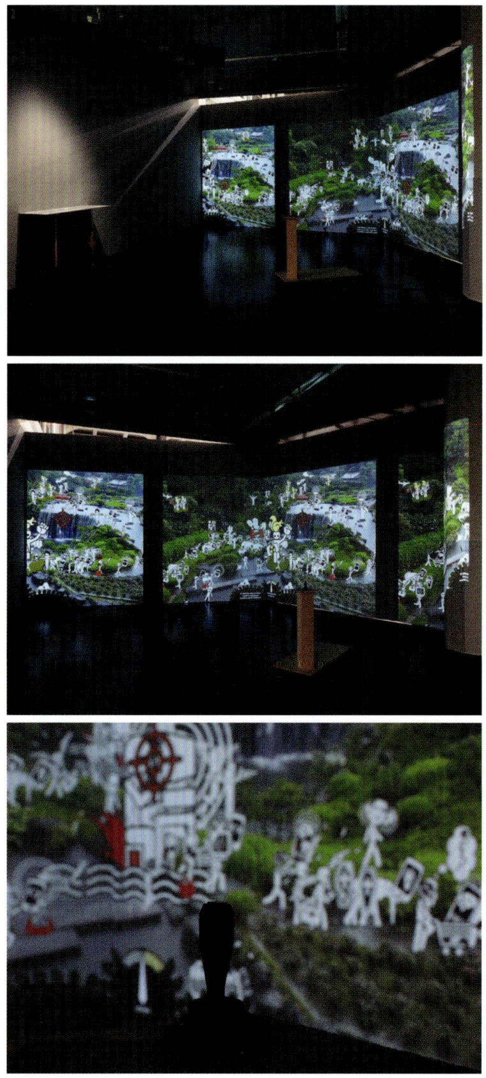

Garden of Error and Decay, 2019, data-driven interactive installation. Installation views, ZKM | Karlsruhe, 2019.

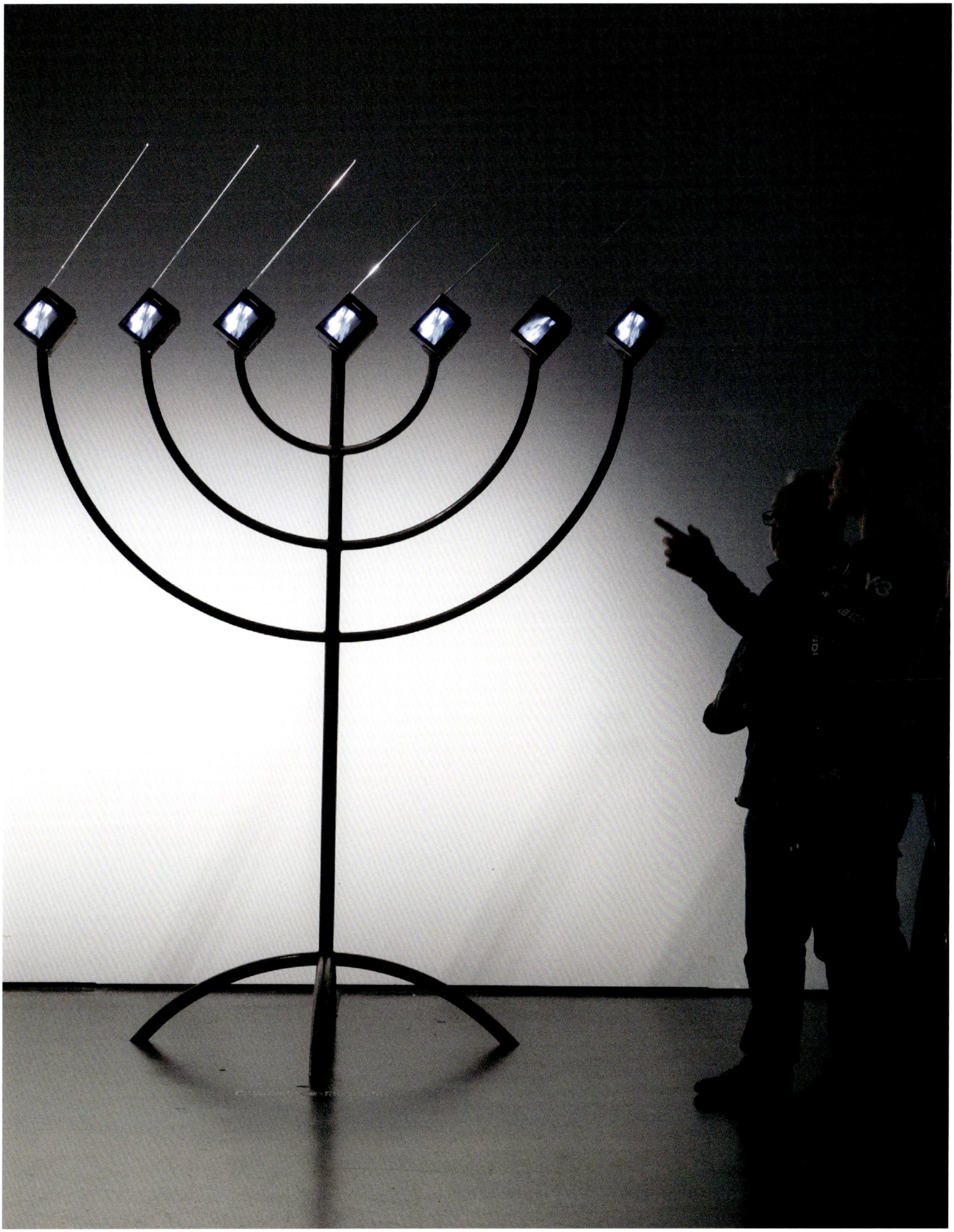

Menorah/Inventory, 1989, video sculpture. Installation view, ZKM | Karlsruhe, 2019.

1 In a unique action, Nam June Paik, together with curator Stephan von Wiese, allowed his students to show their works together on *Fish Flies on Sky*.
2 See Tiziana Caianiello, *Der "Lichtraum (Hommage à Fontana)" und das "Creamcheese" im museum kunst palast. Zur Musealisierung der Düsseldorfer Kunstszene der 1960er Jahre*, (Bielefeld: transcript, 2005), 15-17.
3 For more about the layout and design of the Creamcheese, see. esp. Caianiello, 95-122.
4 Ferdinand Kriwet and Günther Uecker, *Creamcheese-Manifesto*, 1968, offset print on paper, 105 × 70 cm, Kunstpalast, Düsseldorf, here: Ferdinand Kriwet. Translated from the German.
5 Stephan von Wiese, "Fluxus an der Akademie. Düsseldorf auf der biographischen Landkarte von Nam June Paik," in *Mixed Pixels: Students of Paik 1978-95*, eds. Susanne Rennert and Stephan von Wiese (Düsseldorf: Kunstmuseum Düsseldorf, 1996), 11-13, here 11. Translated from the German.
6 The title is a reference to Marcel Duchamp's painting *Nude Descending a Staircase, No. 2* (1912).
7 The magazine was published in the mid-1980s by Michael Schürmann.
8 On Paik as a teacher, see Susanne Rennert, "Mixed Pixels. Siebzehn Jahre Klasse Paik," in *mixed pixels - nam june paik*, http://paik.cultd.net/text/rennert.htm. Also interesting in this context are the comments of the artist and professor at the State Academy of Fine Arts Stuttgart, Rainer Ganahl. Drawing on his own art studies at the academies in Vienna (Peter Weibel) and Düsseldorf (Nam June Paik), among other places, Ganahl described and humorously compared the different teaching concepts. His personal résumé was: "Weibel's influence on my learning and understanding, despite the disharmony between us, was rather strong. This stands in contrast to the experience with my next principle [sic] art teacher, Nam June Paik at the Academy of Fine Arts in Düsseldorf. He was a love affair for anyone who encountered him. [...] But I felt I didn't really learn more than that which had been already communicated through his work and all books about him." Rainer Ganahl, "Strange Teaching: The Artist as Excellent and Miserable Teacher," in *Parse*, 1 (Spring 2015): 67-76, here 69.
9 Rennert, "Mixed Pixels." Translated here from the German.
10 Ibid.
11 Nam June Paik taught at the Academy of Fine Arts in Düsseldorf from 1979 to 1996.
12 With his video piece *Fat Corner,* created in collaboration with Ricardo Peredo in 1987.
13 Here, he was presented with his video work *Paik - I'm an Experimentalist*, 1987.
14 Wulf Herzogenrath, "Versuche, die verdammte Kiste abzuschaffen - oder: die Anfänge eines Kunstmediums in Europa mit Fluxus," in *Videokunst in Deutschland 1963-1982: Videobänder, Videoinstallationen, Video-Objekte, Videoperformances, Fotografien*, ed. Wulf Herzogenrath (Stuttgart: Hatje, 1982), 26-29, here 26. Translated from the German.
15 The term "deep time" was coined, in the media-historical context, by media theorist Siegfried Zielinski in *Deep Time of the Media: Toward an Archaeology of Hearing and Seeing by Technical Means* [2002], trans. Gloria Custance (Cambridge, MA: The MIT Press, 2006).
16 See the interview of Peter Weibel and Michael Bielicky in this publication.
17 See Michael Bielicky, "Prague - A Place of Illusionists," in *Future Cinema: The Cinematic Imaginary after Film*, eds. Peter Weibel and Jeffrey Shaw (Cambridge, MA: The MIT Press, 2003), 96-101, here 96.
18 See Vít Havránek, "Laterna Magika, Polyekran, Kinoautomat," in *Future Cinema*, 102-107.
19 See Gershom Scholem, *Judaica II* (Frankfurt am Main: Suhrkamp, 1970), 77-87.
20 See, on the link between religion and technology in Michael Bielicky's oeuvre, Peter Weibel's remarks in the interview with Bielicky printed in this publication.
21 Mel Alexenberg and Norman Lamm, "Light, Vision and Art in Judaism: A Dialogue," in *LightsOROT: Essays and Catalog of an Exhibition at the Yeshiva University Museum in New York City*, eds. Mel Alexenberg and Otto Piene (New York: CAVS; Cambridge, MA: The MIT Press, 1988), 22-29, here 22.
22 See the interview of Peter Weibel and Michael Bielicky in this publication.

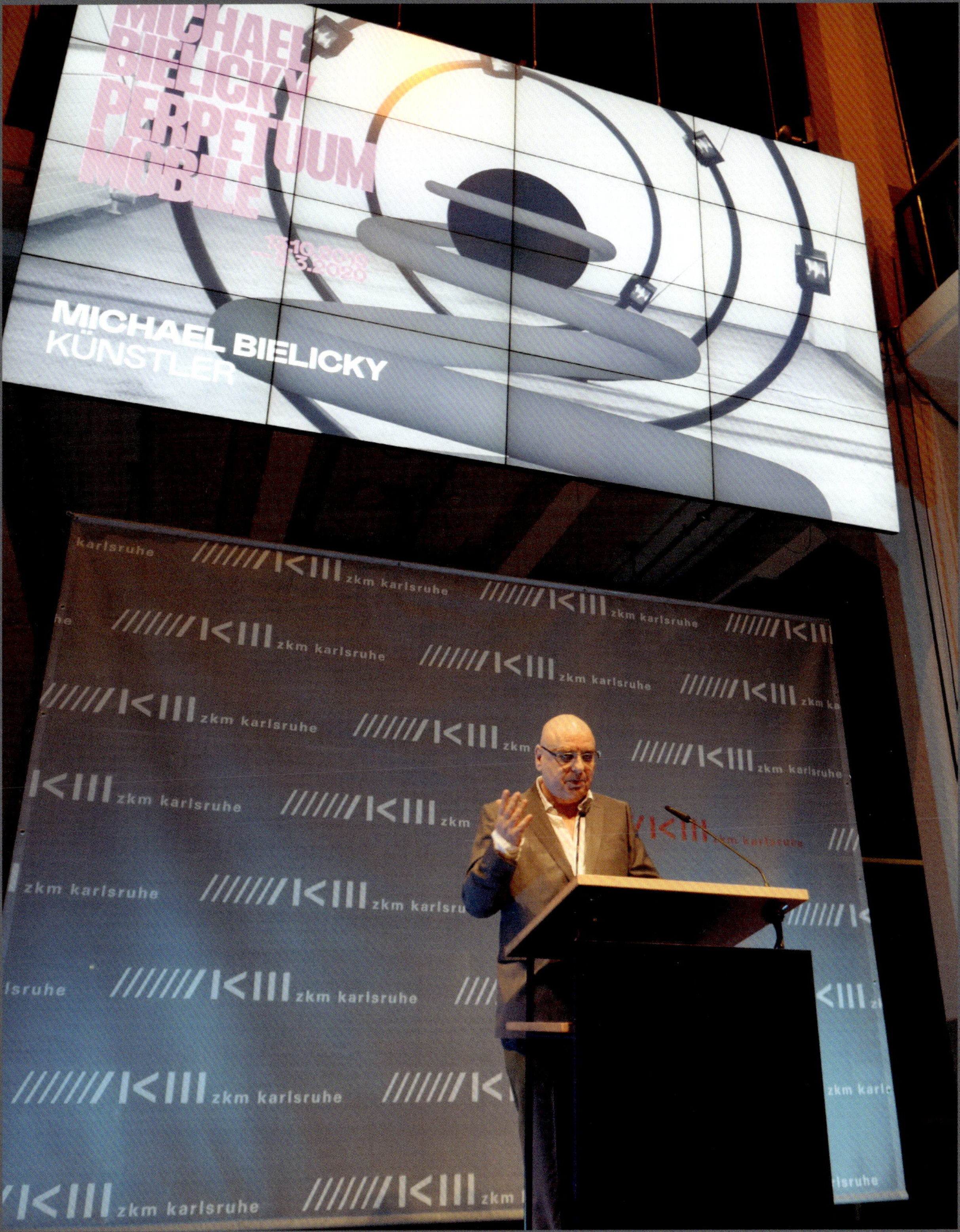

Michael Bielicky, opening of his exhibition at ZKM | Karlsruhe, 2019.

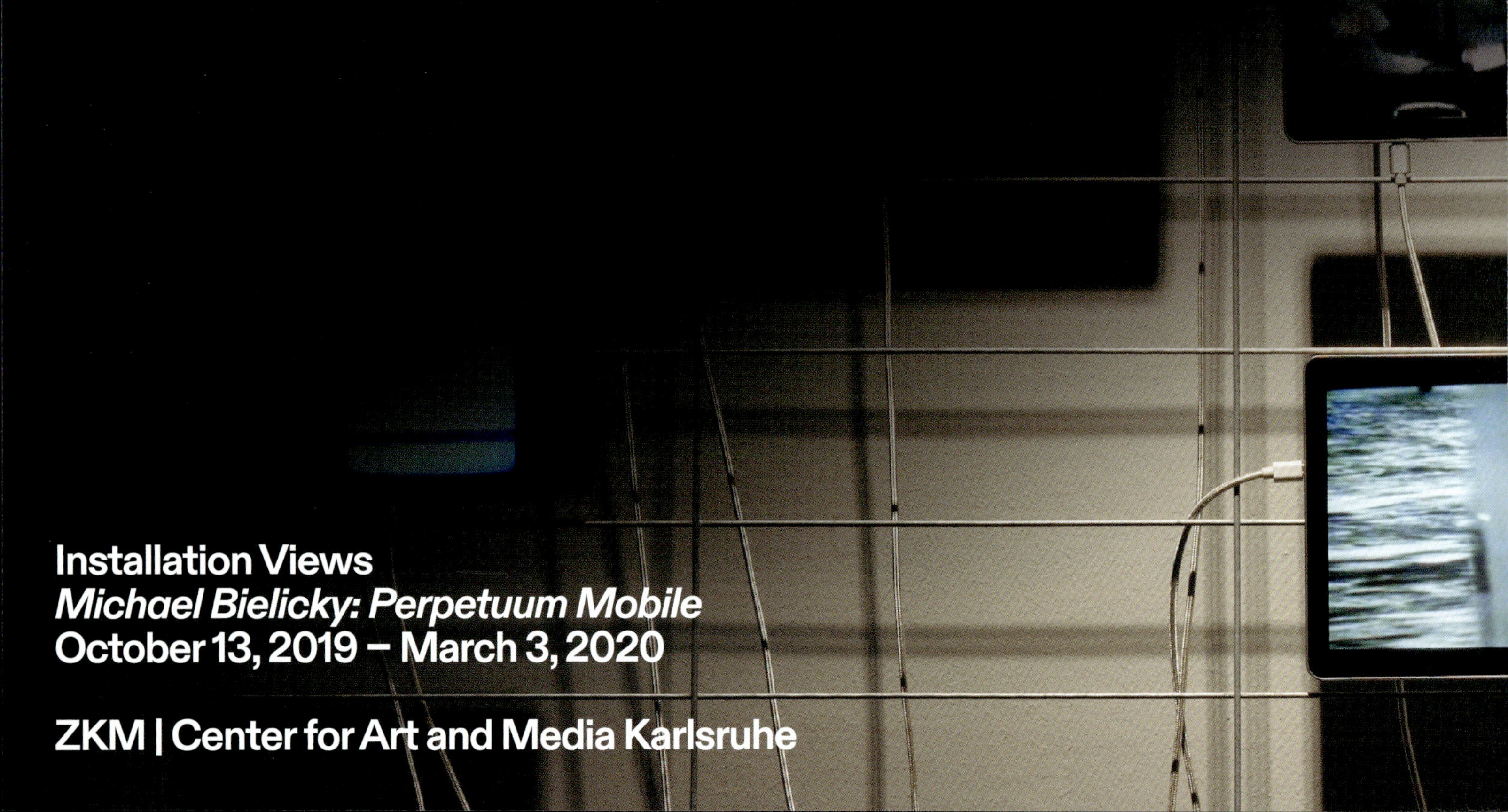

Installation Views

Michael Bielicky: Perpetuum Mobile

October 13, 2019 – March 3, 2020

ZKM | Center for Art and Media Karlsruhe

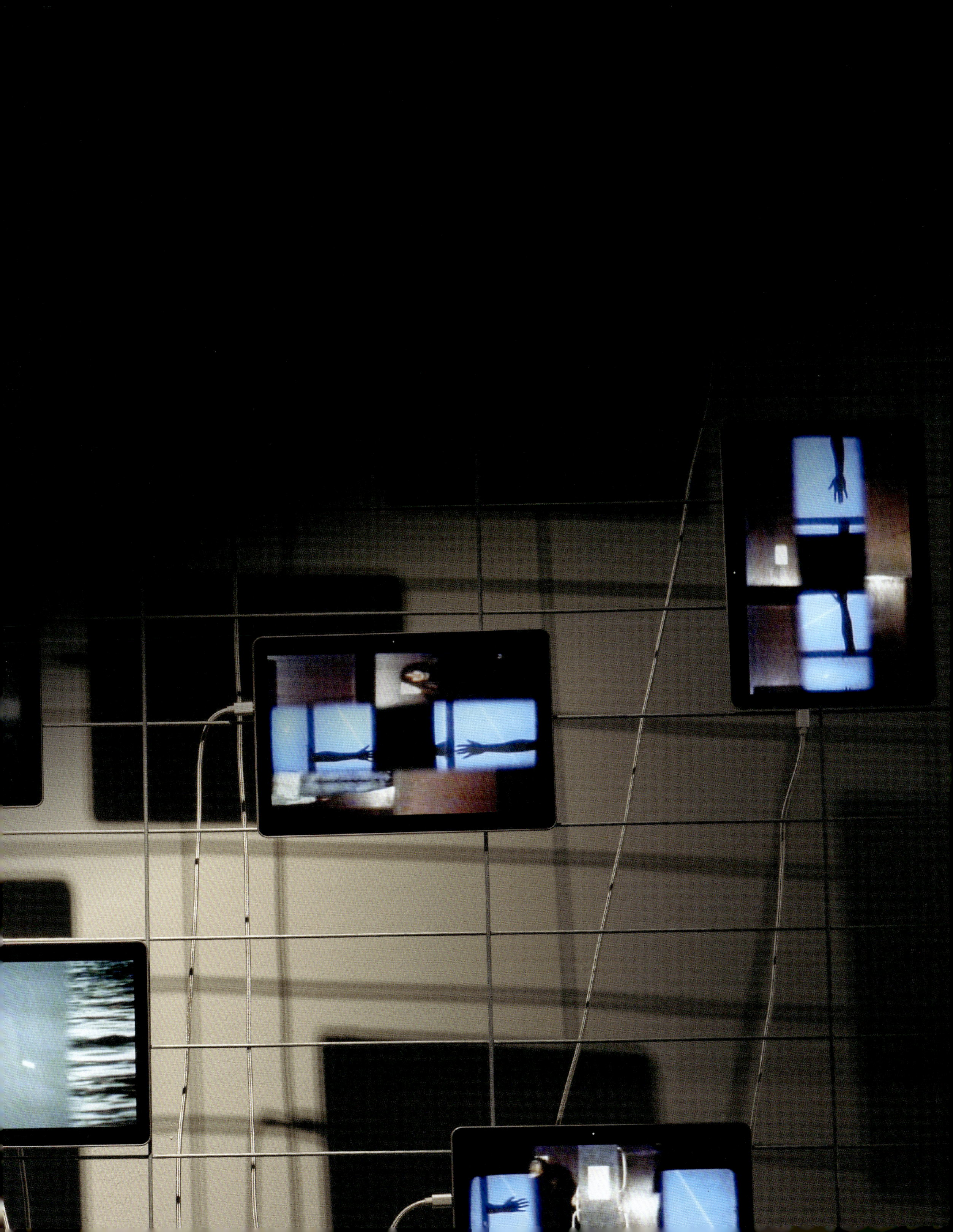

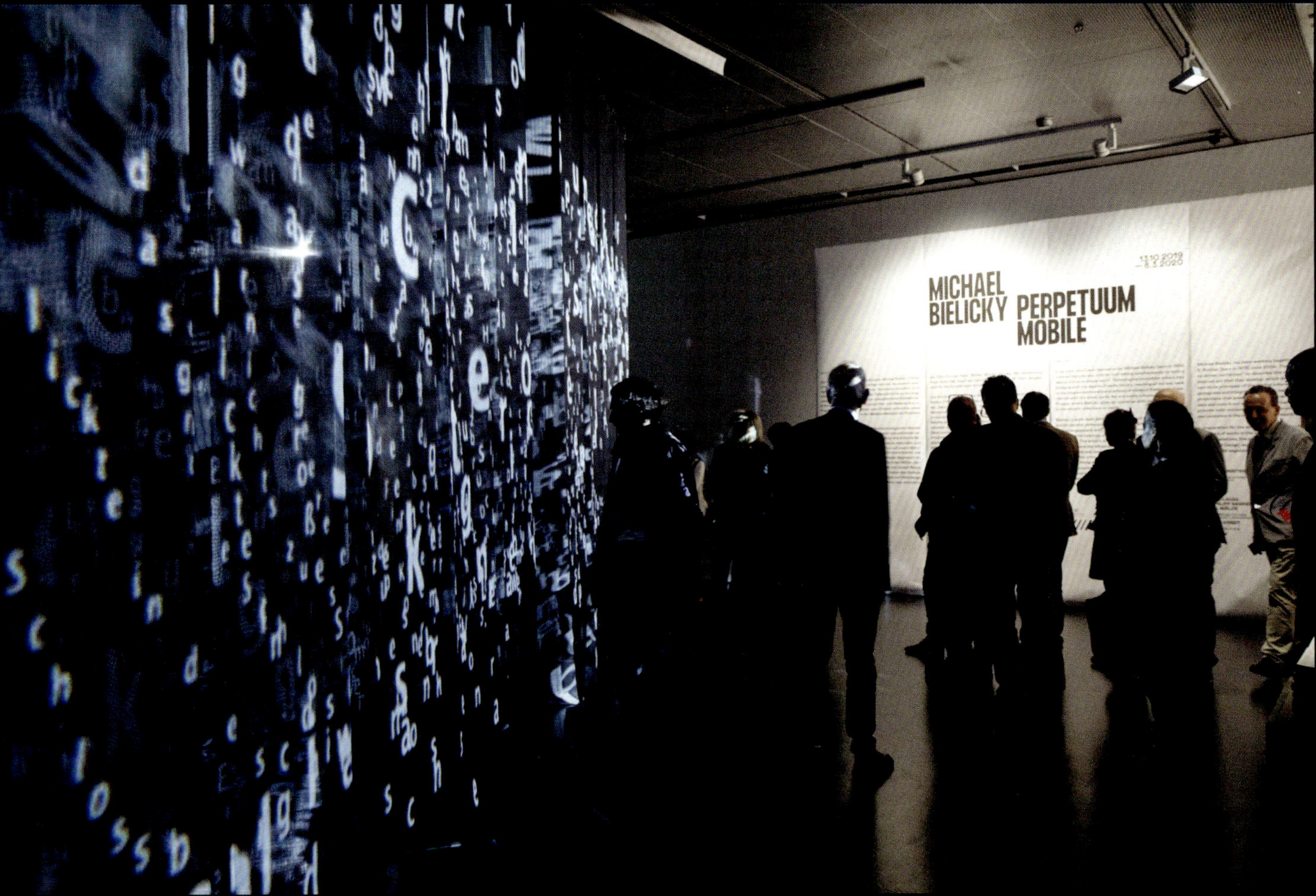
MICHAEL
BIELICKY
PERPETUUM
MOBILE

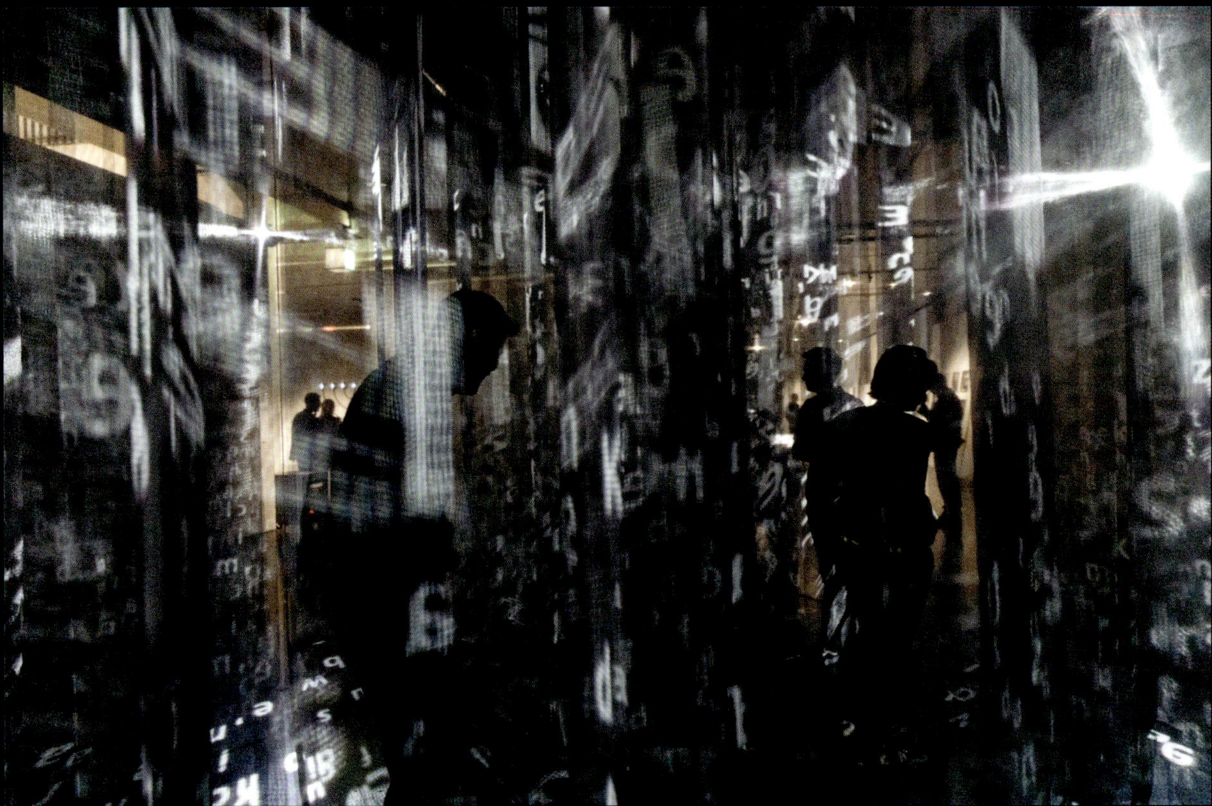

03

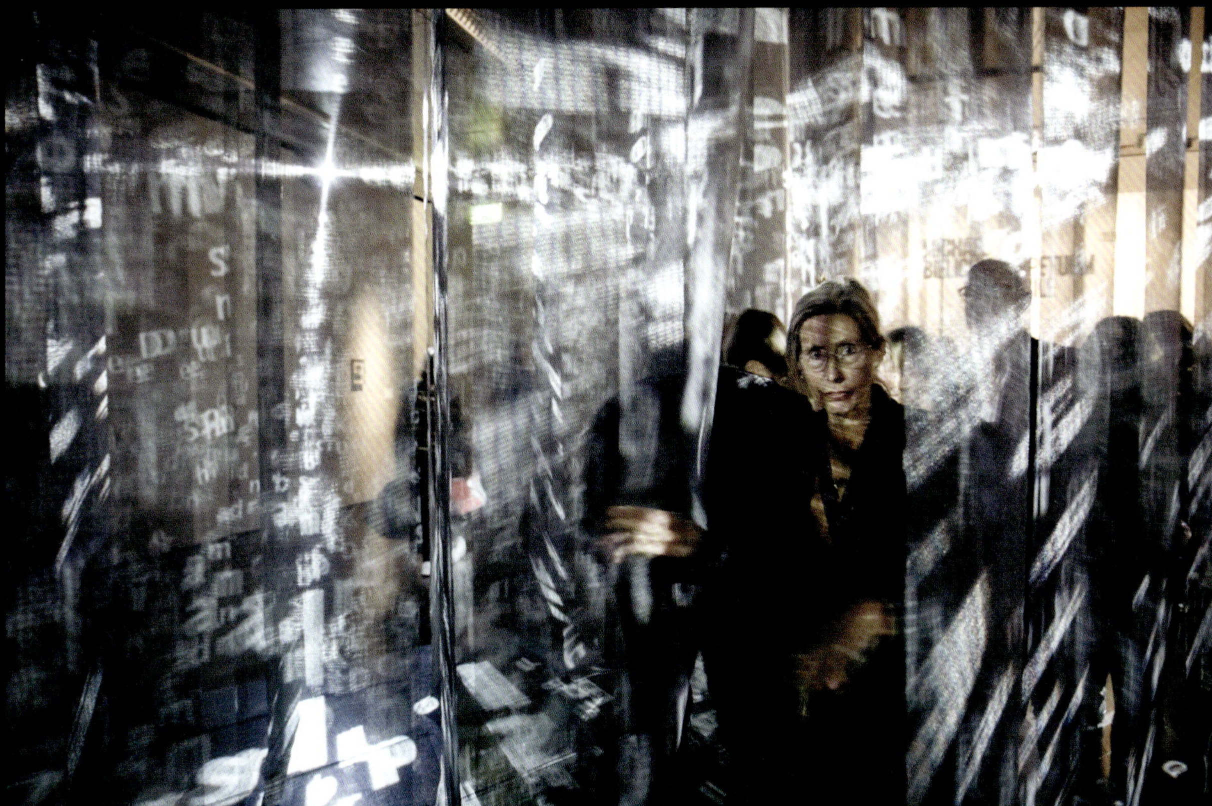

04

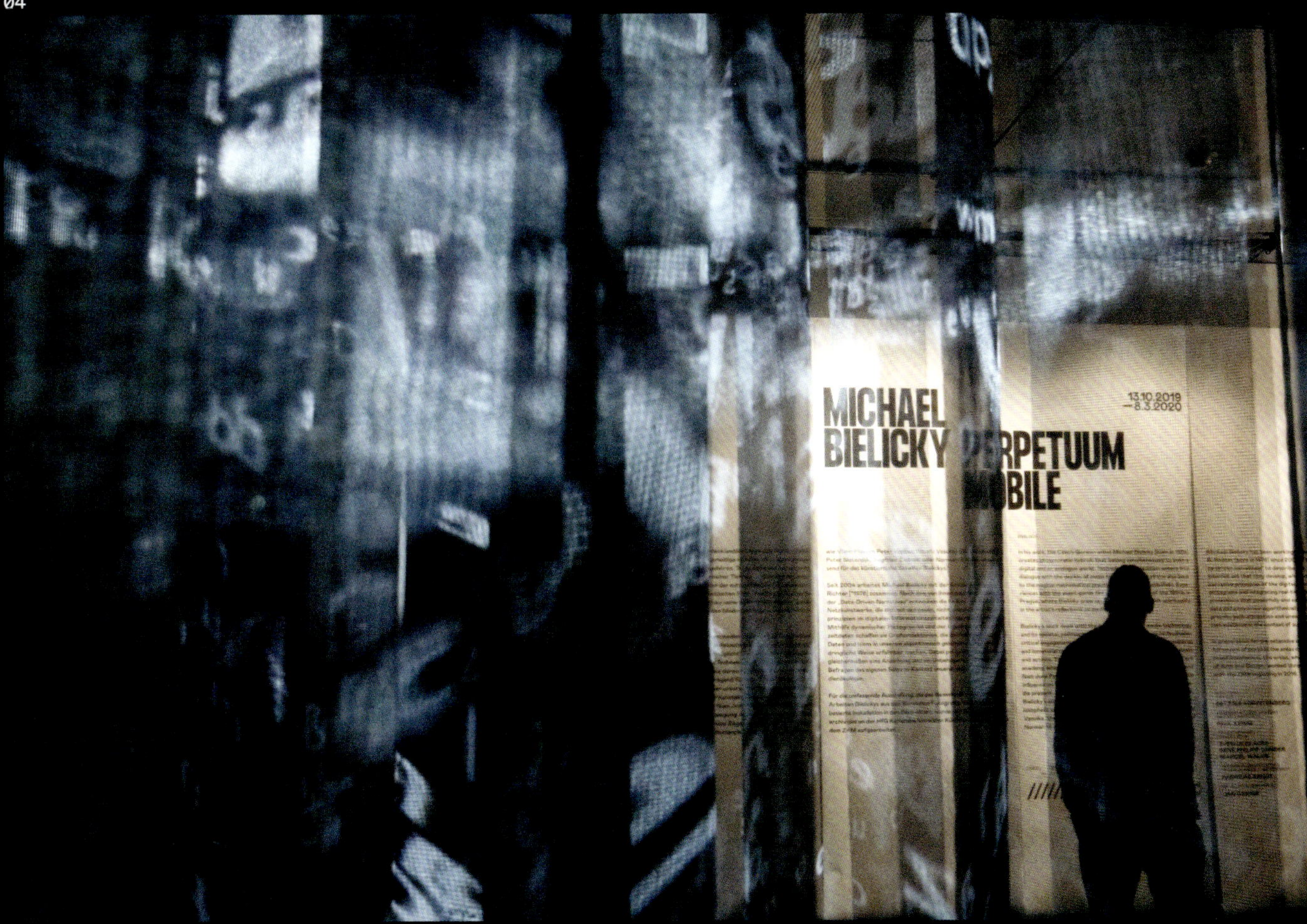

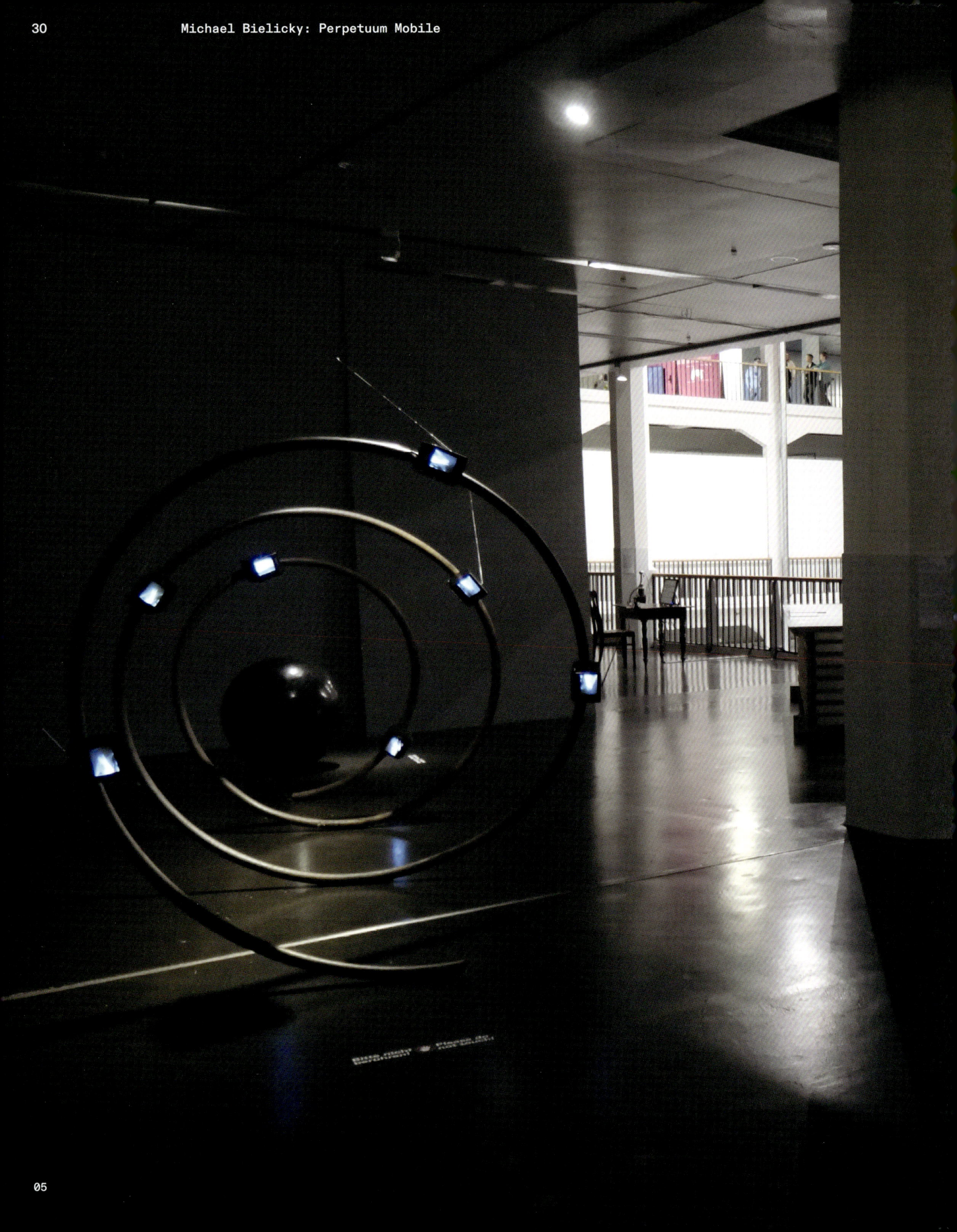

05

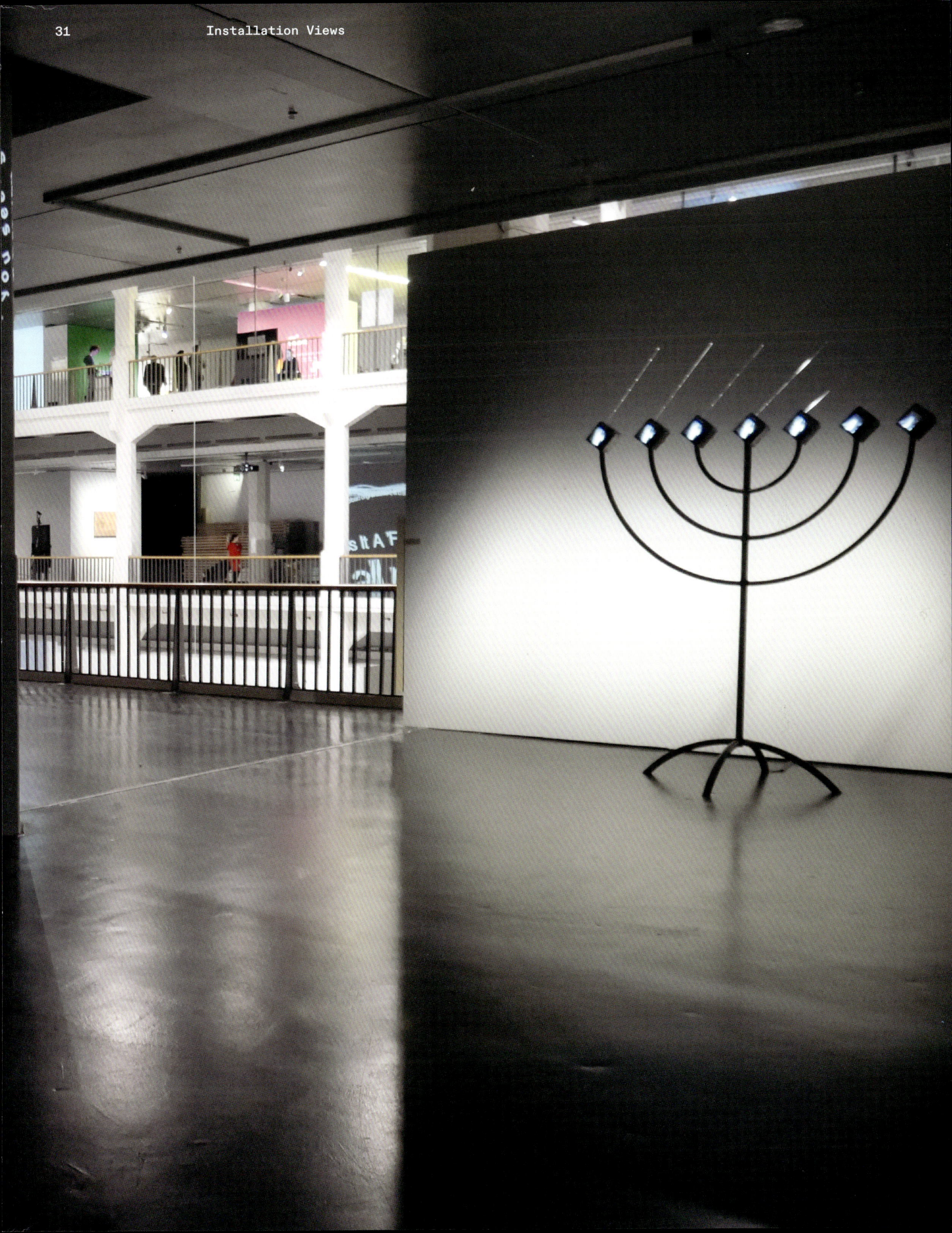

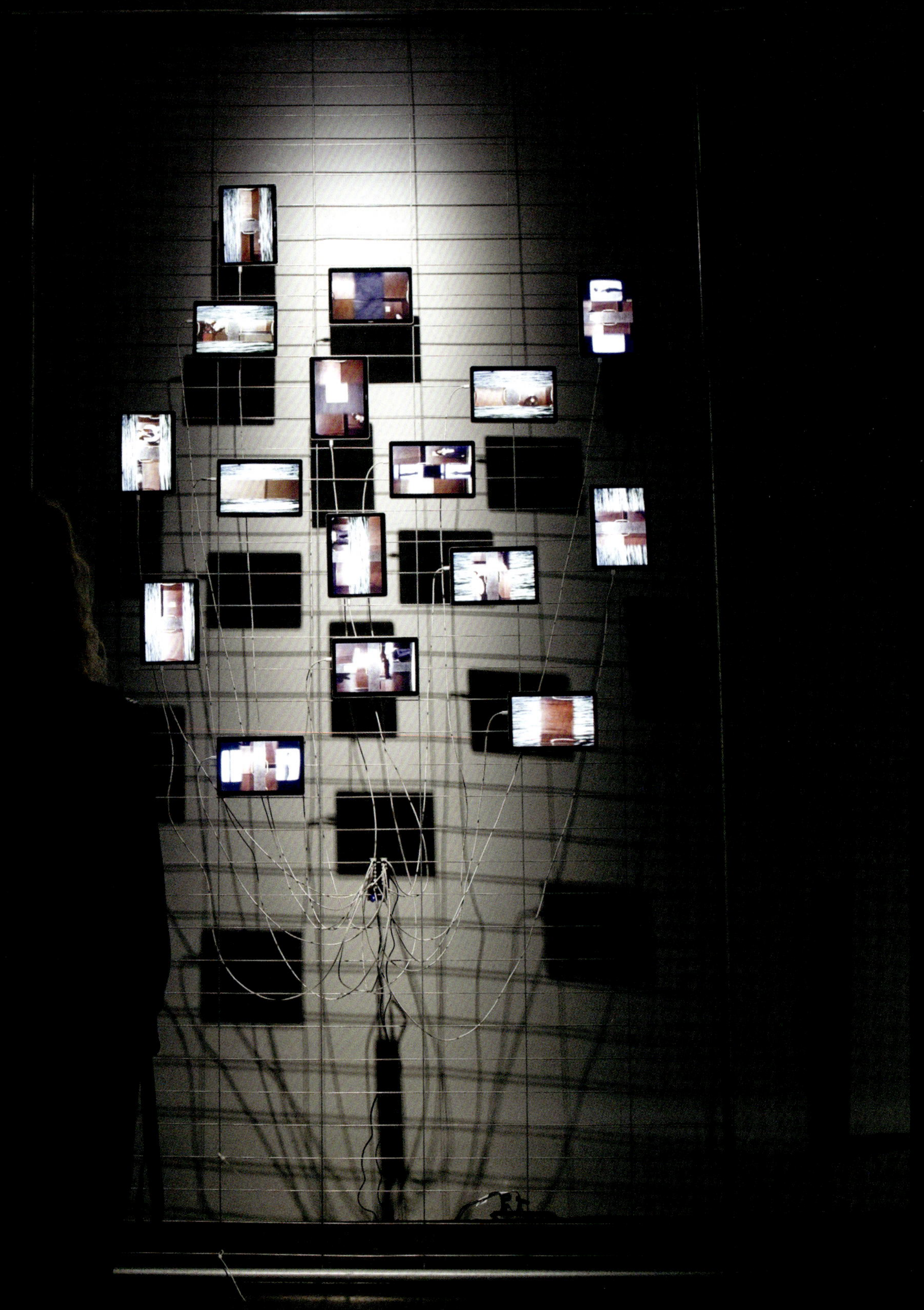

06

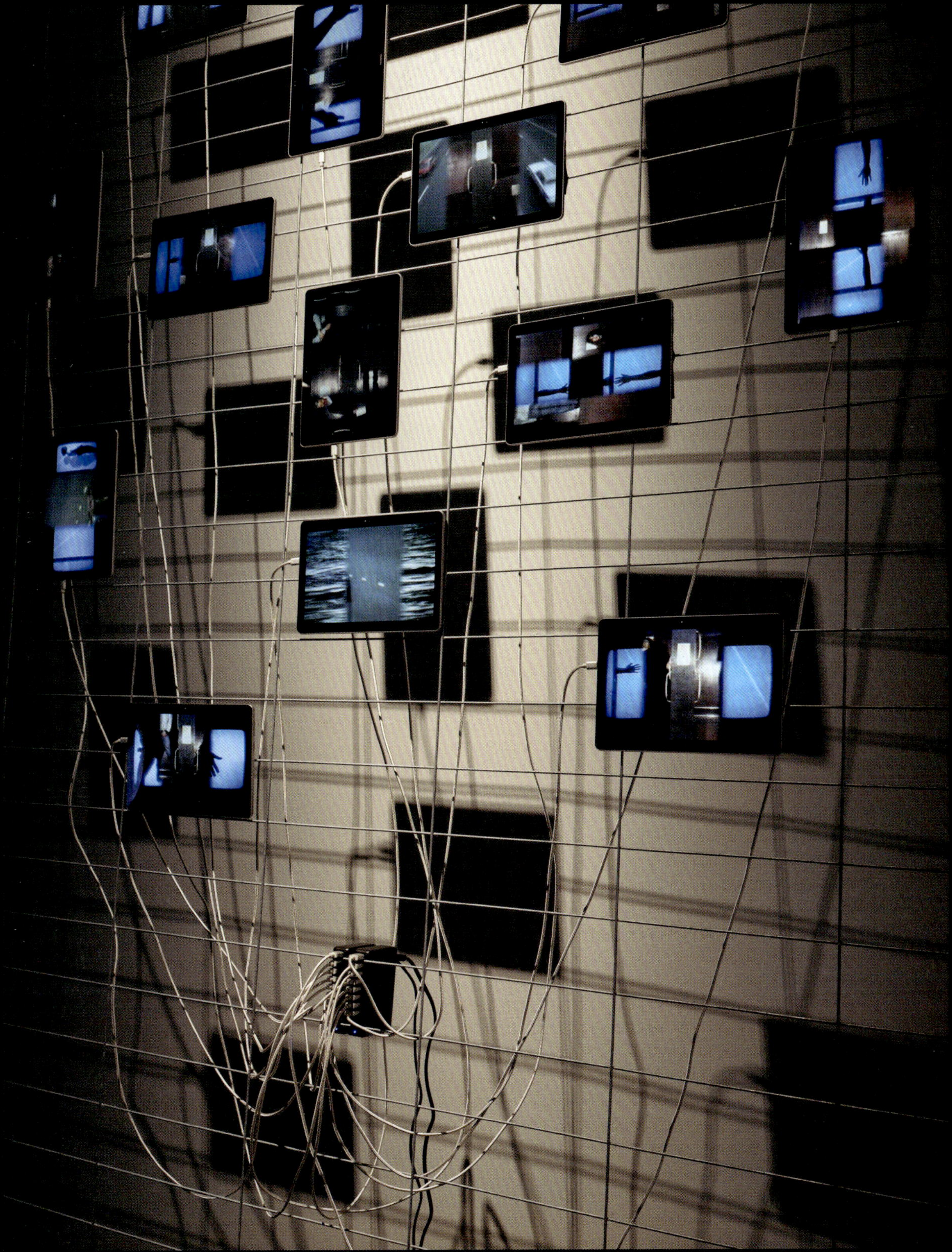

07

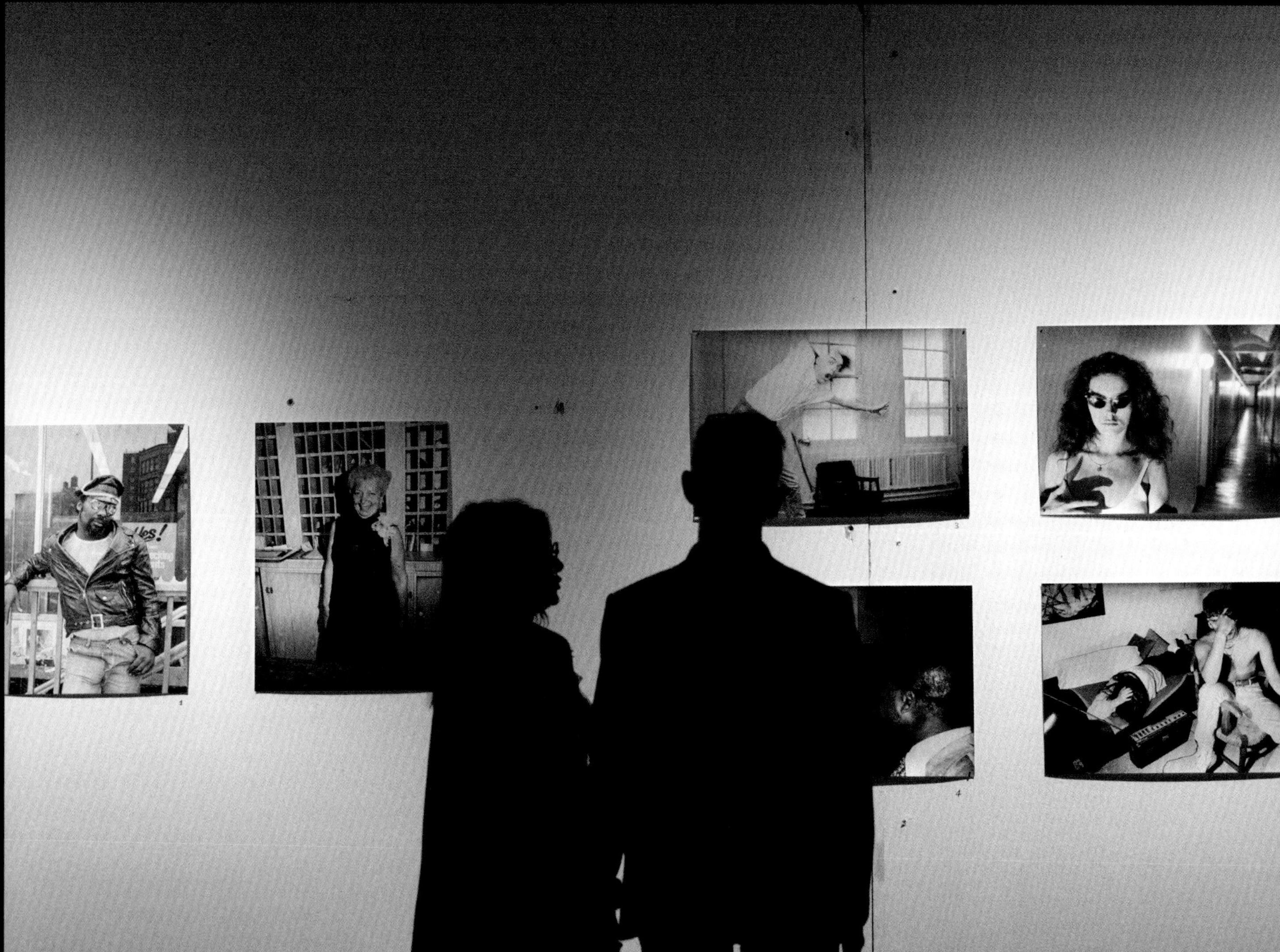

08

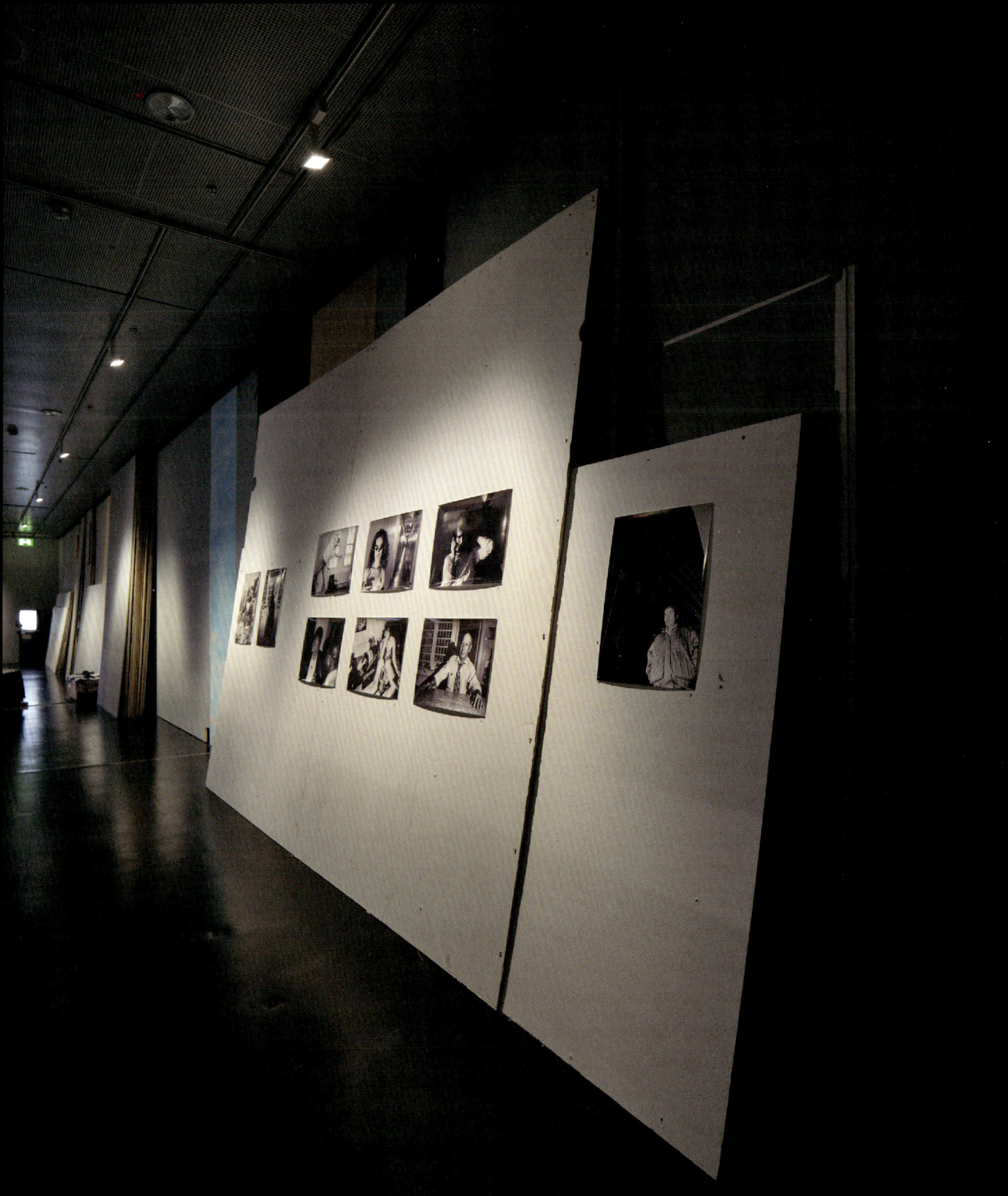

09

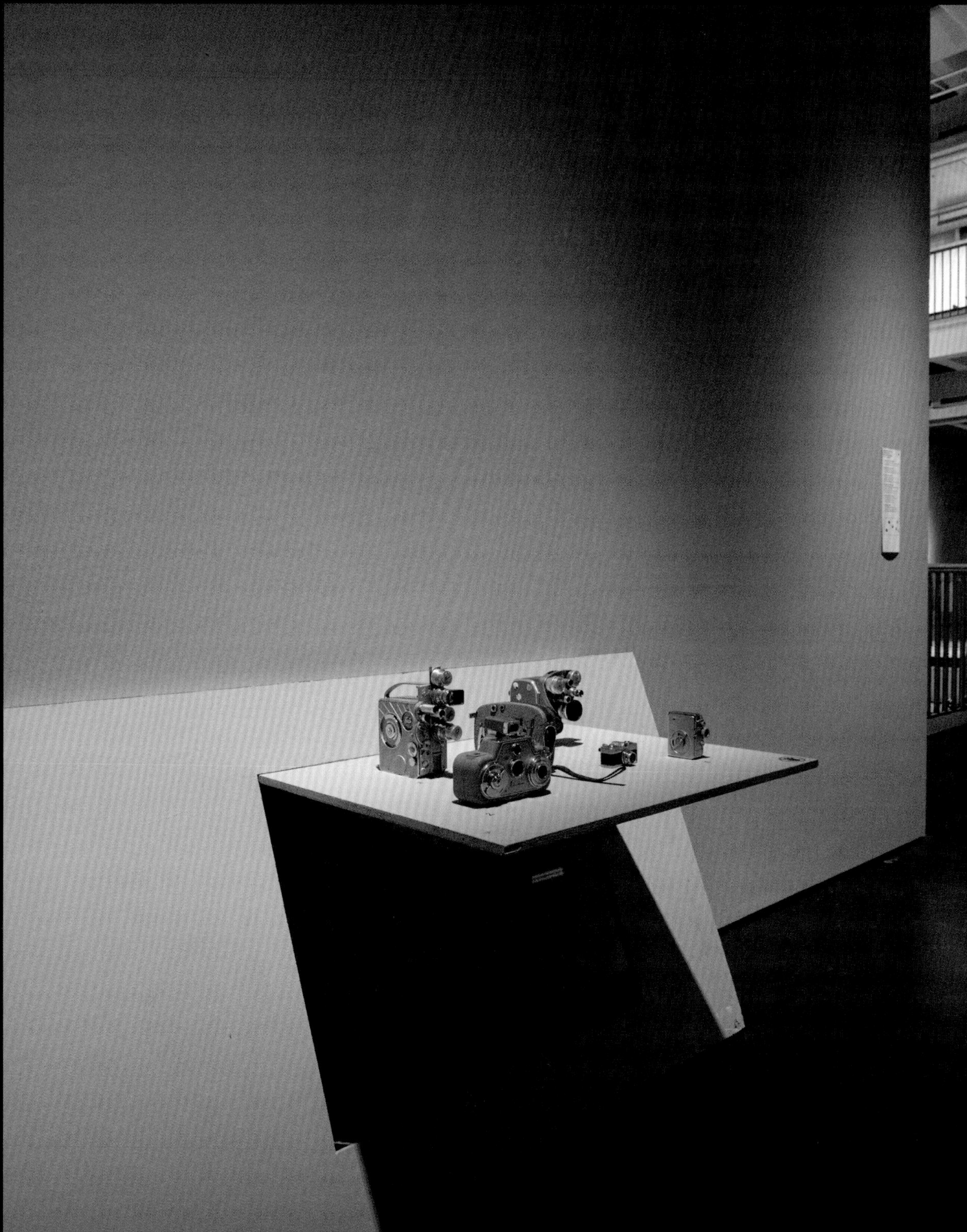

10

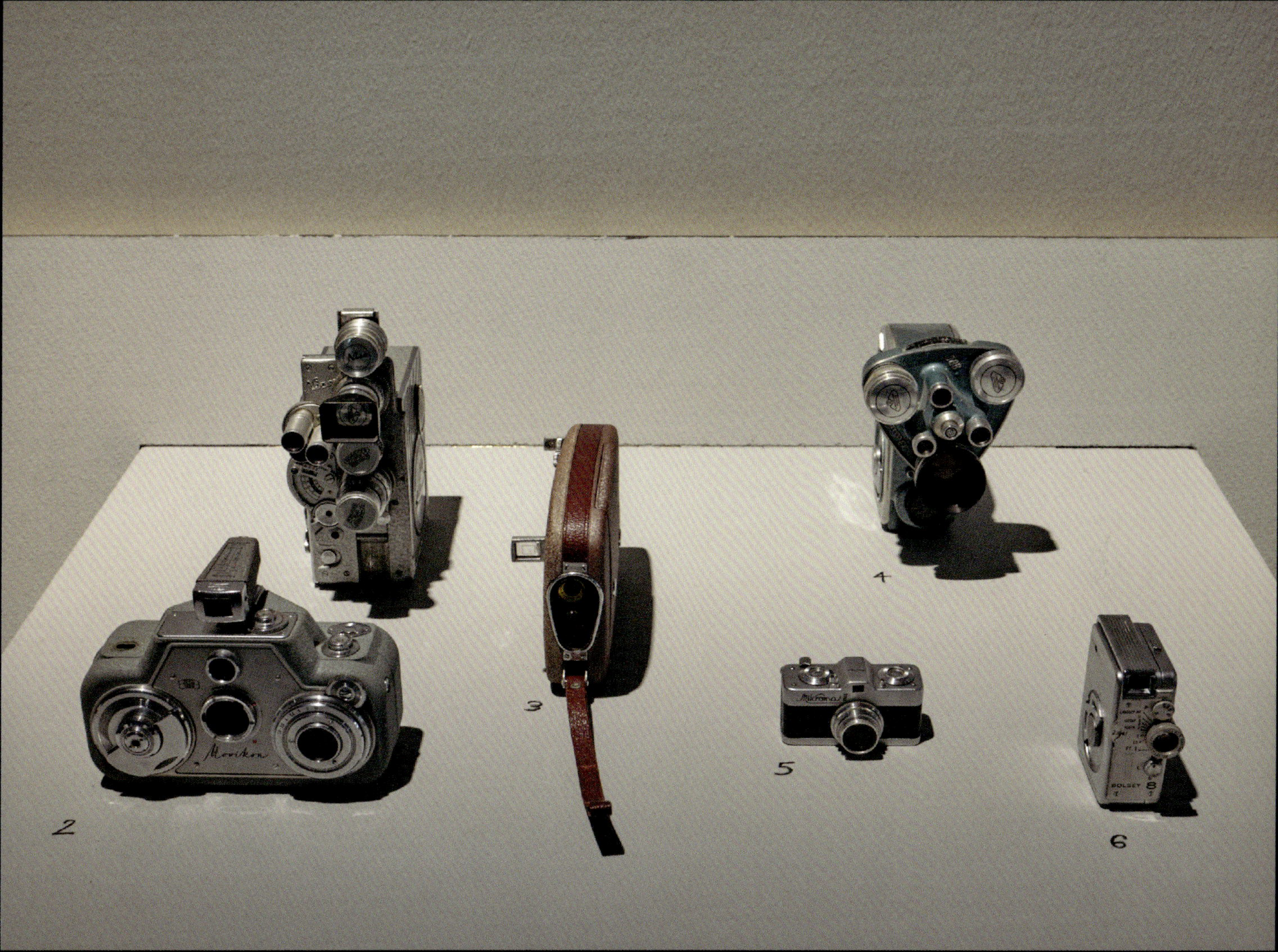
2
3
4
5
6

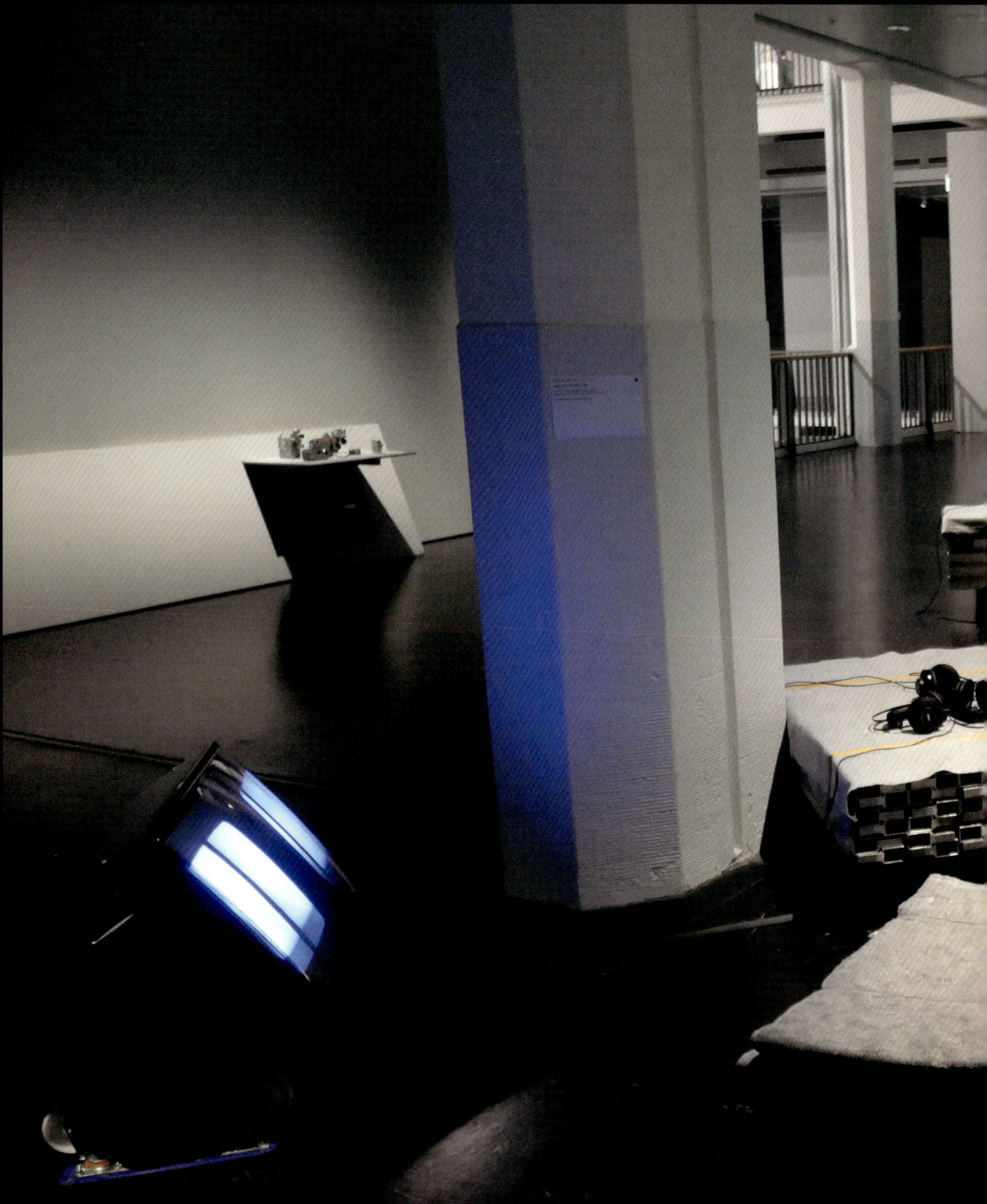

12

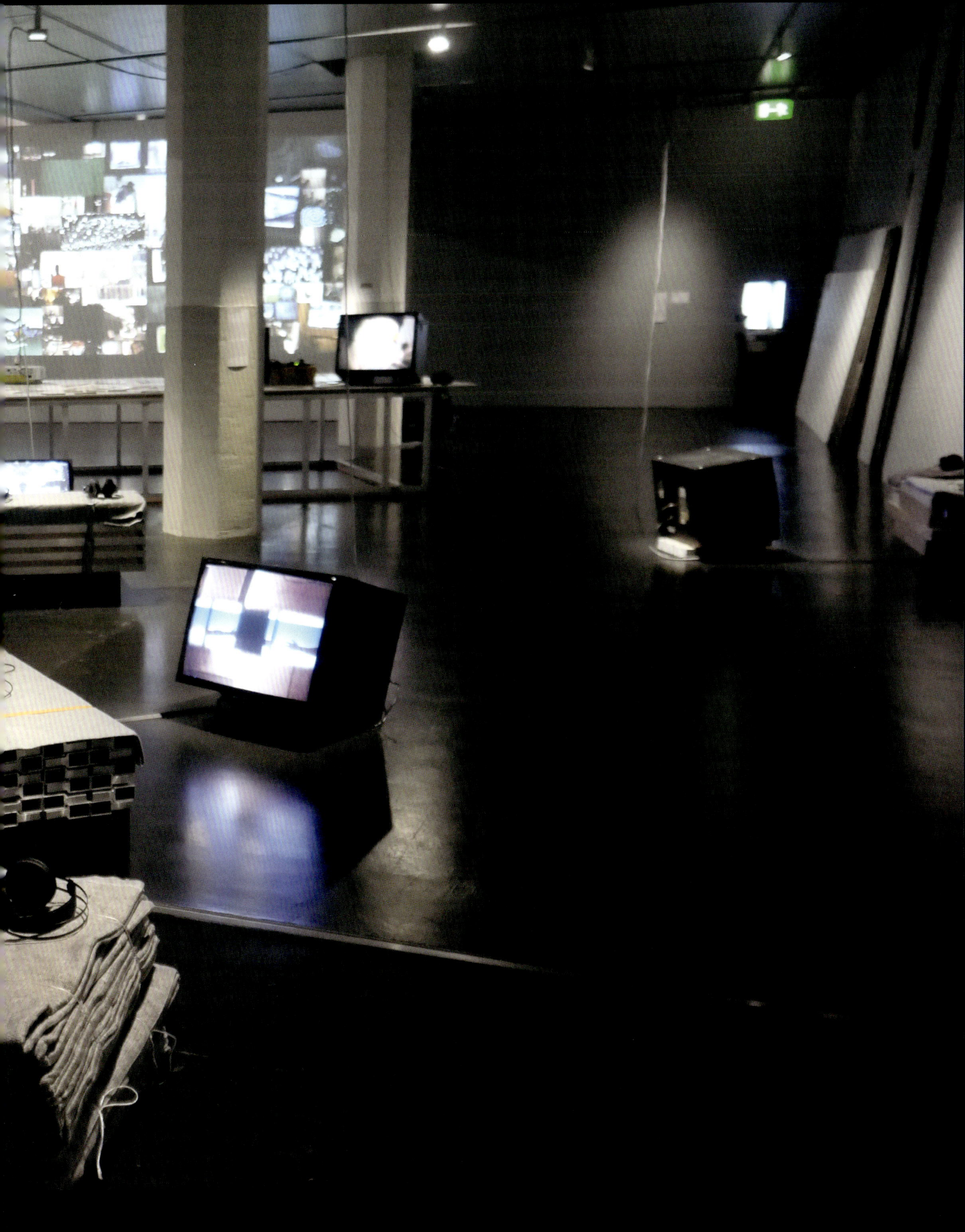

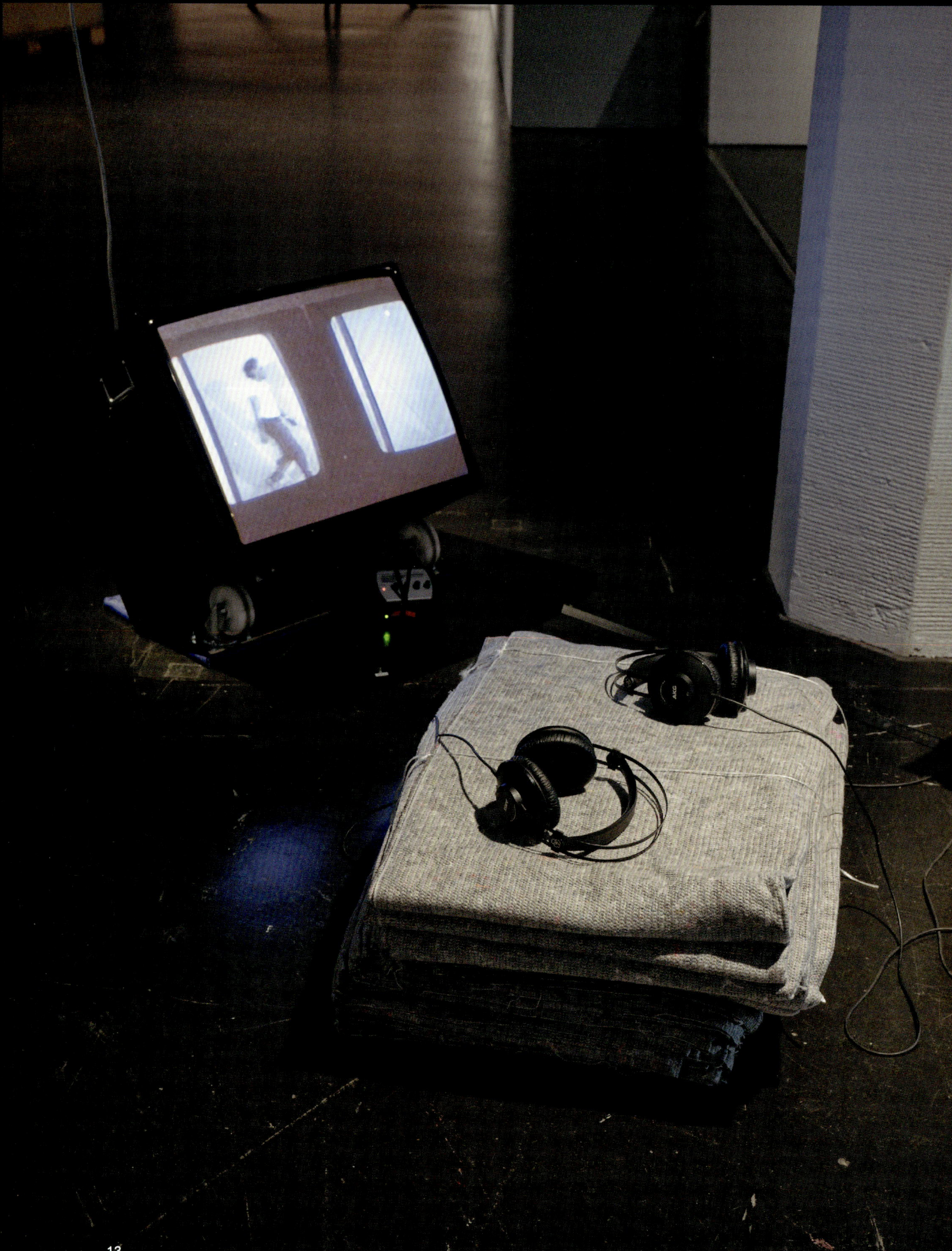

13

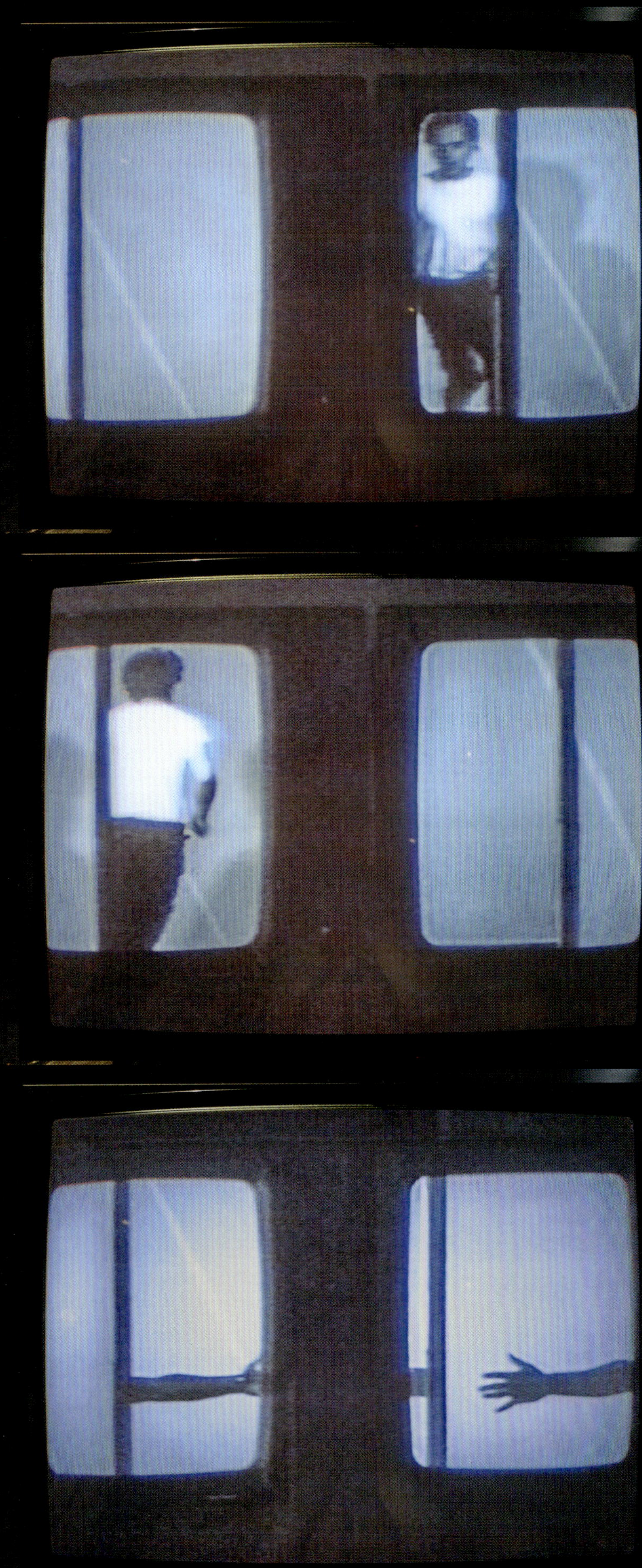

14

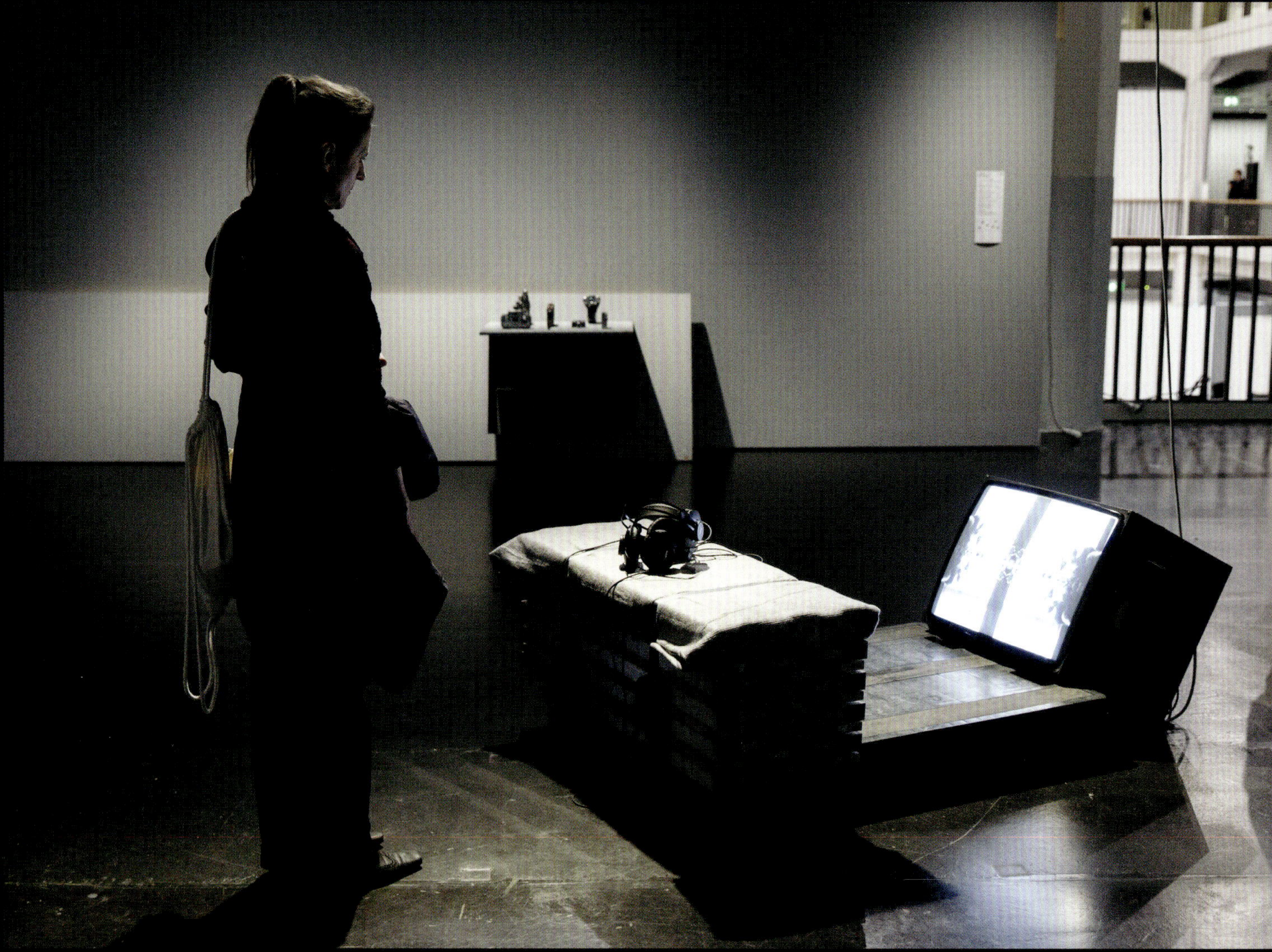

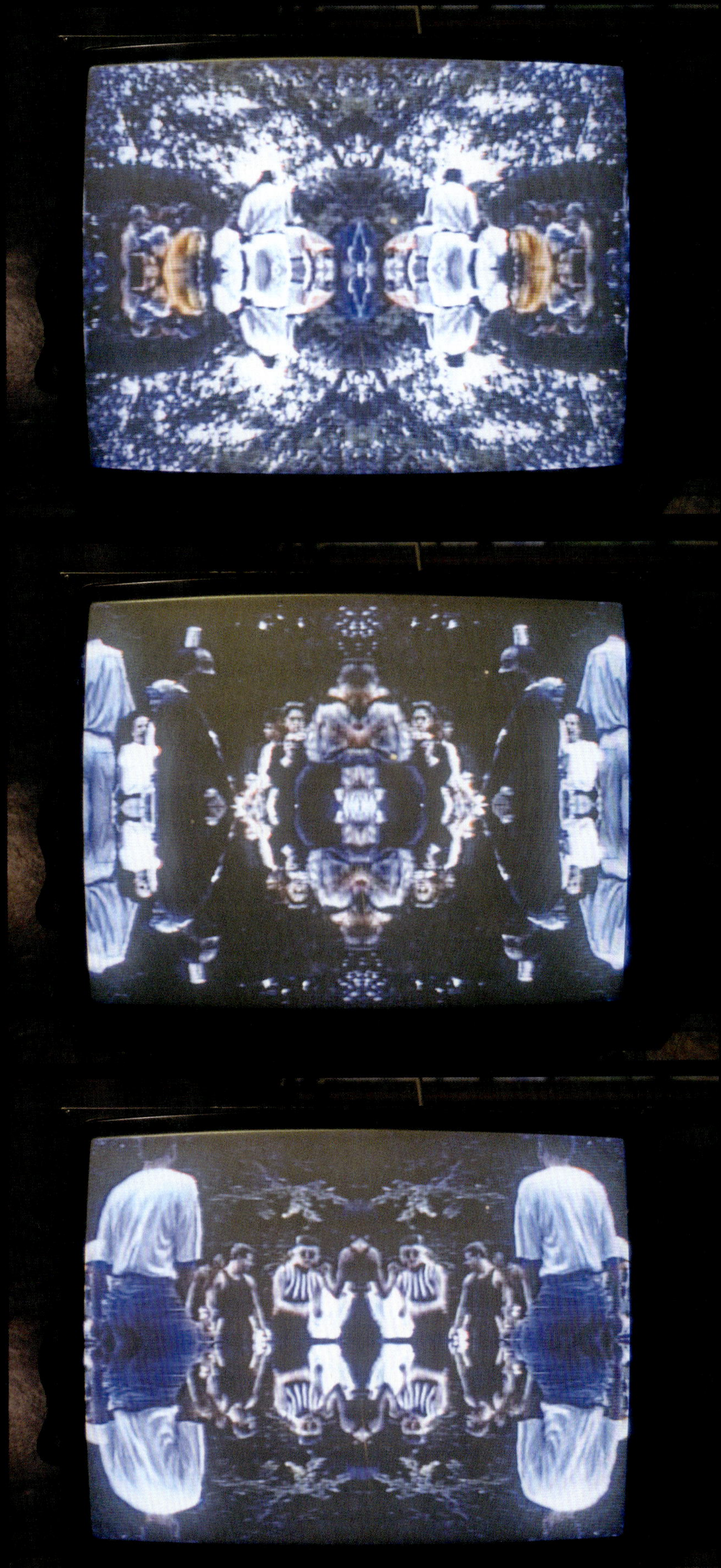

16

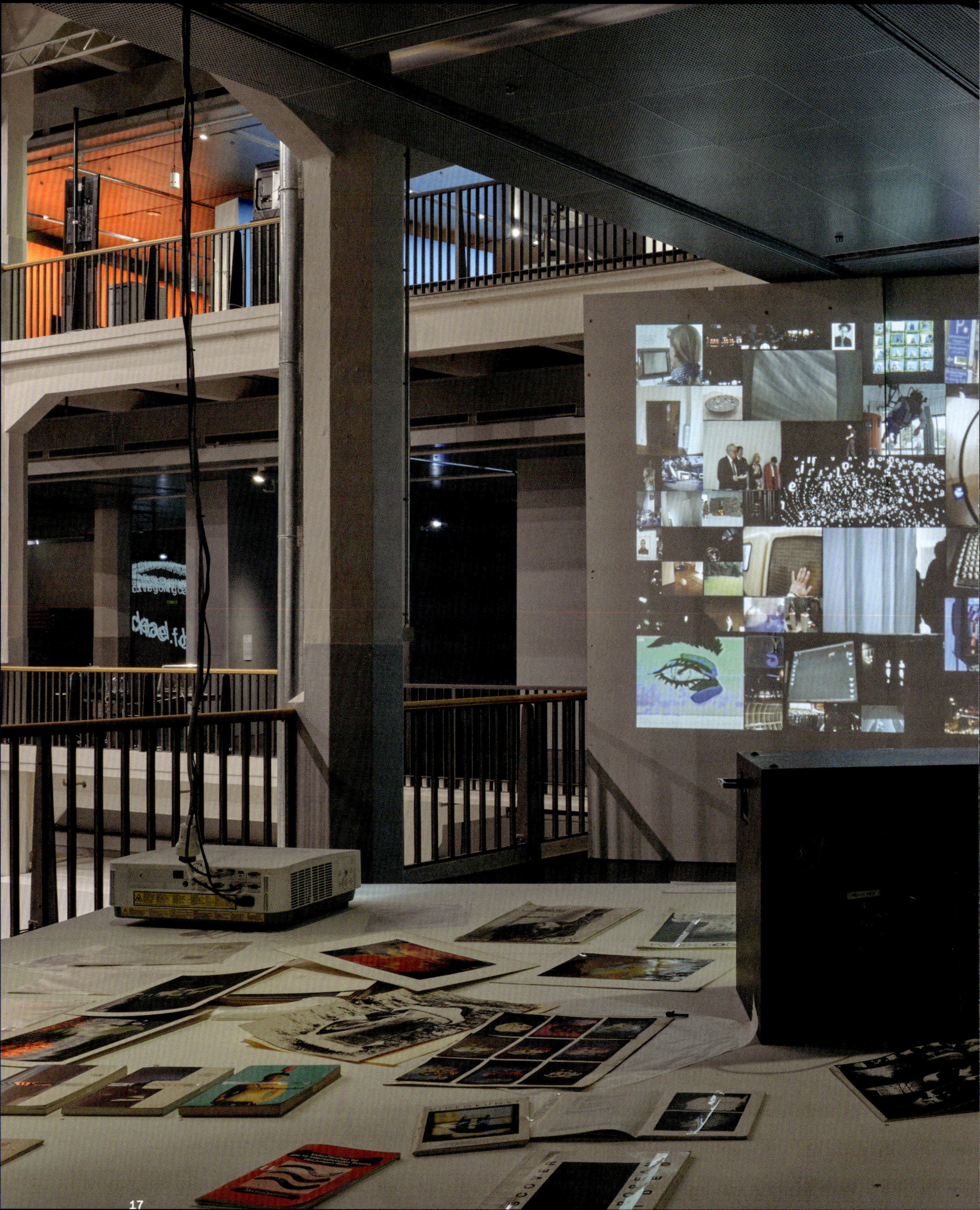

17

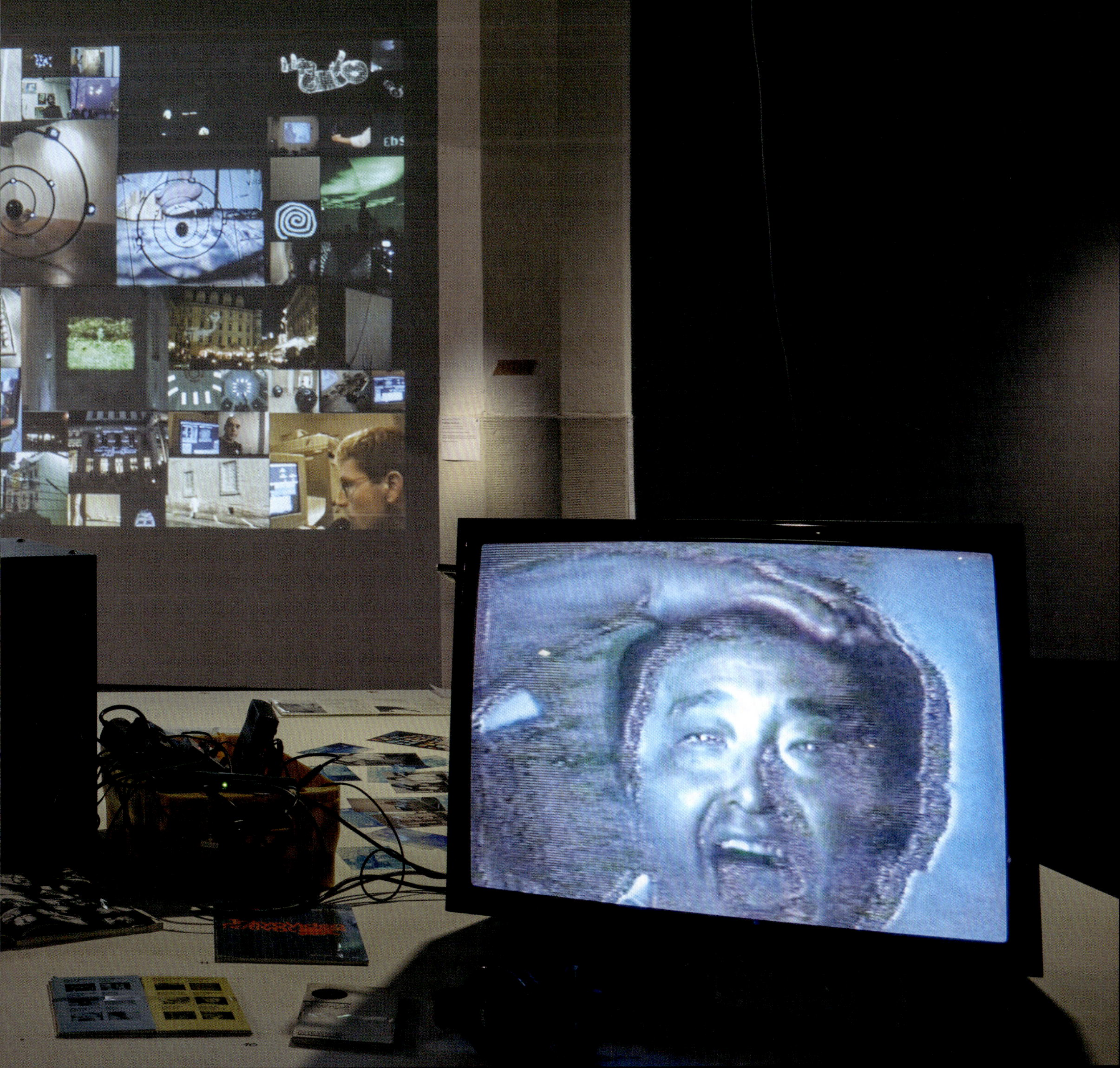

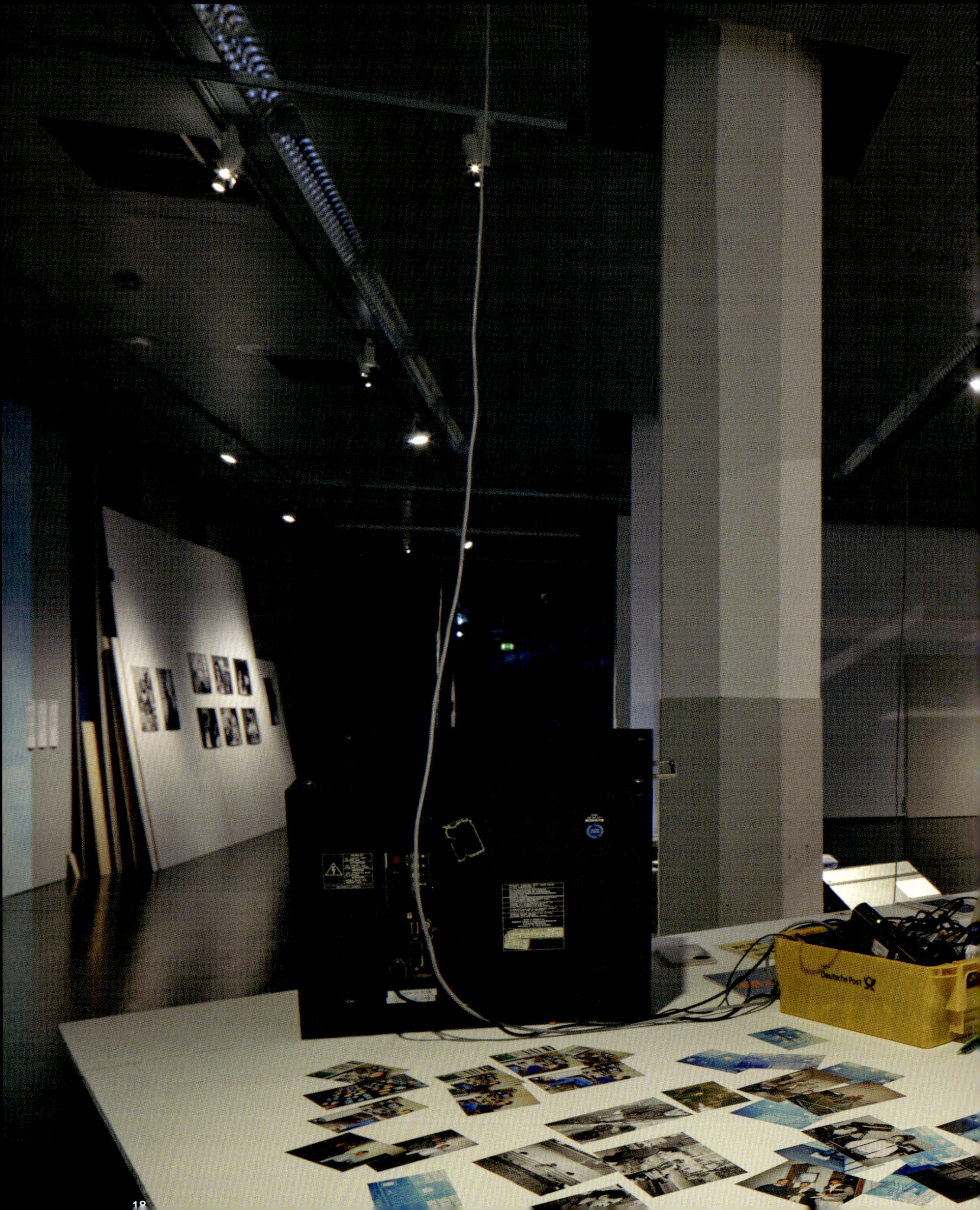

18

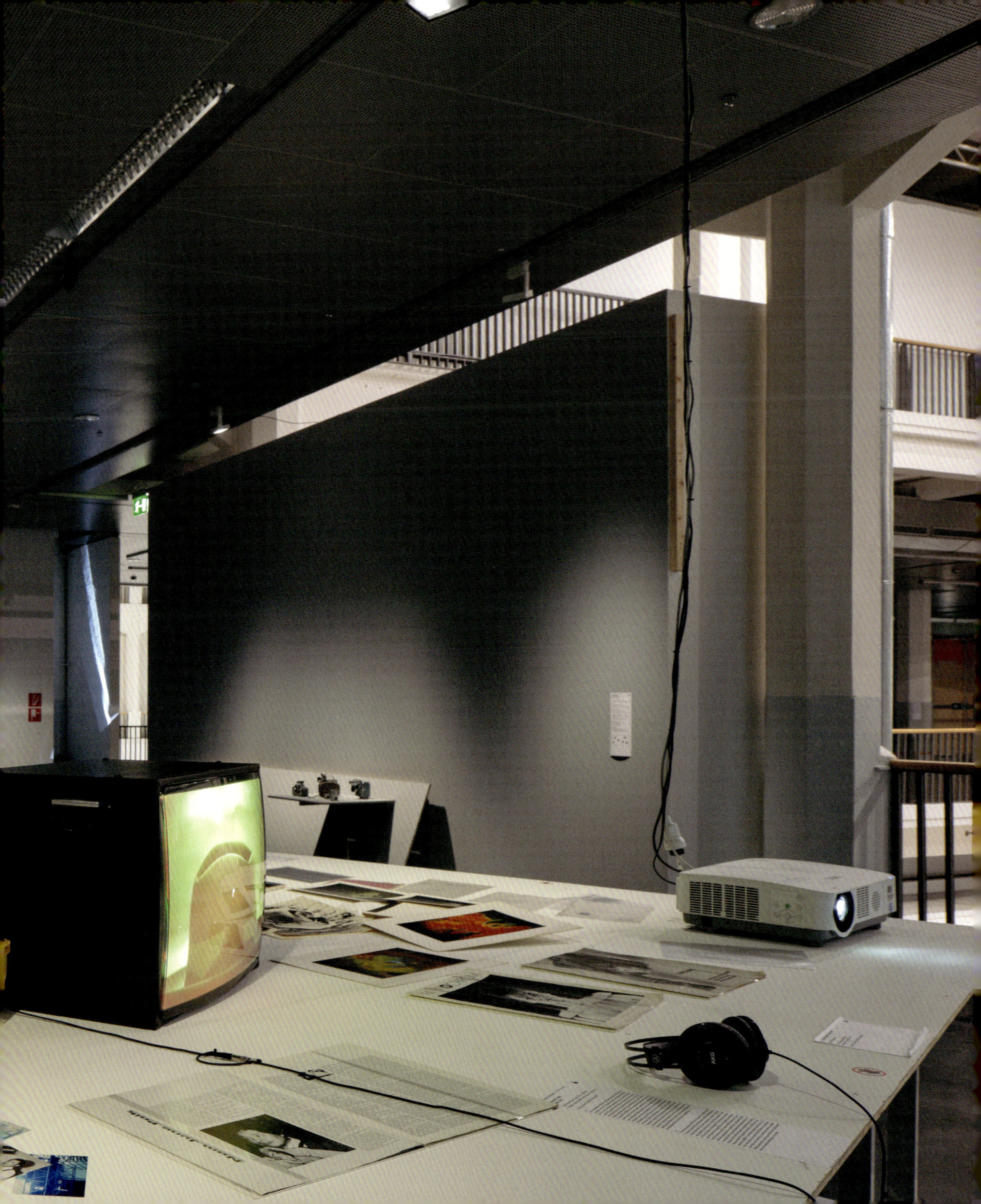

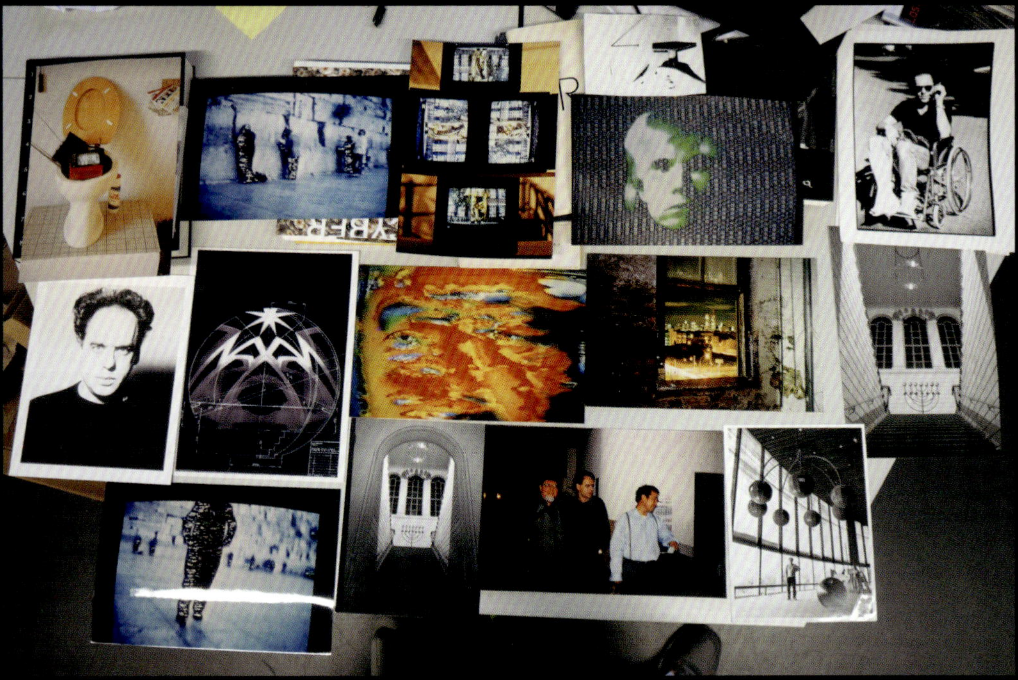

19

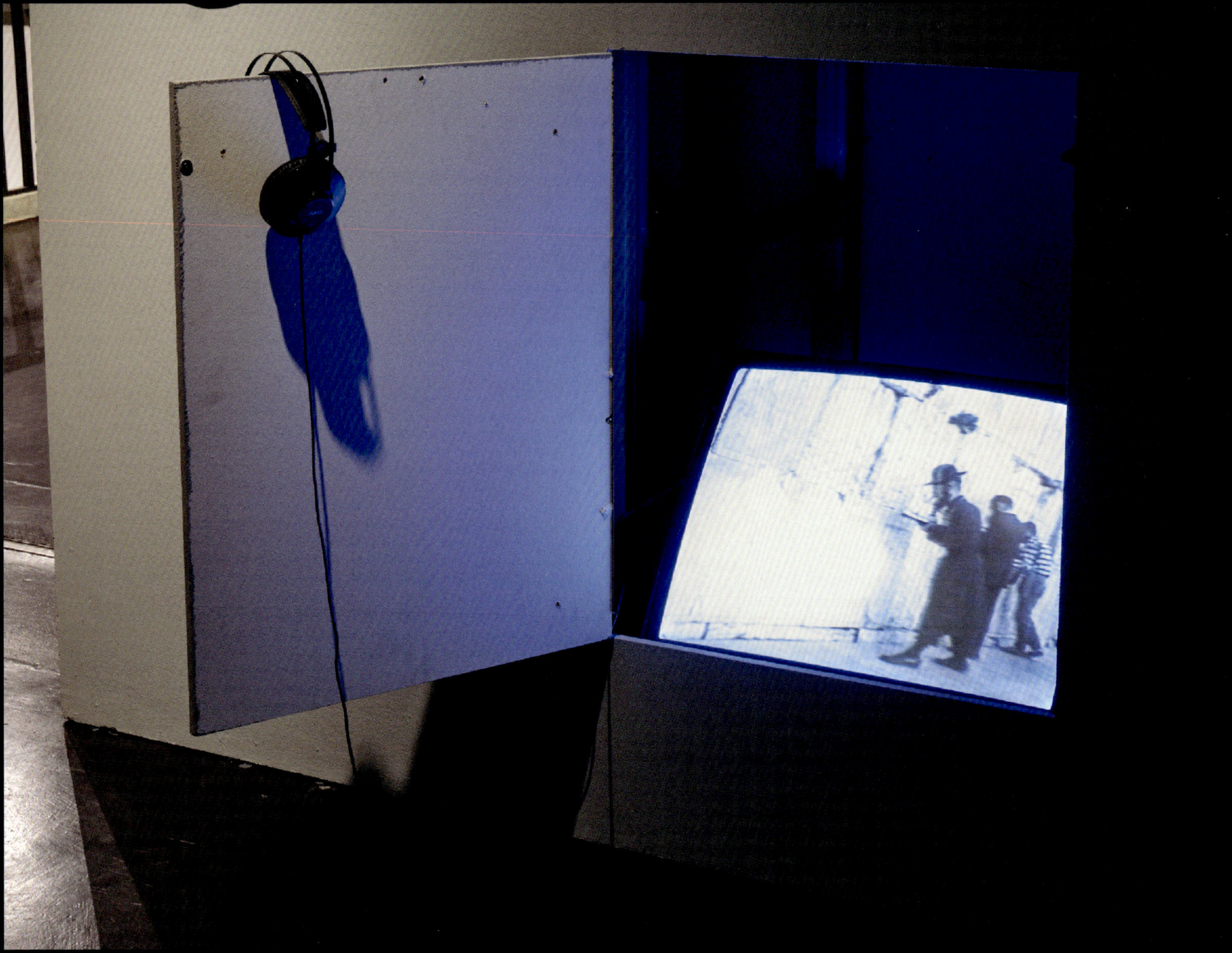

20

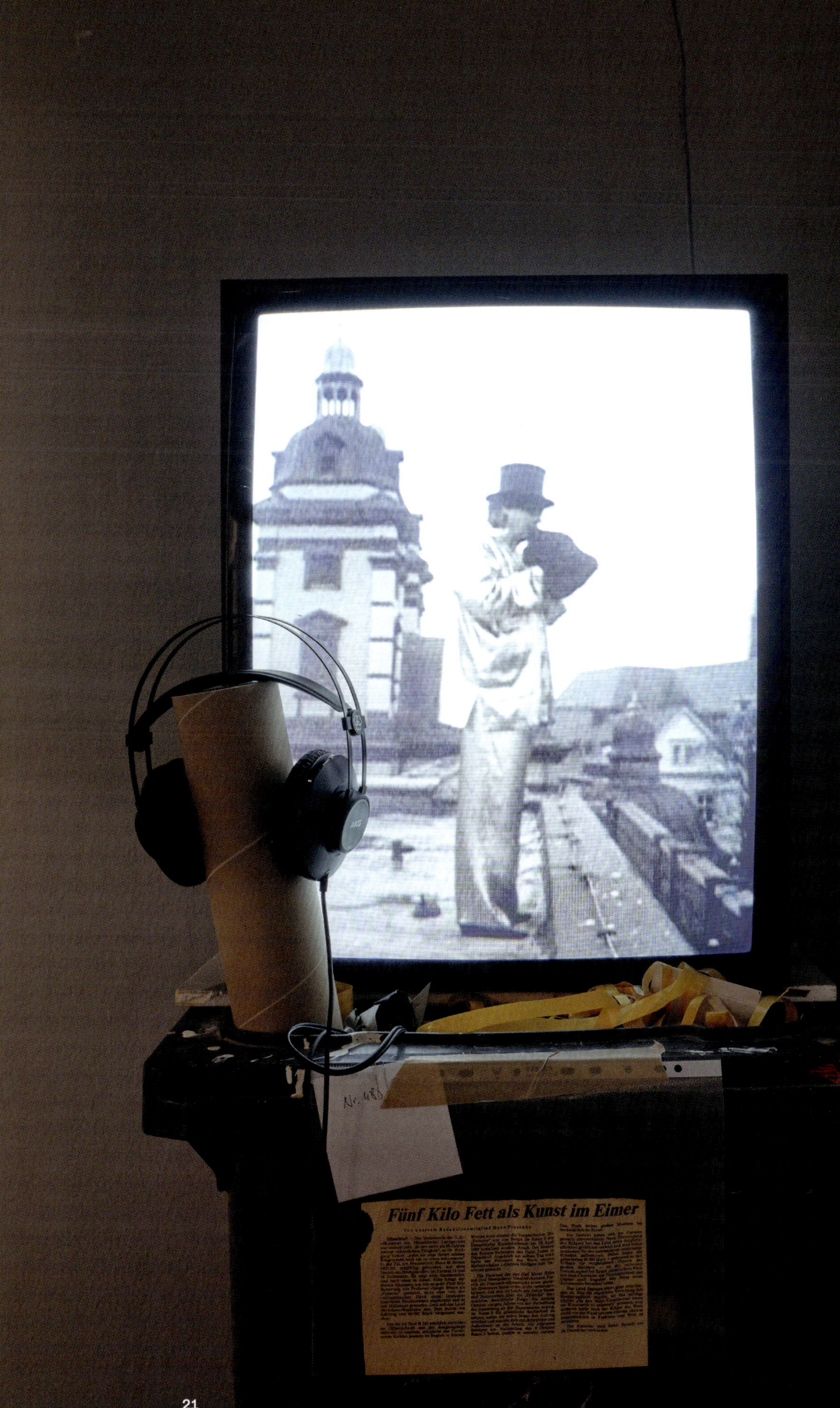
Fünf Kilo Fett als Kunst im Eimer

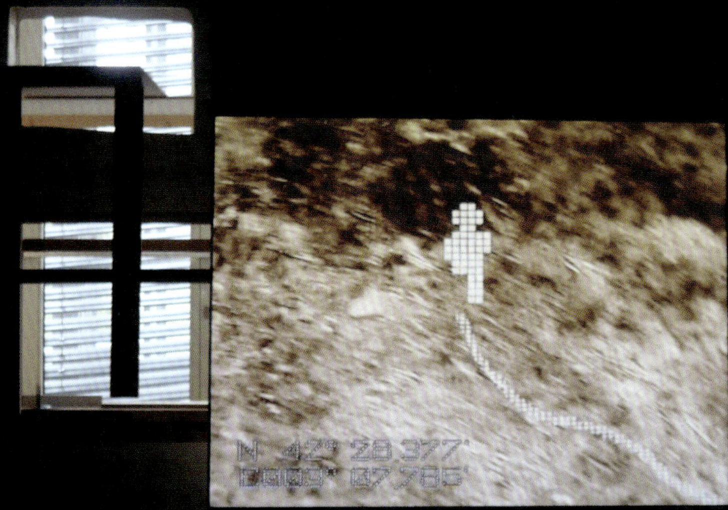

22

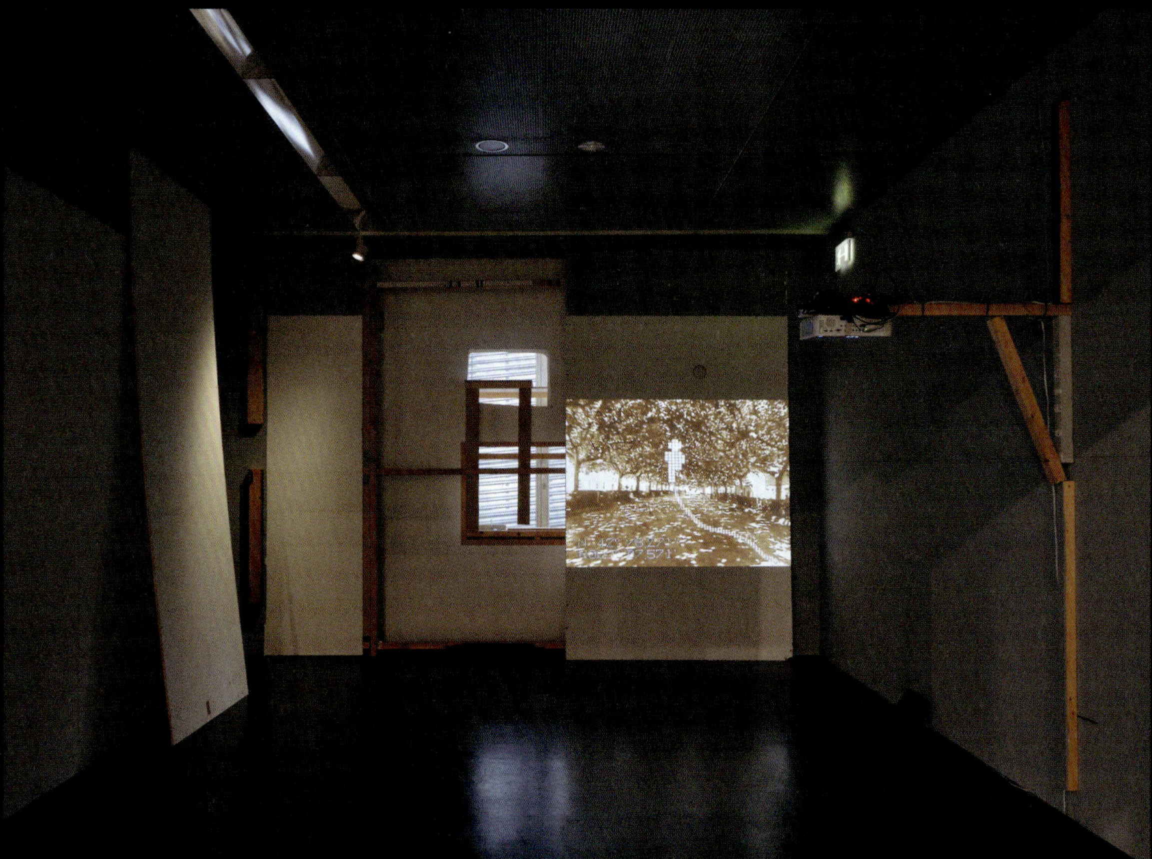

23

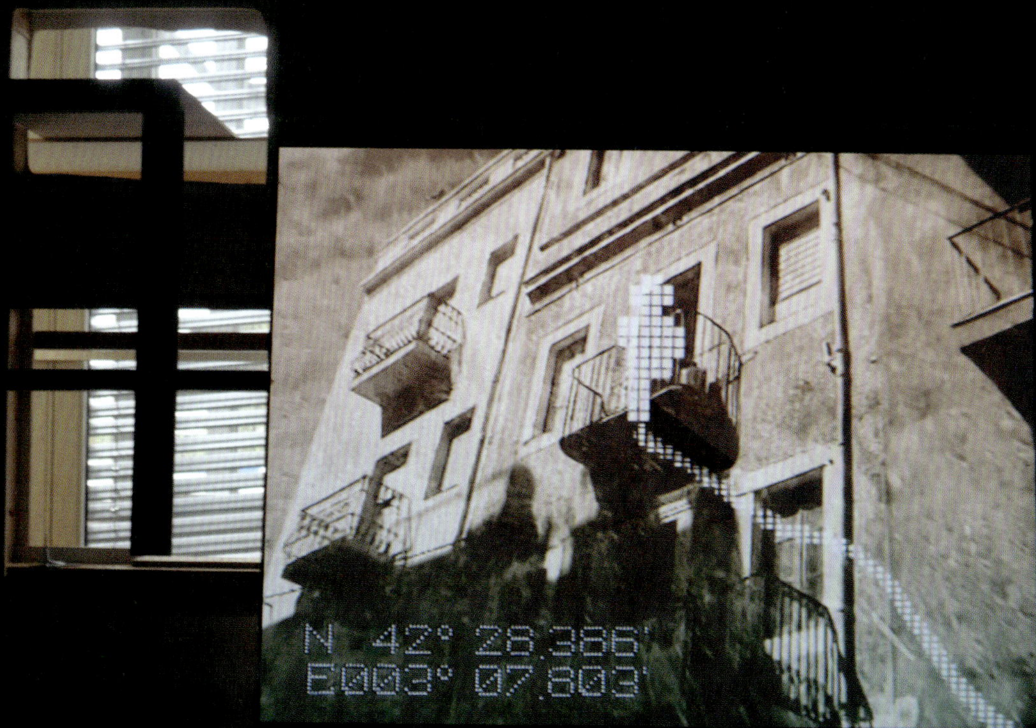

24

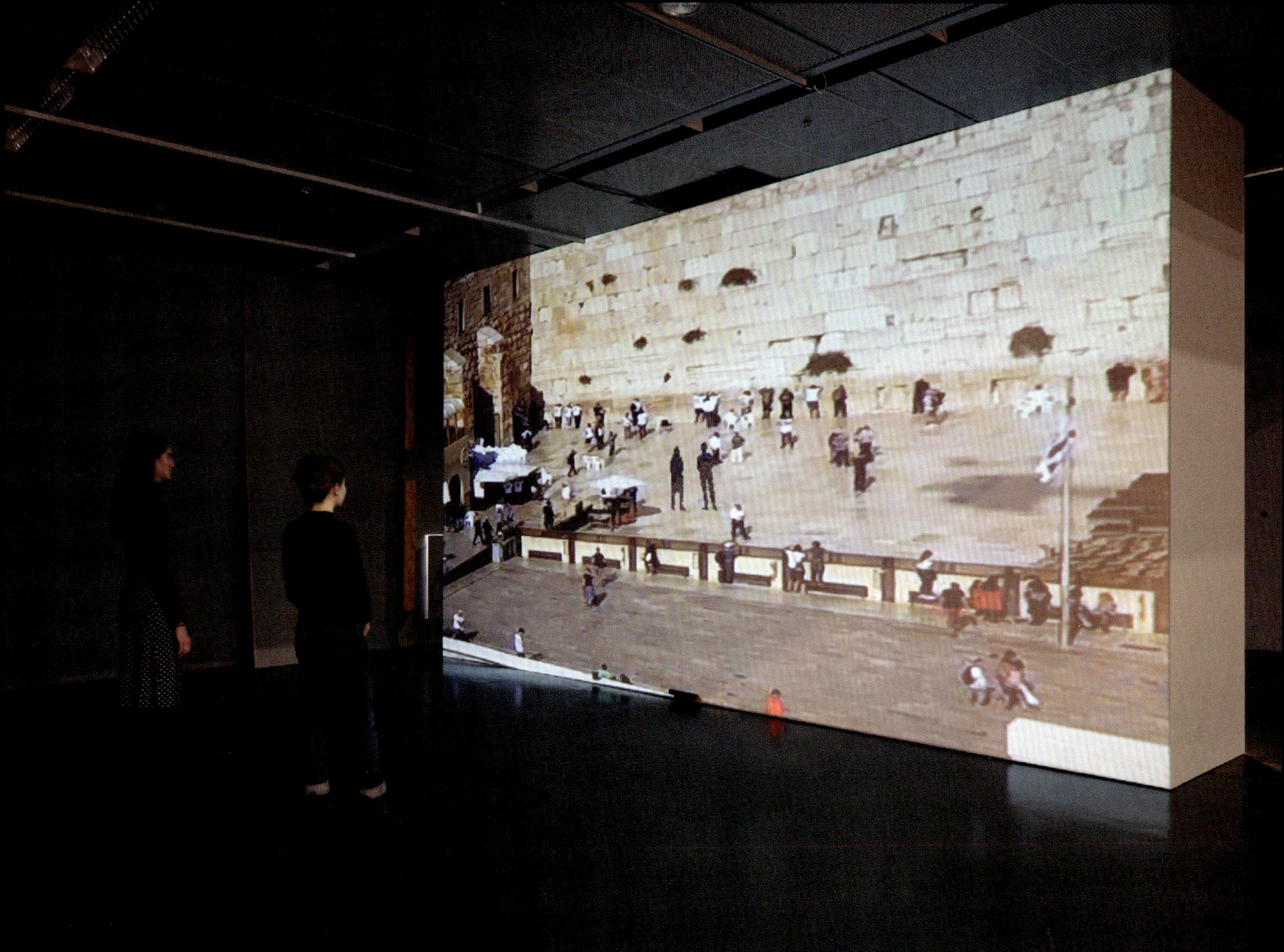

25

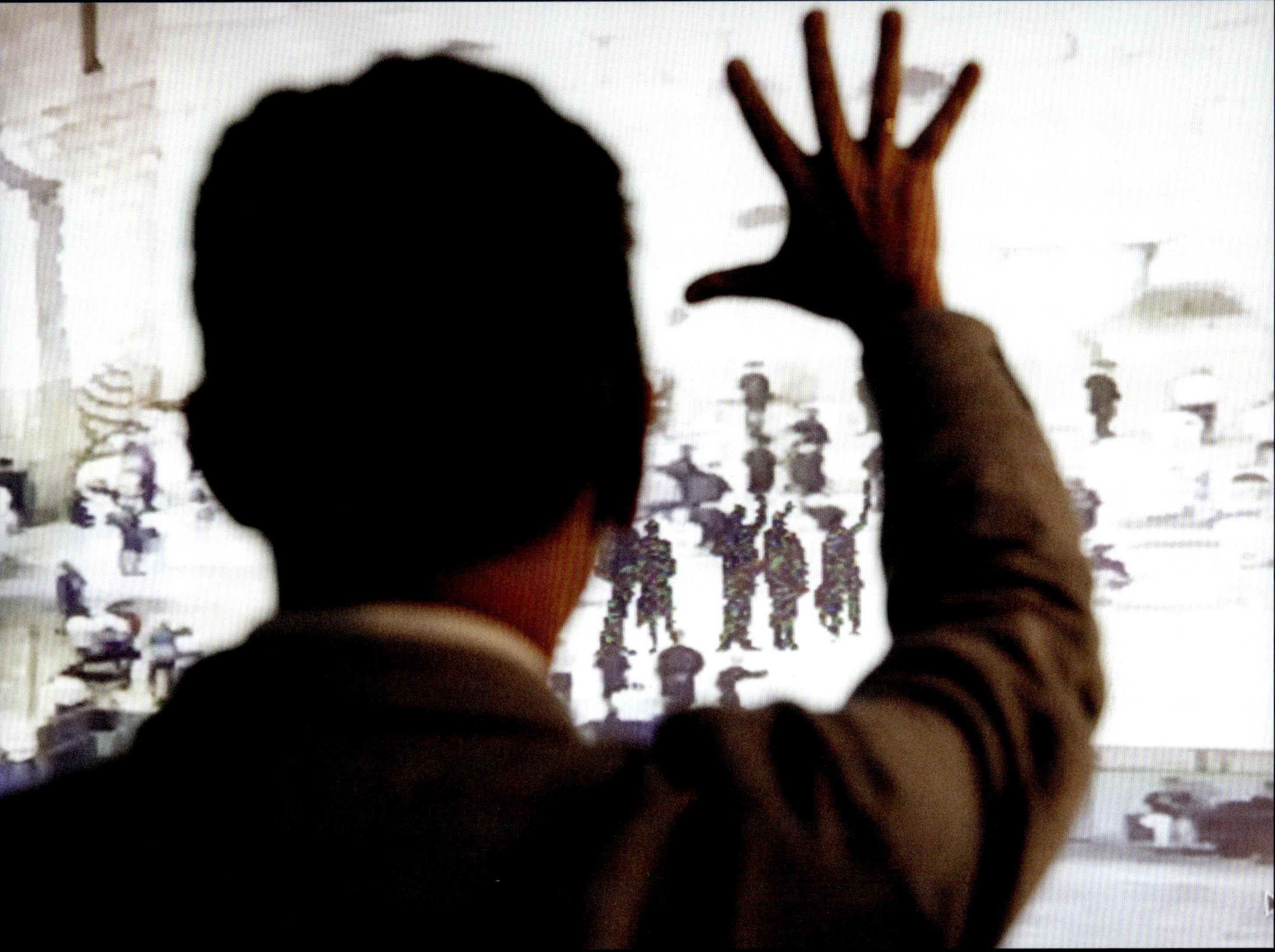

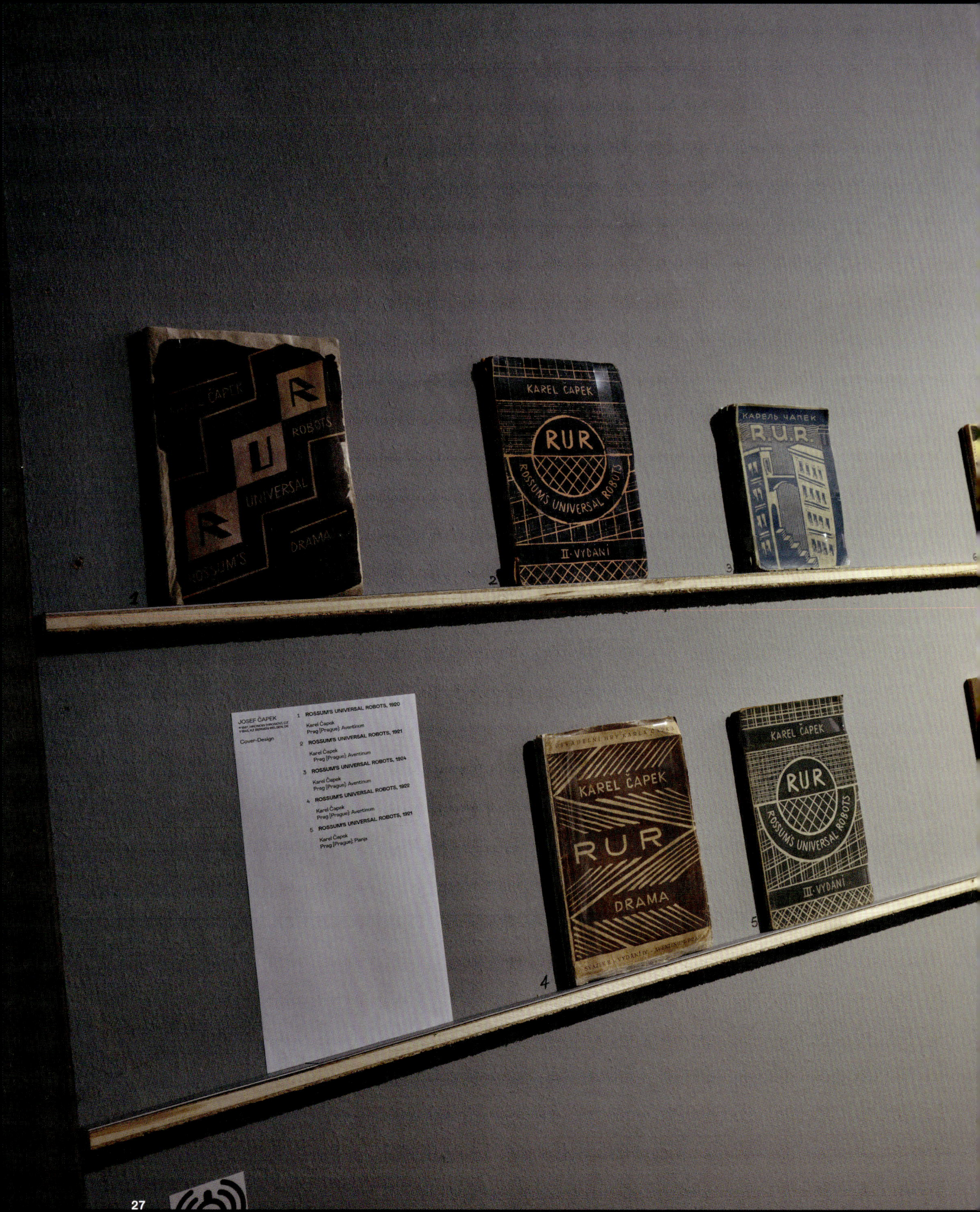
KAREL ČAPEK
RUR
ROSSUM'S UNIVERSAL ROBOTS
DRAMA
KAREL ČAPEK
RUR
ROSSUMS UNIVERSAL ROBOTS
II·VYDÁNÍ
КАРЕЛЬ ЧАПЕК
R.U.R.
JOSEF ČAPEK
Cover-Design
1 ROSSUM'S UNIVERSAL ROBOTS, 1920
Karel Čapek
Prag [Prague]: Aventinum
2 ROSSUM'S UNIVERSAL ROBOTS, 1921
Karel Čapek
Prag [Prague]: Aventinum
3 ROSSUM'S UNIVERSAL ROBOTS, 1924
Karel Čapek
Prag [Prague]: Aventinum
4 ROSSUM'S UNIVERSAL ROBOTS, 1922
Karel Čapek
Prag [Prague]: Aventinum
5 ROSSUM'S UNIVERSAL ROBOTS, 1921
Karel Čapek
Prag [Prague]: Planja
KAREL ČAPEK
RUR
DRAMA
KAREL ČAPEK
RUR
ROSSUMS UNIVERSAL ROBOTS
III·VYDÁNÍ

27

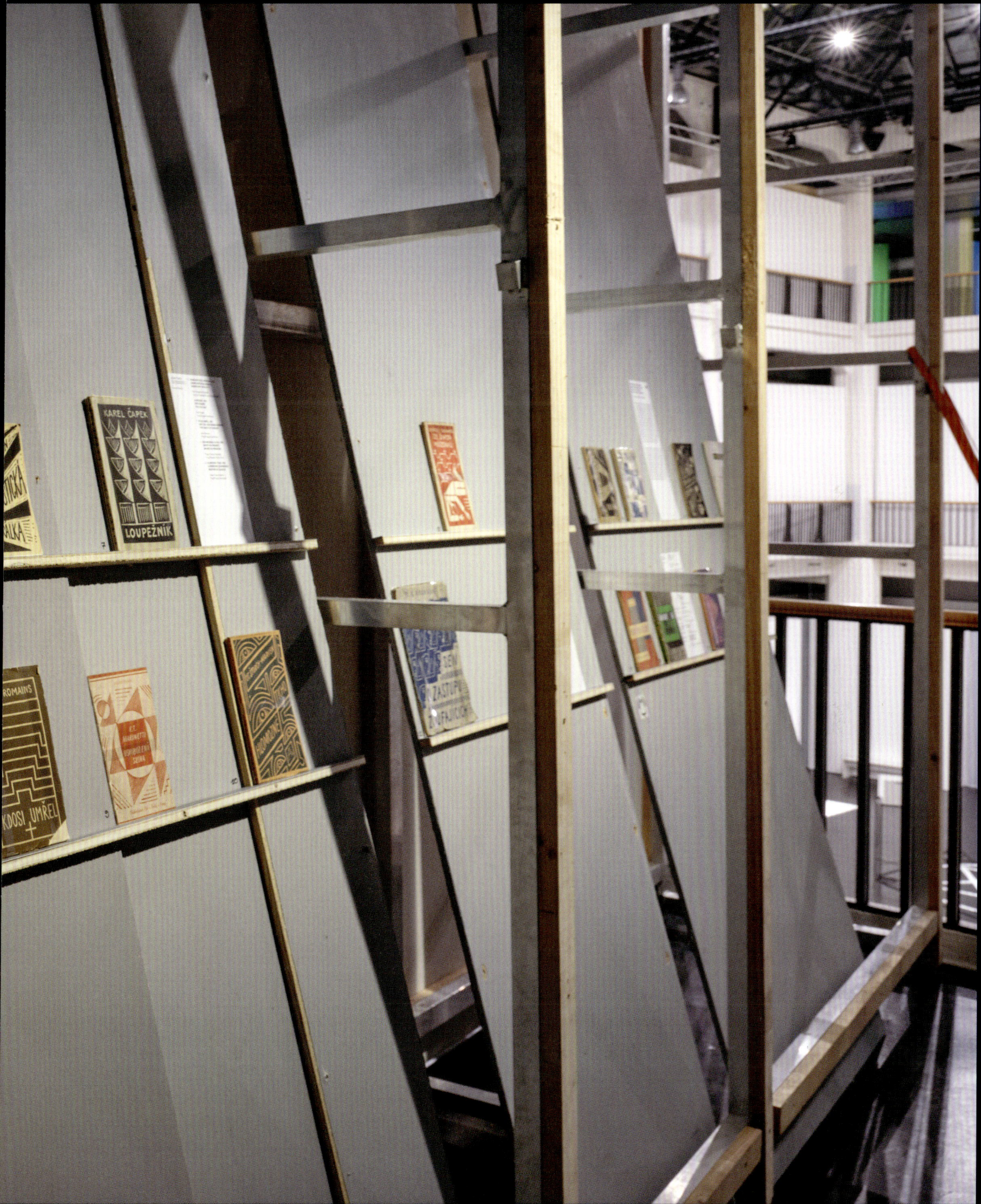
KAREL ČAPEK
LOUPEŽNÍK
ROMAINS
KDOSI UMŘEL

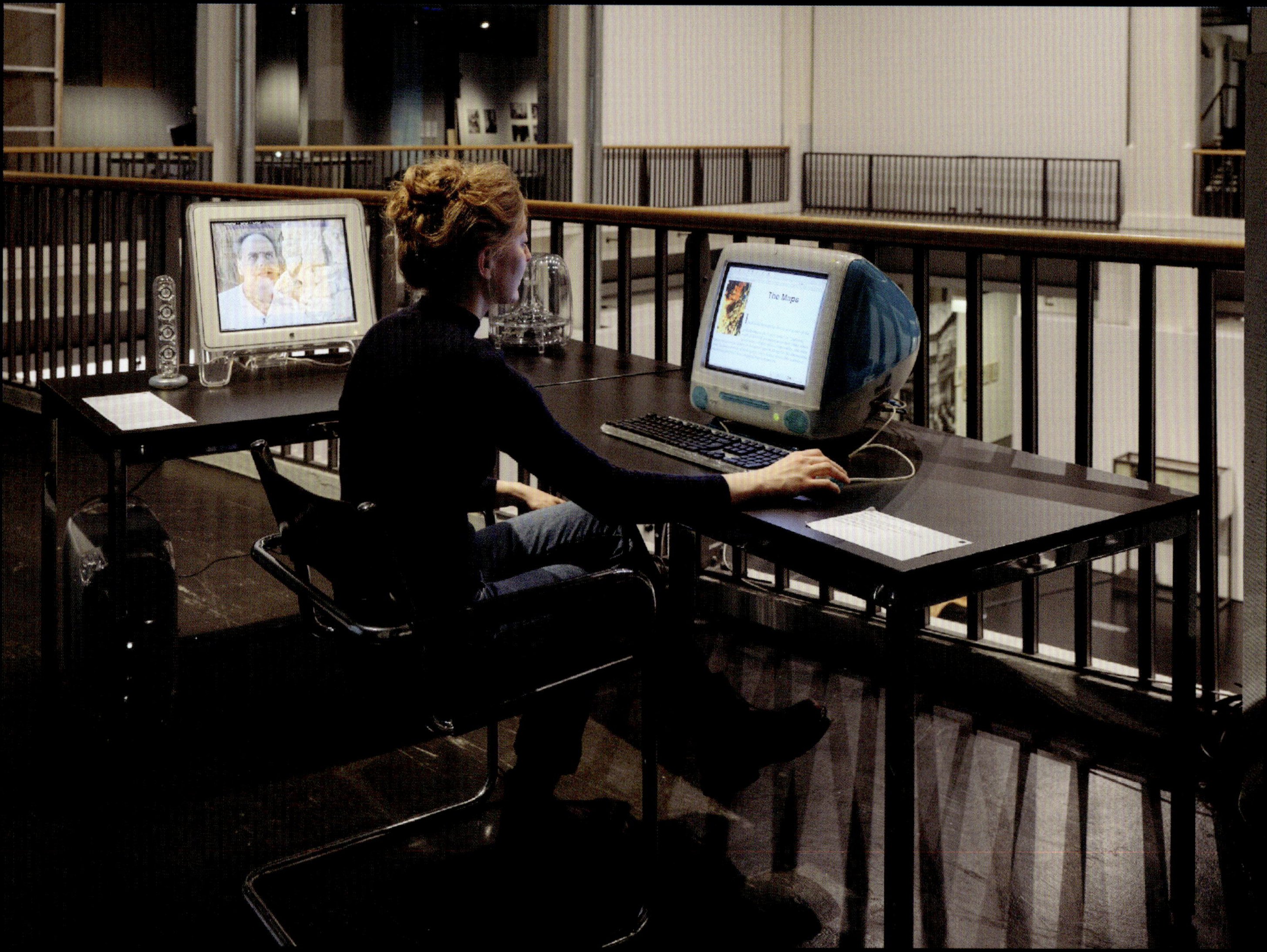

28

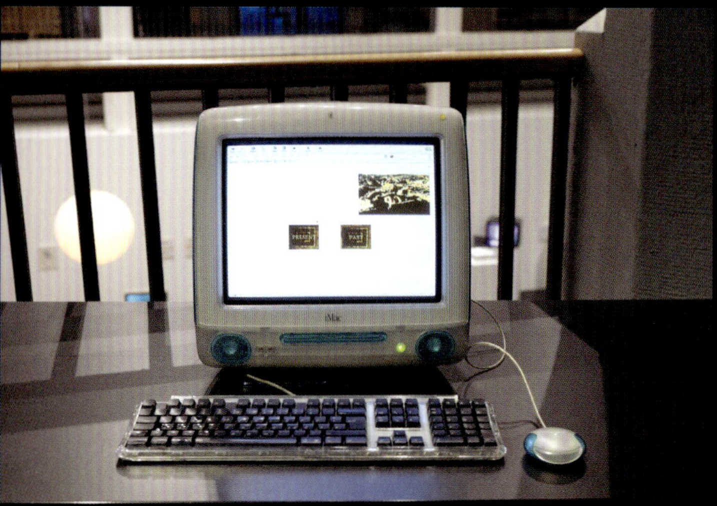

29

30

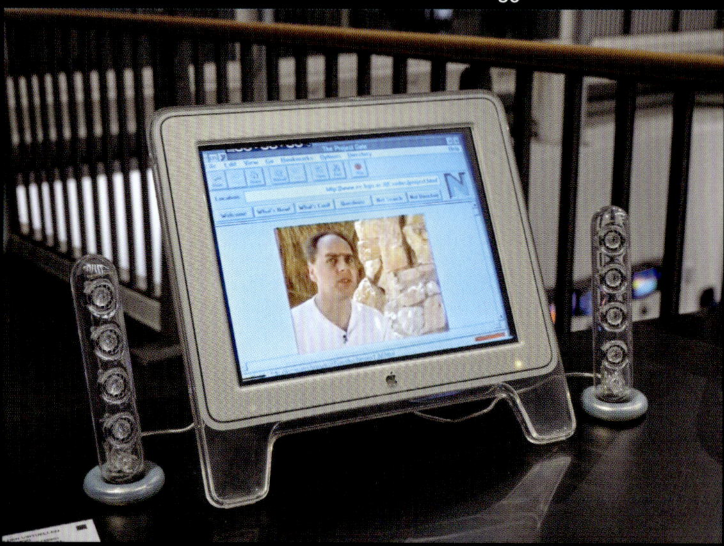

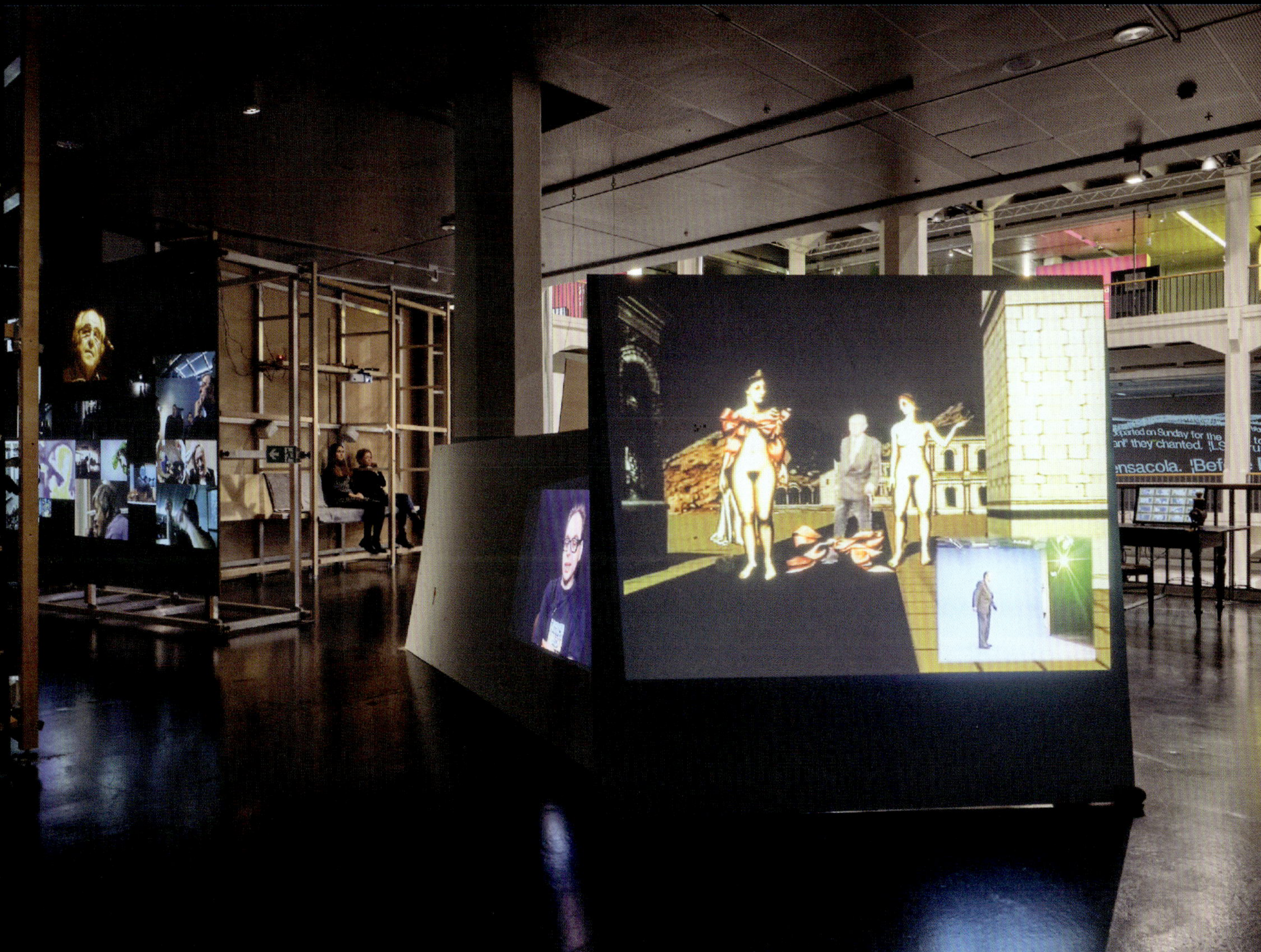

31

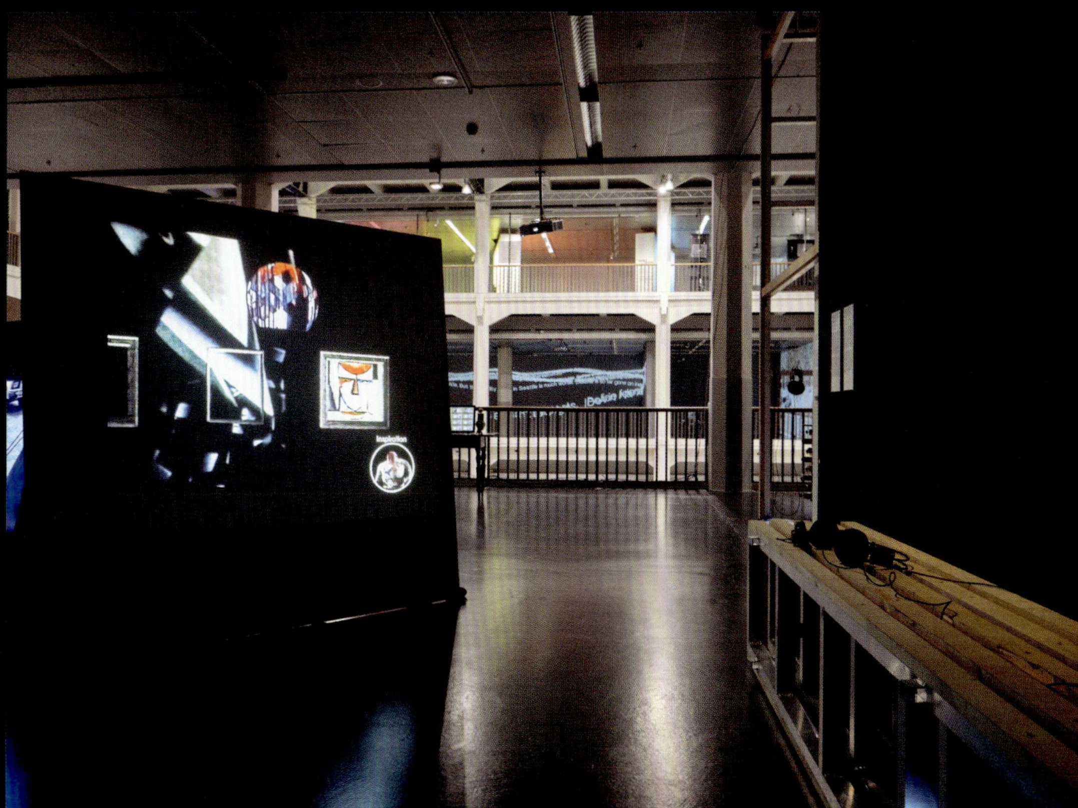

32

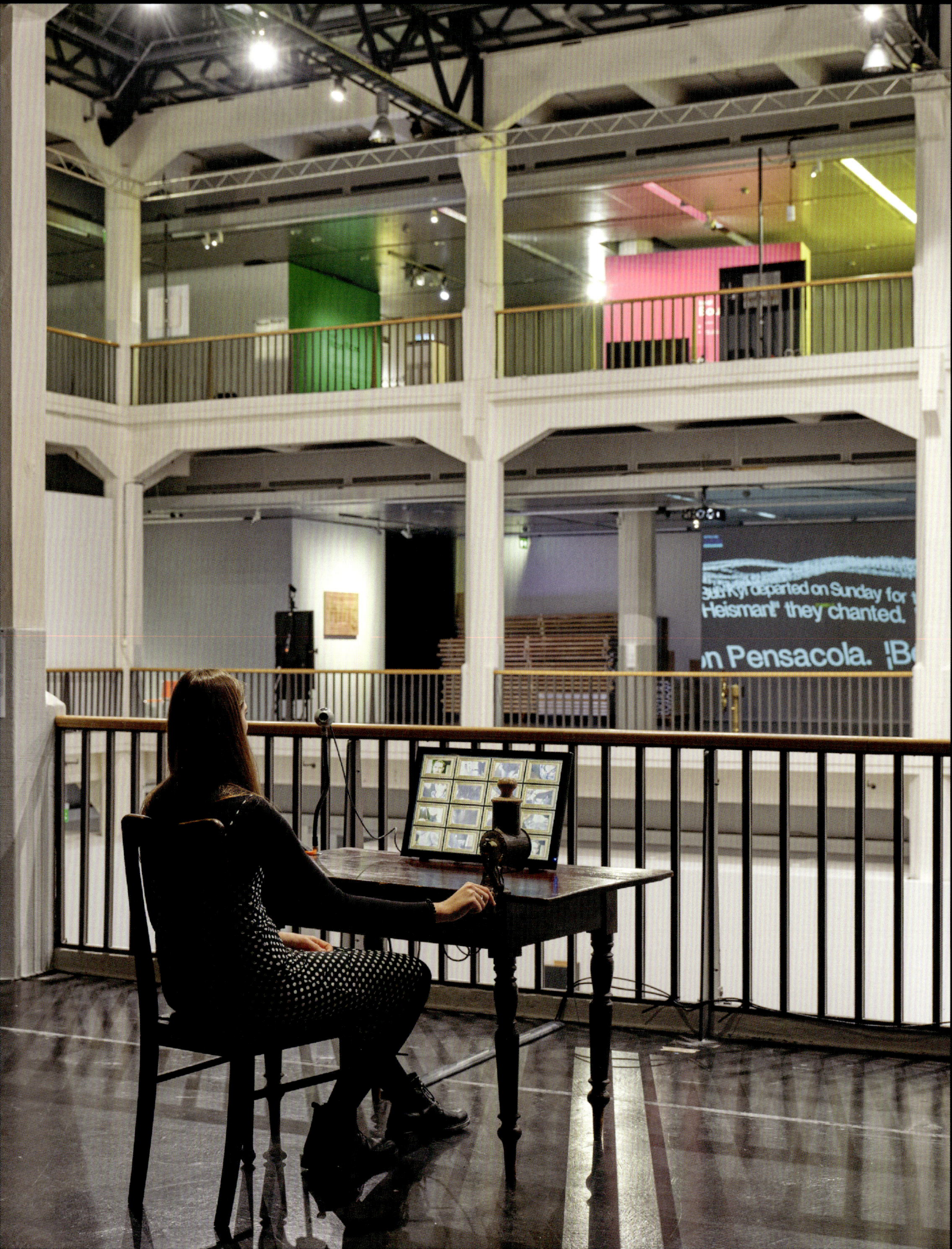
departed on Sunday for
Heisman!" they chanted.
Pensacola.

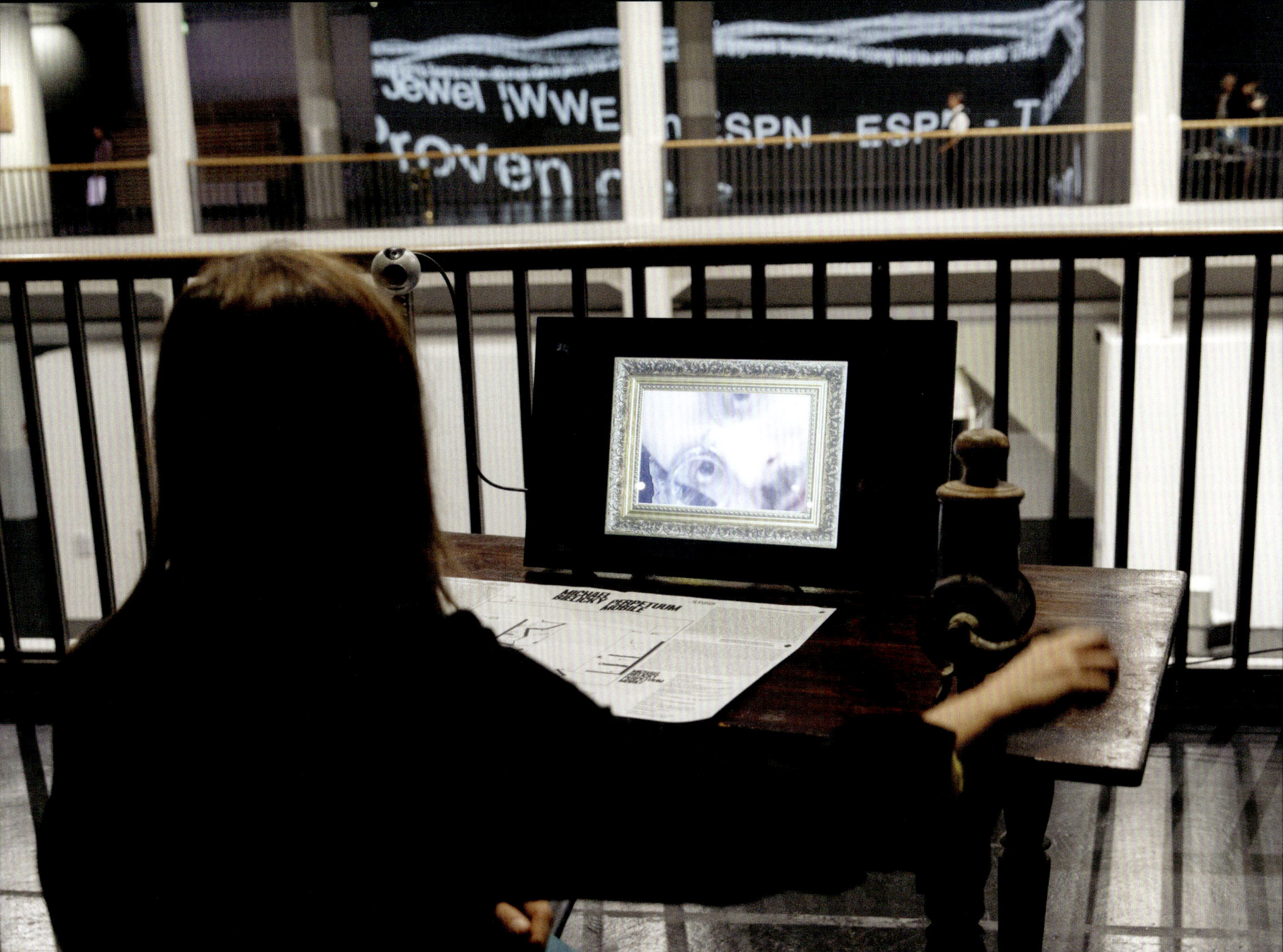
Jewel
WWE
ESPN
Proven

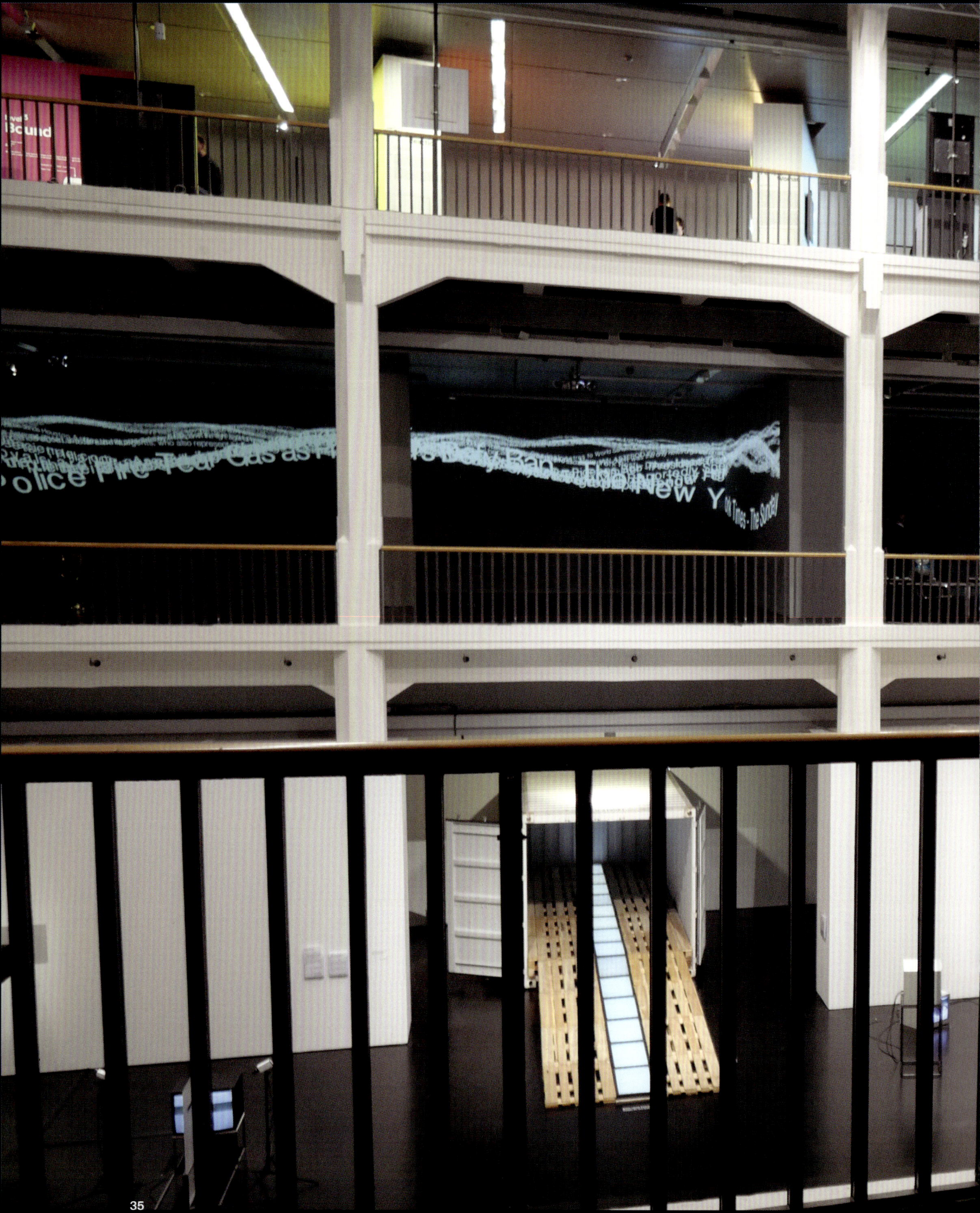

35

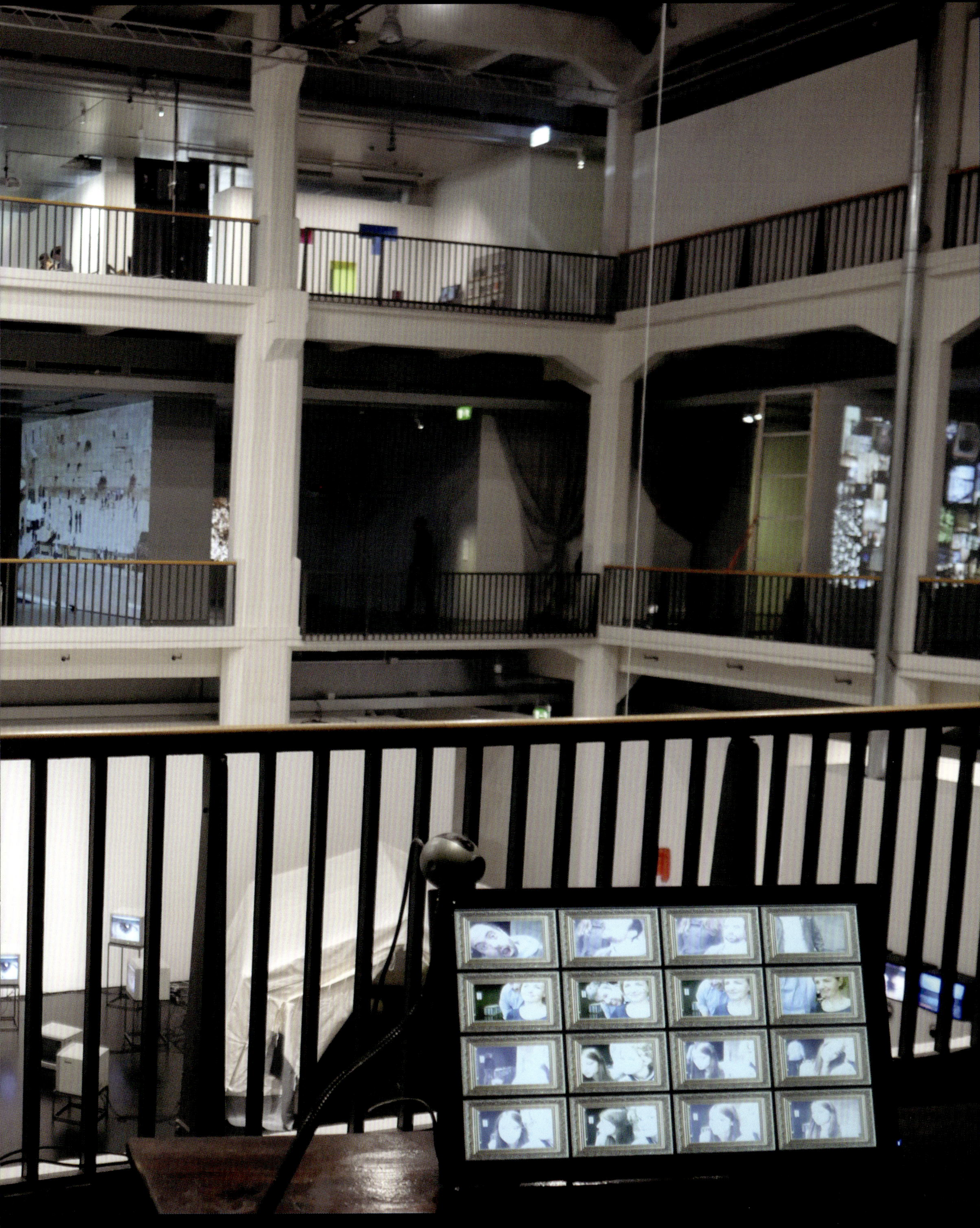

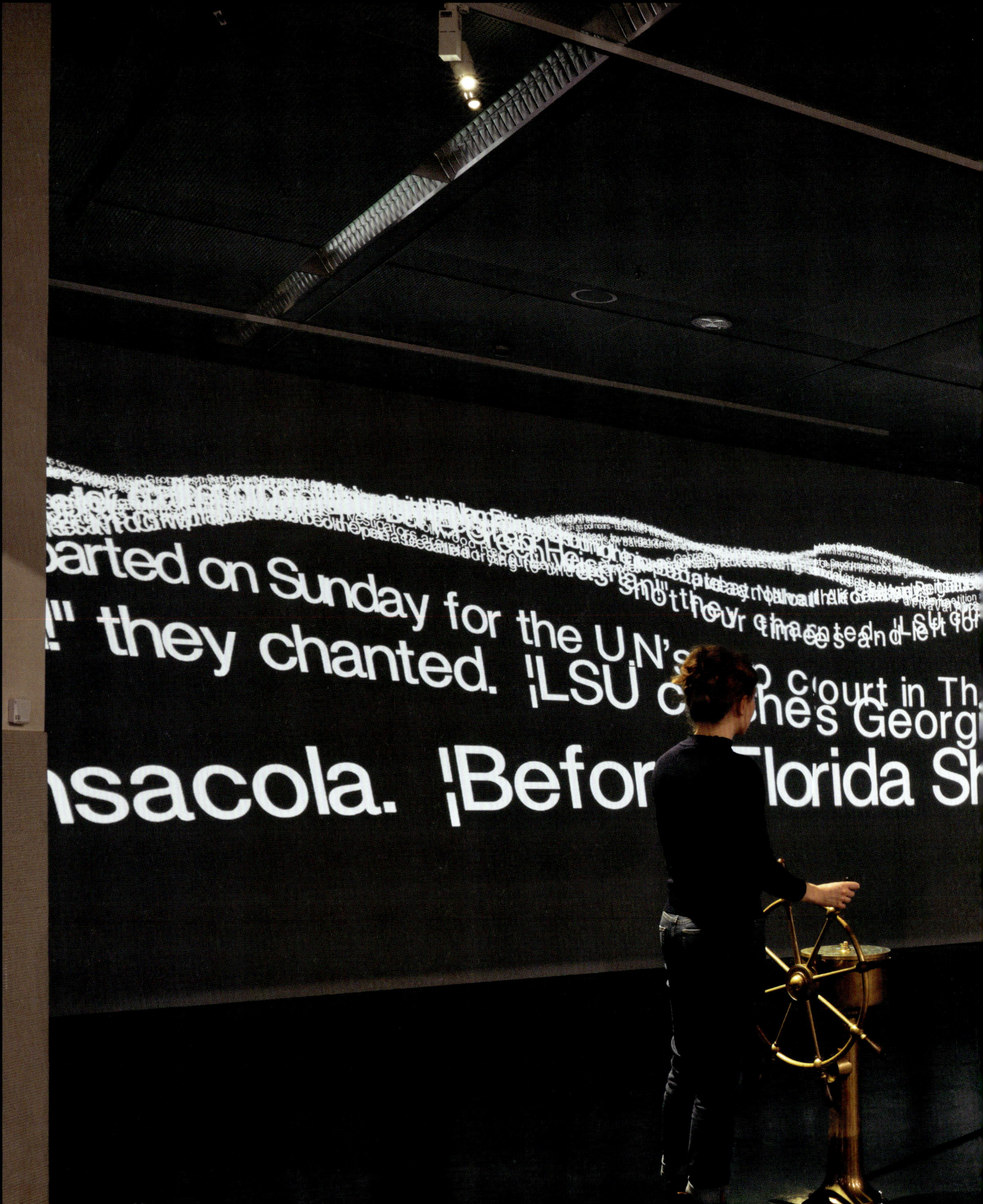
parted on Sunday for the UN's
" they chanted. ¡LSU
ourt in Th
he's Georg
nsacola. ¡Befor
lorida Sh

36

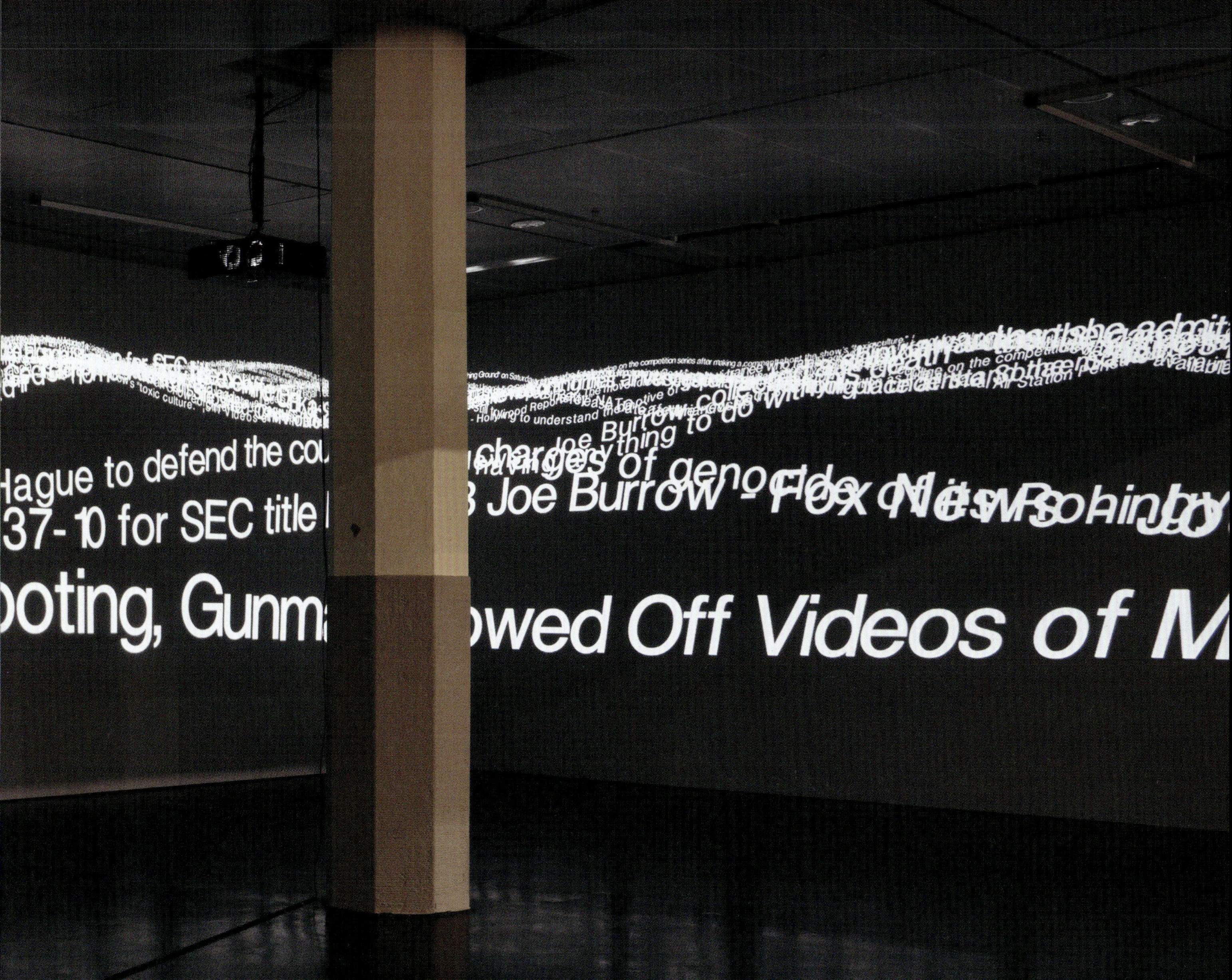
Hague to defend the cou
37-10 for SEC title
Joe Burrow - Fox News
ooting, Gunma
owed Off Videos of M

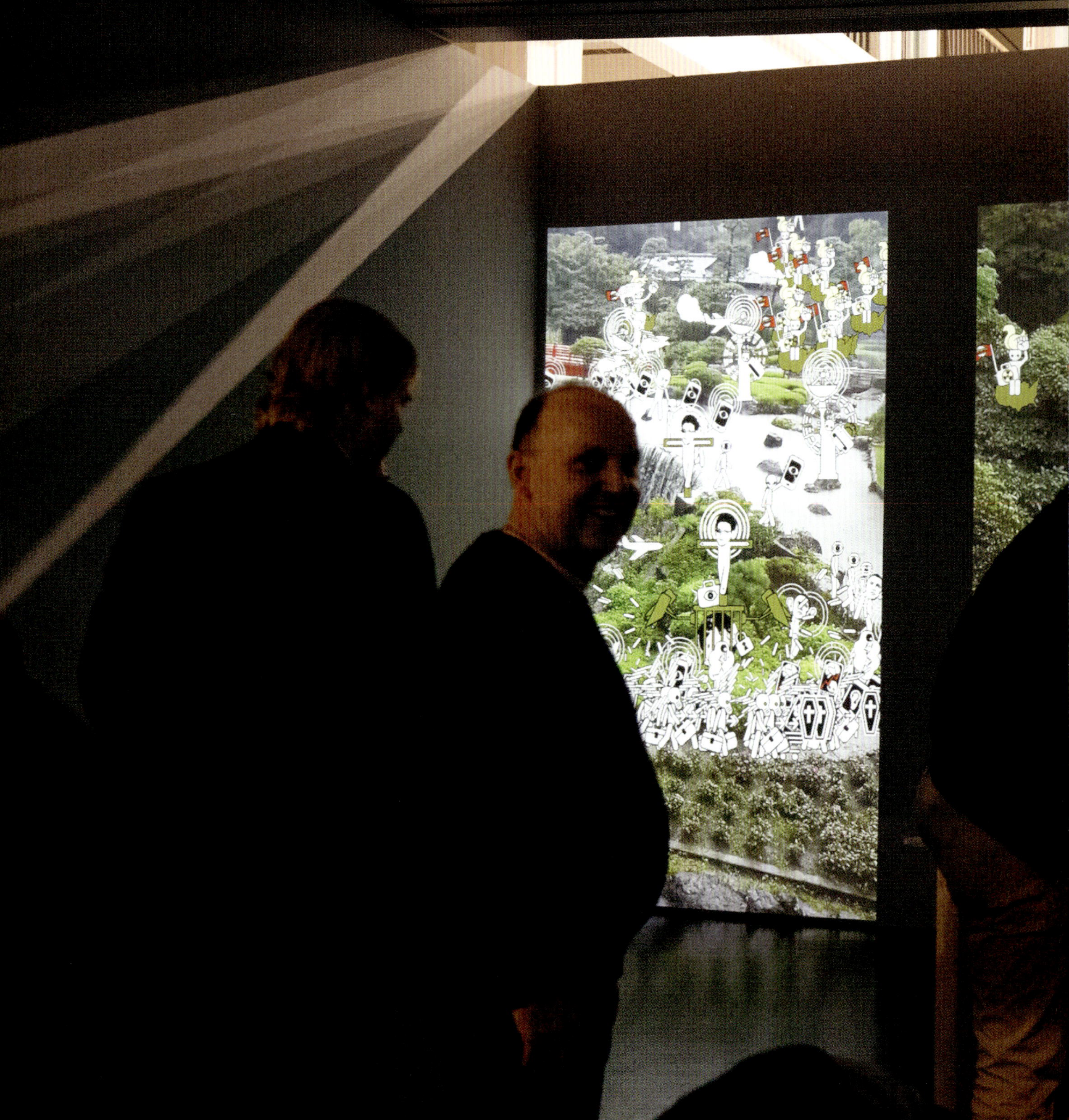

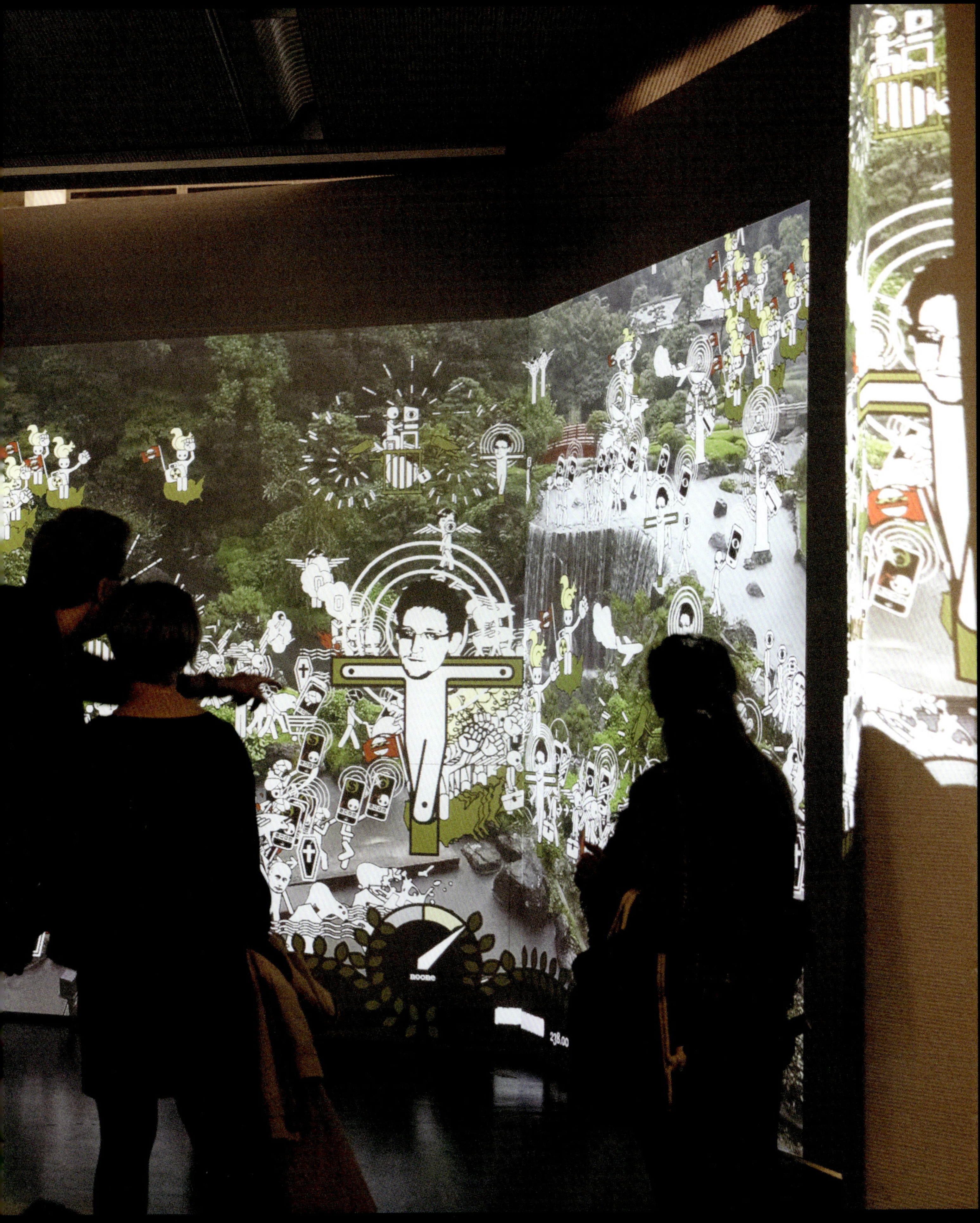

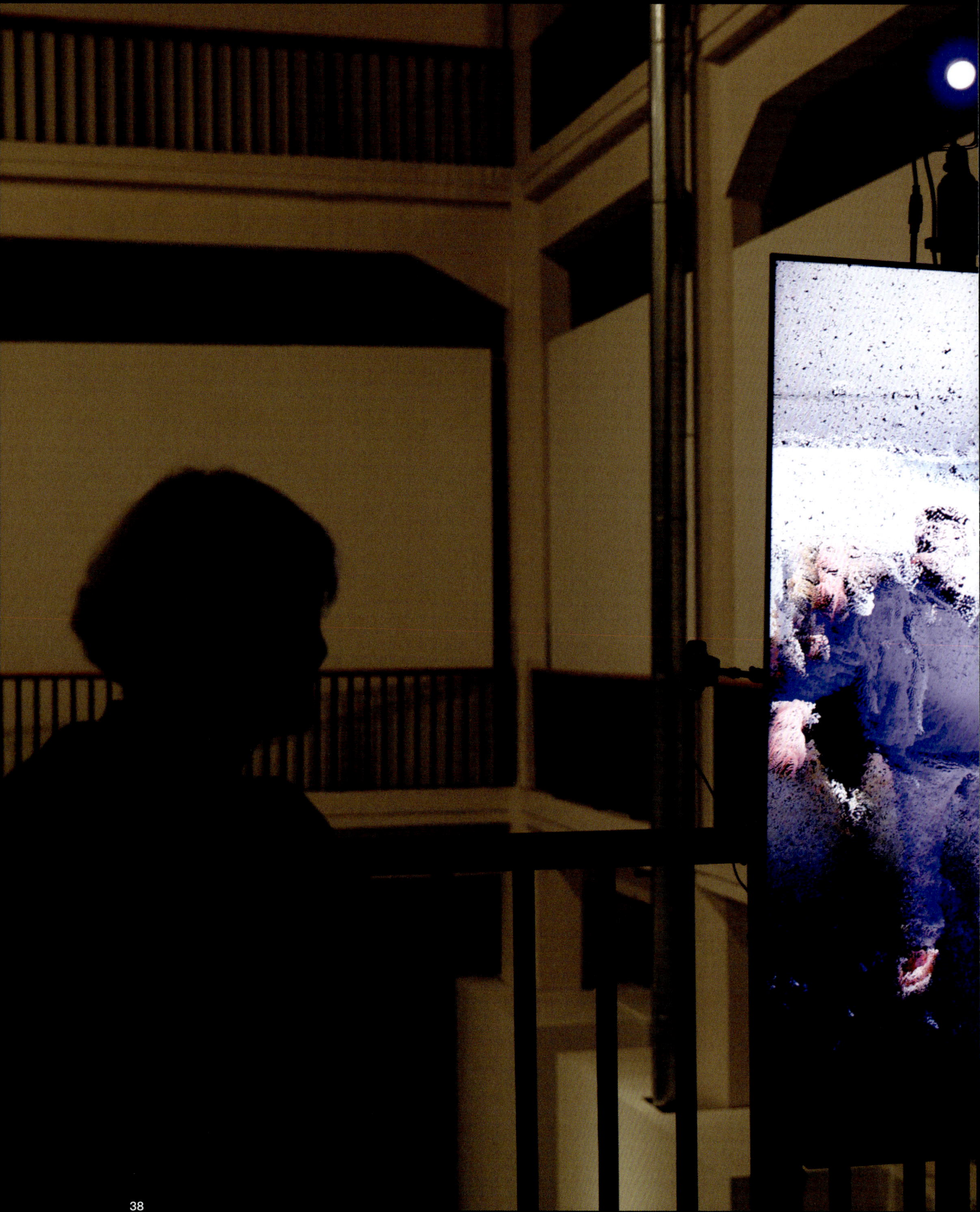

38

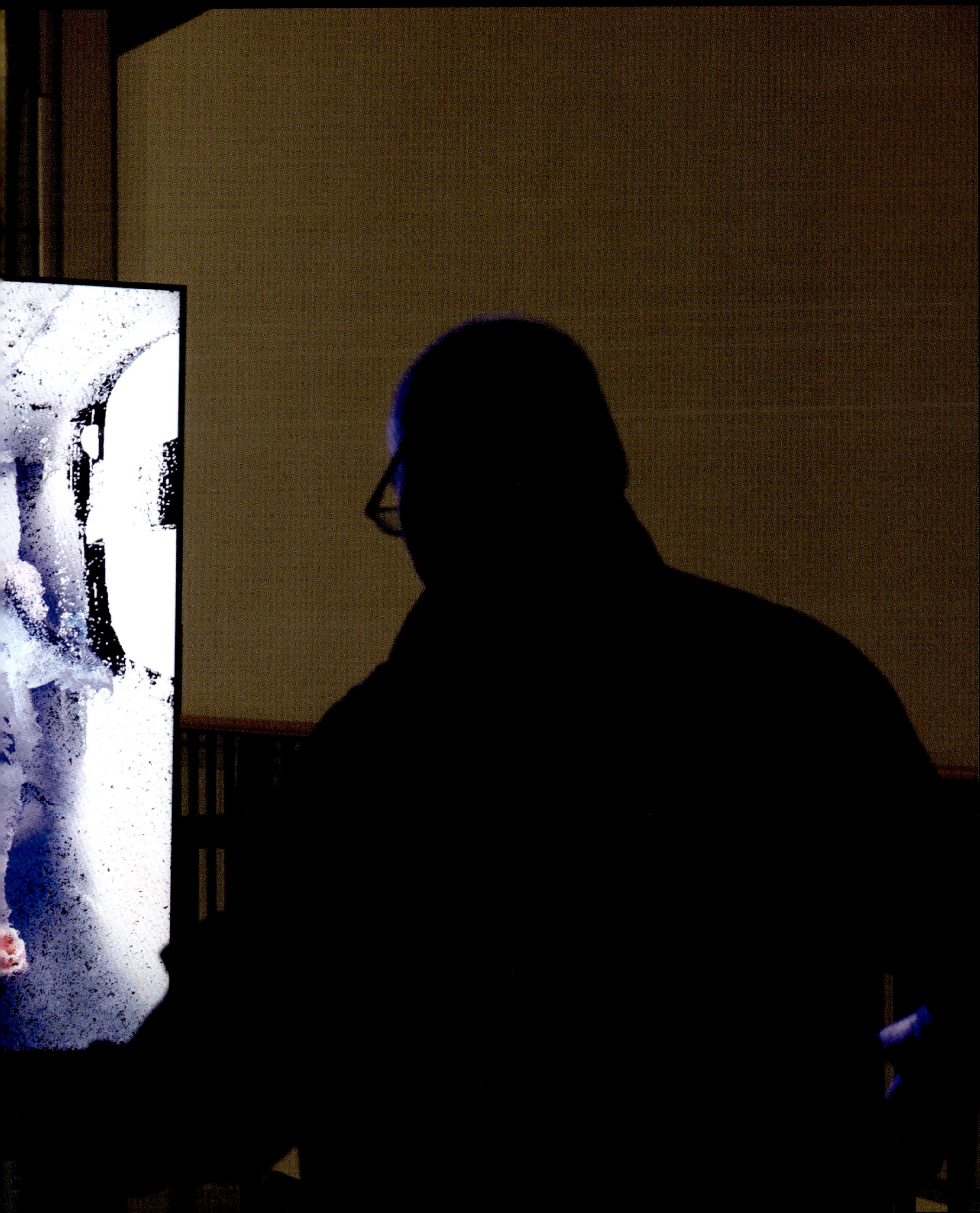

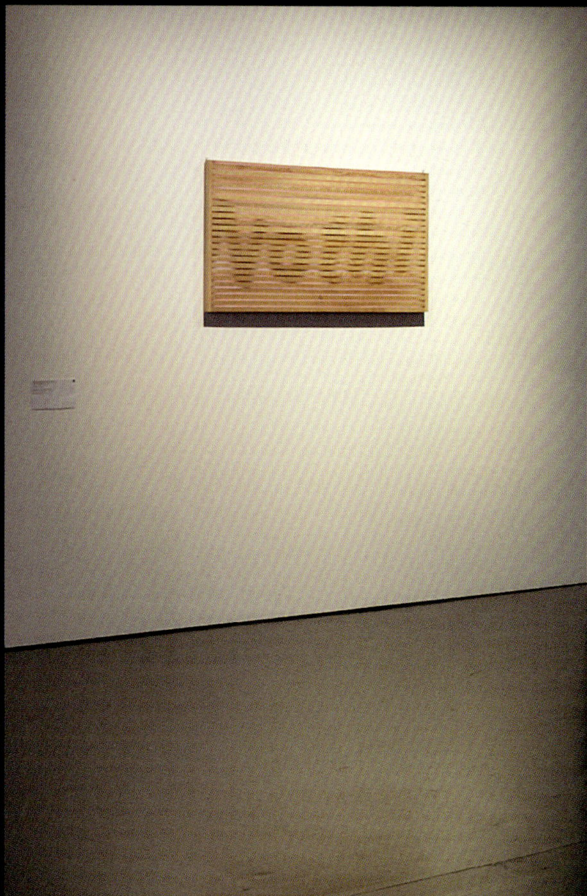

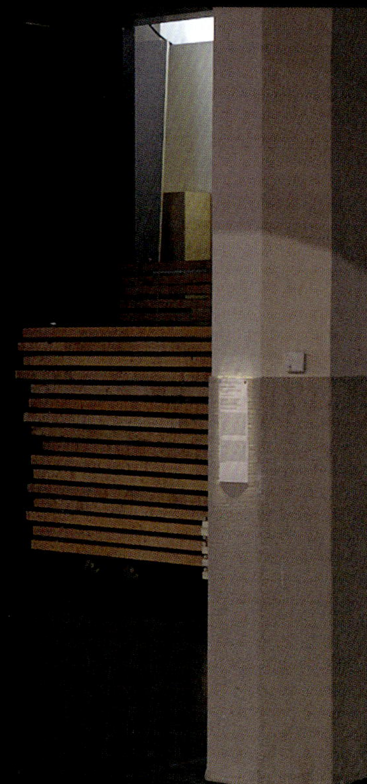

39

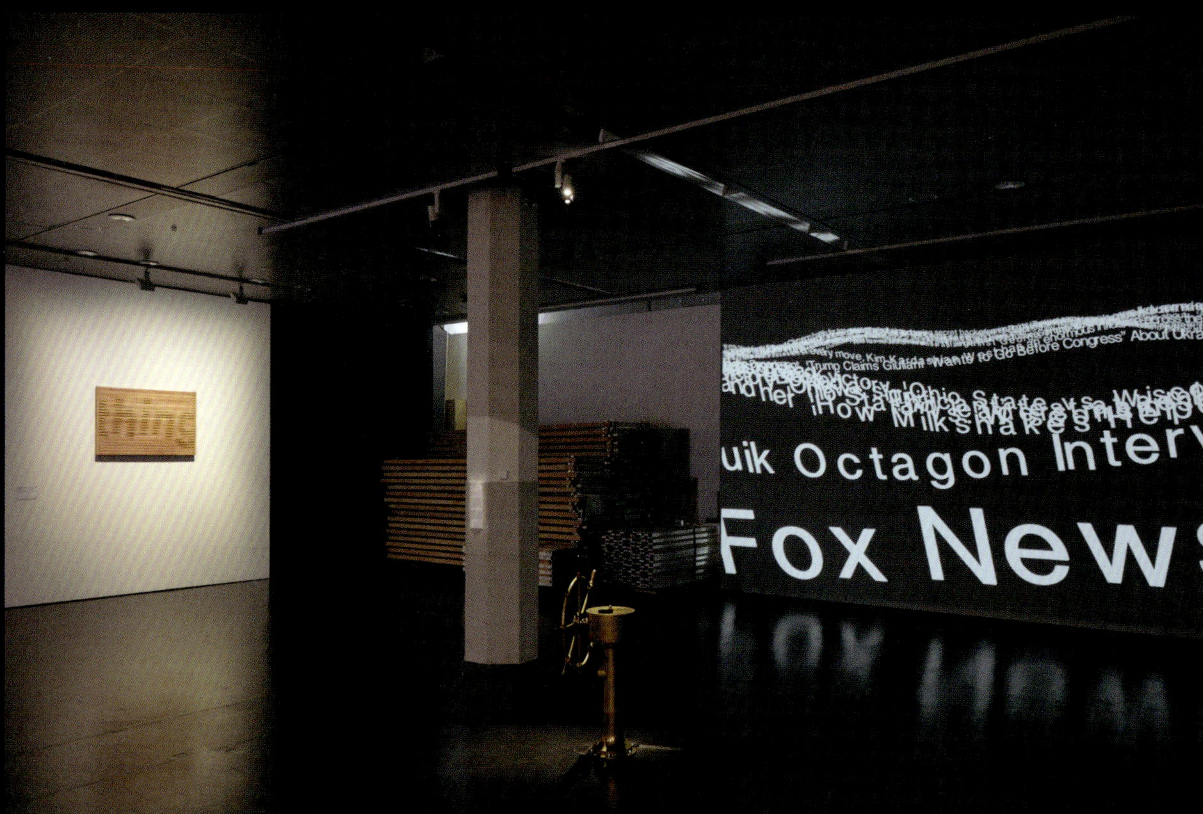

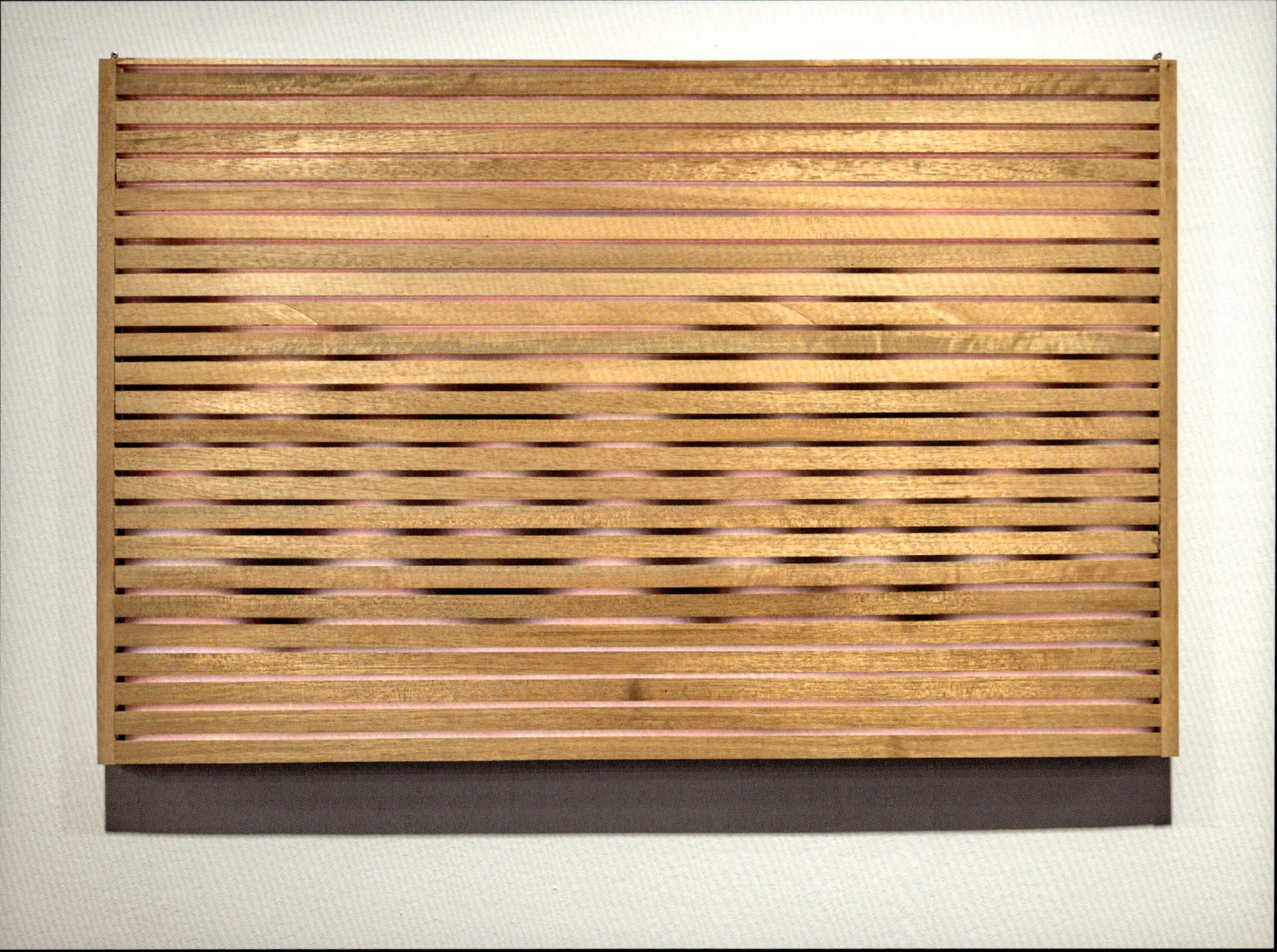

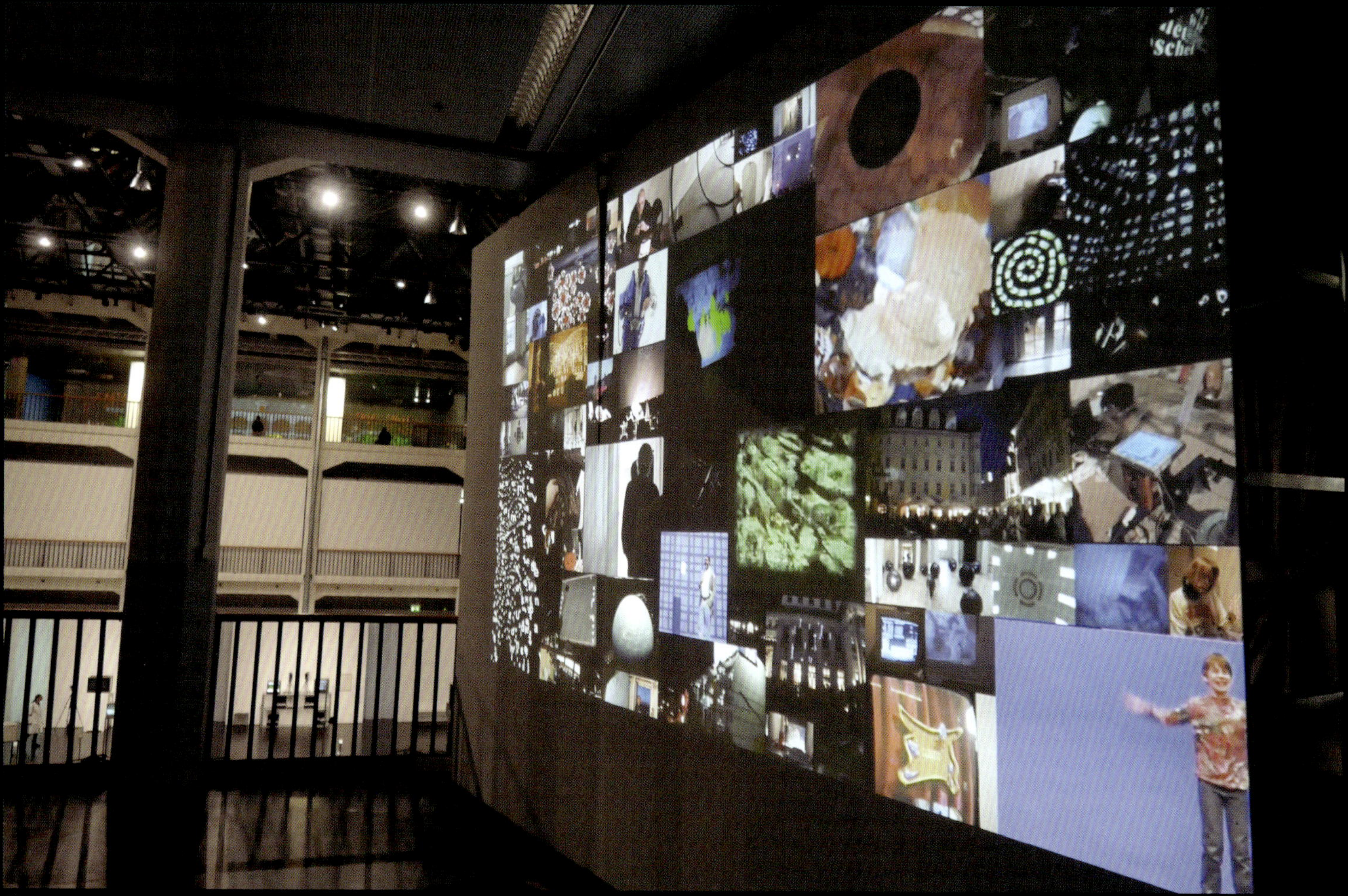

42

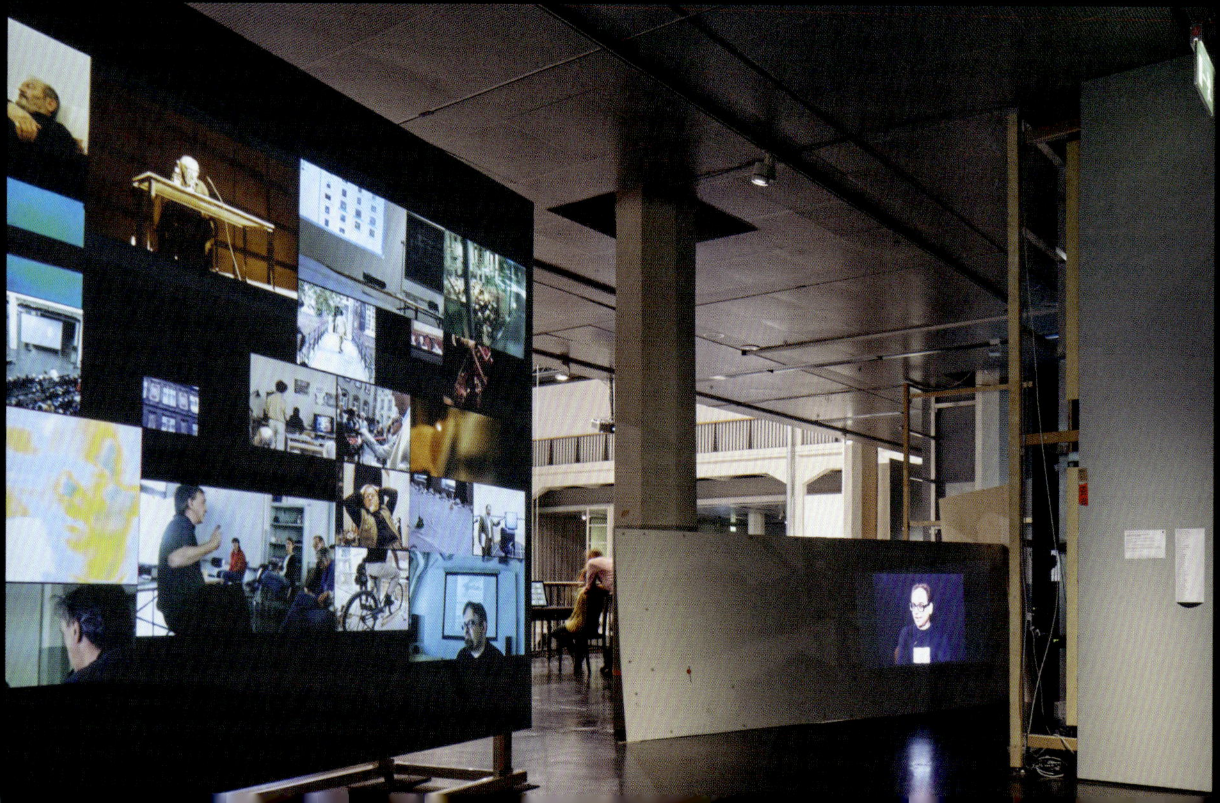

43

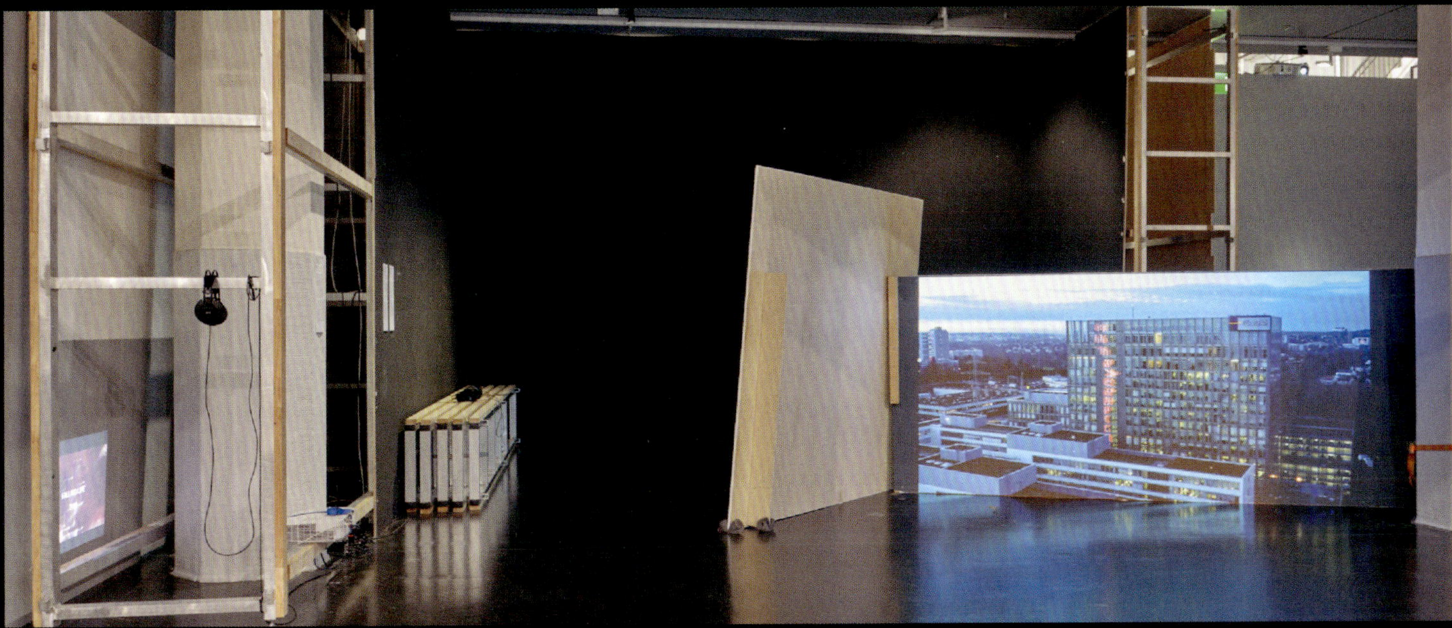

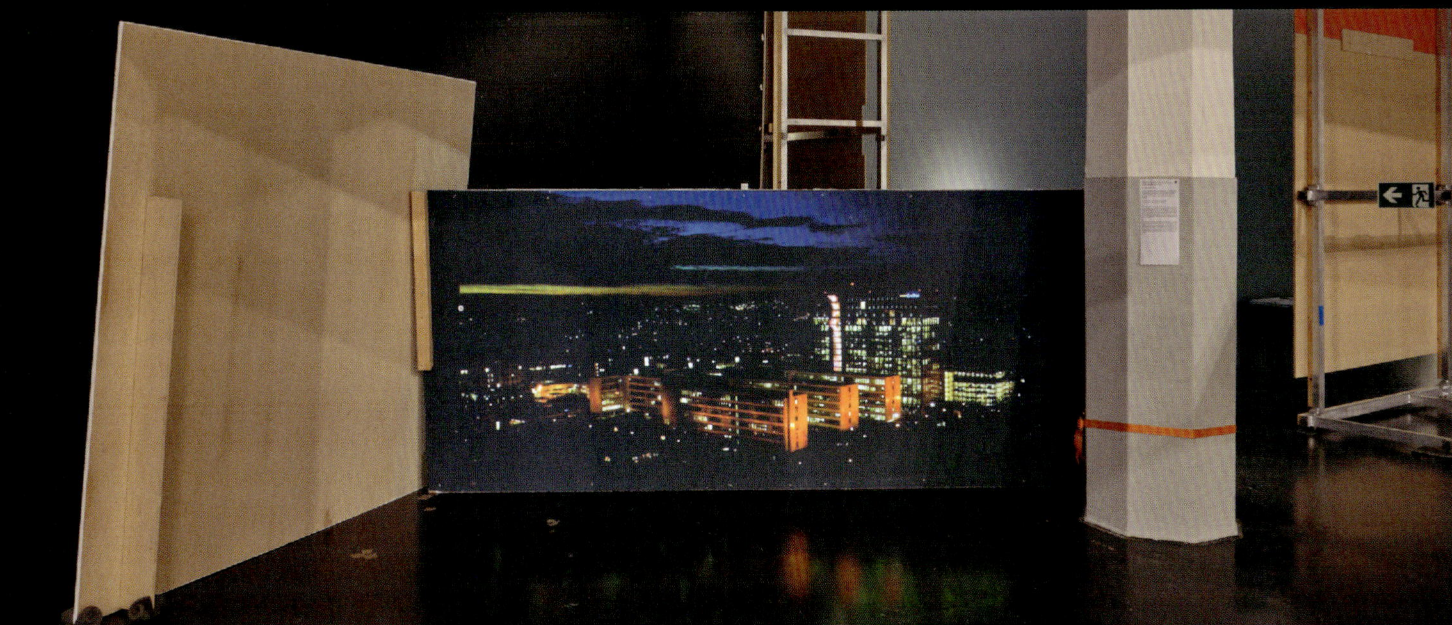

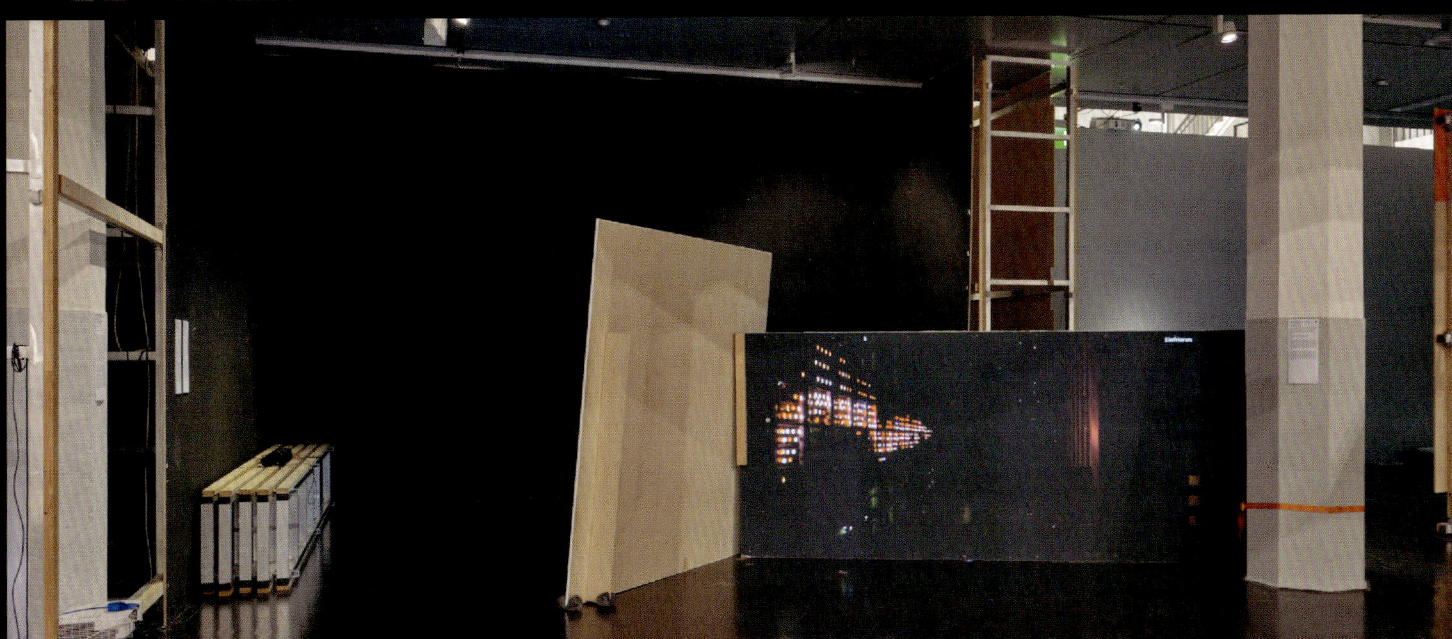

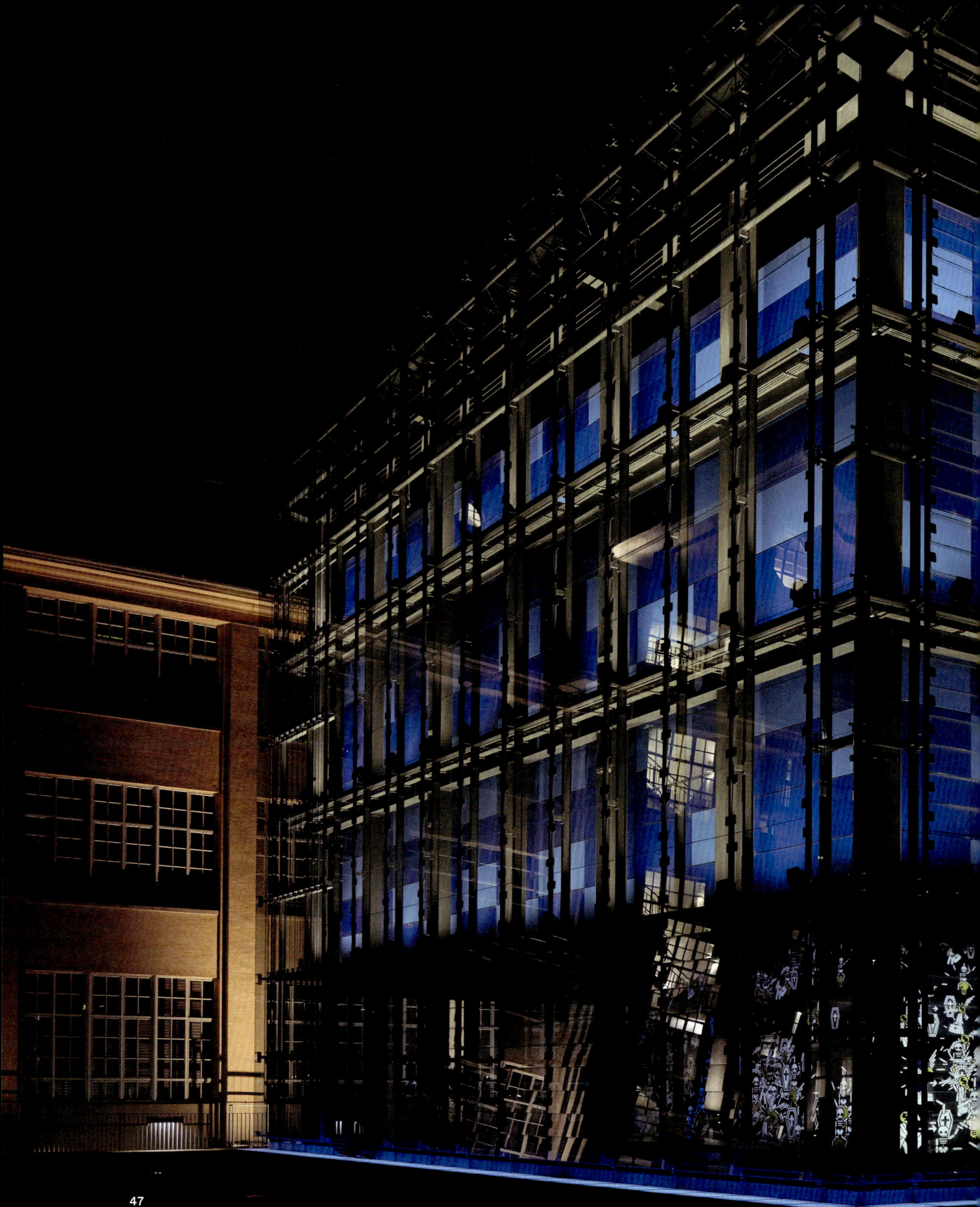

47

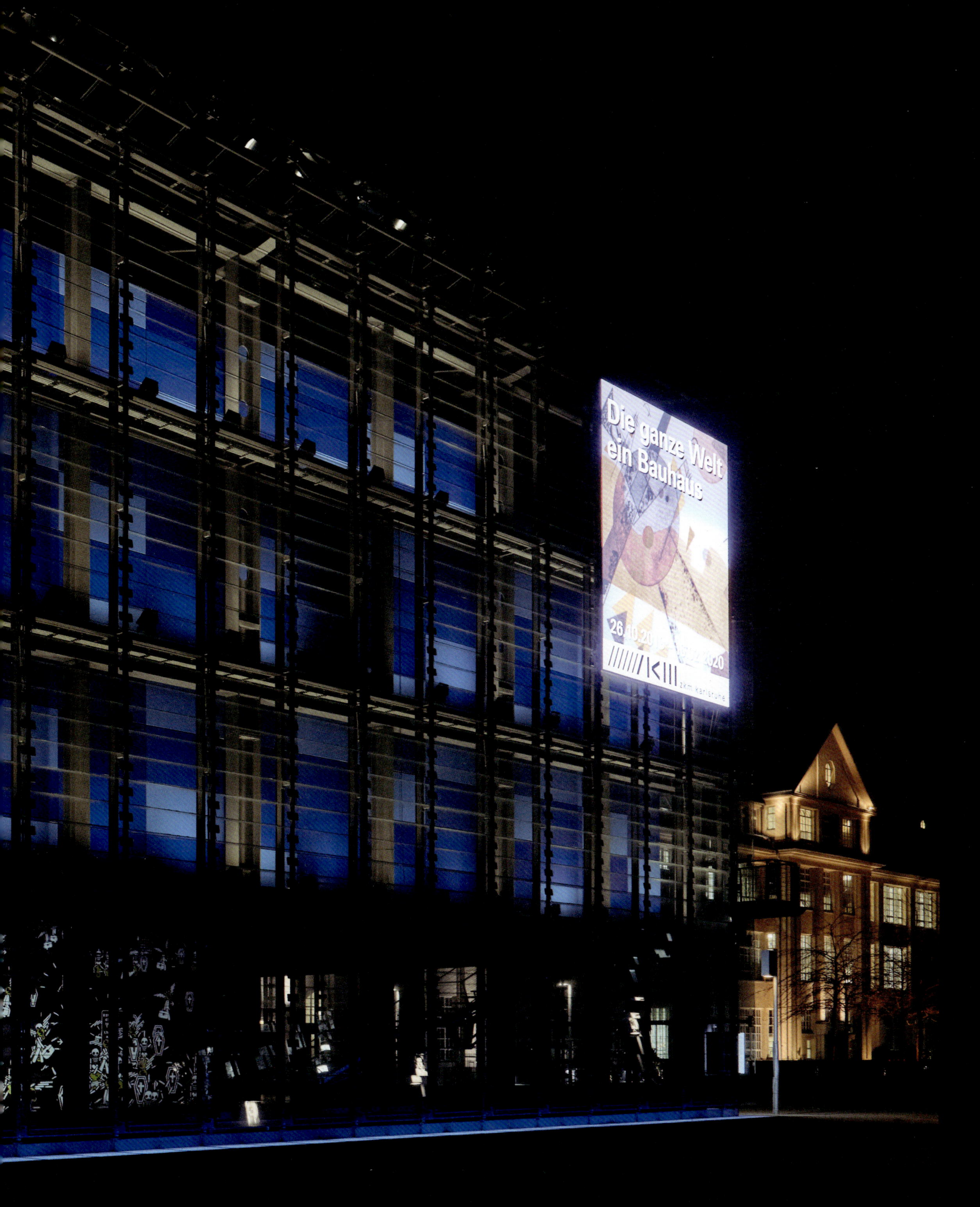
Die ganze Welt
ein Bauhaus
zkm karlsruhe

[01]–[04] *Data Labyrinth*, 2016, data-driven installation.
[05] left: *The Name,* 1990, video sculpture; right: *Menorah/Inventory,* 1989, video sculpture.
[06]–[07] *Perpetuum Mobile*, 2019, video sculpture.
[08]–[09] *Untitled*, 1980–85, analog photographs.
[10]–[11] Analog 8 mm film cameras collection.
[12] Works related to Michael Bielicky's studies with Nam June Paik, 1984–90.
[13]–[14] *Circulus Viciosus*, 1985, single-channel video.
[15]–[16] *Perpetuum Mobile II*, 1990, single-channel video.
[17]–[19] Exhibits related to Michael Bielicky's studies with Nam June Paik, 1984–90.
[20] *Next Year in Jerusalem (Homage to Rabbi Loew)*, 1988, single-channel video.
[21] *Fat Corner*, with Ricardo Peredo, 1987, single-channel video.
[22]–[24] *Crossings: The Last Path of Walter Benjamin*, 2002, single-channel video.
[25]–[26] *This Year in Jerusalem*, 2019, real-time telematic installation.
[27] Book collection with focus on the Czech authors Josef Čapek, Karel Teige, Zdeněk Pešánek, and others.
[28] –[30] *Exodus,* 1995, teleperformance. Documentation by Israeli television.
[31] *Delvaux's Dream*, 1998–99, immersive virtual reality environment. Documentation.
[32] *Room with a View*, 2000, immersive interactive installation. Documentation.
[33]–[34] *Exhibition (On the Net)*, 2019, web-based digital installation.
[35] View into the exhibition space.
[36] *Columbus 2.0*, 2019, data-driven interactive installation.
[37] *Garden of Error and Decay*, 2019, data-driven interactive installation.
[38] *Narcissistic Machine*, 2018, data-driven interactive installation.
[39]–[41] *Ex Nihilo*, 2019, data-driven digital installation.
[42] *Rawmaterial*, 2019, 100-channel video.
[43] *Subjektprojektionen* [subject projections], 2019, 50-channel video.
[44-46] *Flashouse,*2018, data-driven installation on facade. Documentation.
[47] *Lost* (2017), 2019, data-driven immersive installation, ZKM Kubus| Karlsruhe, Germany.

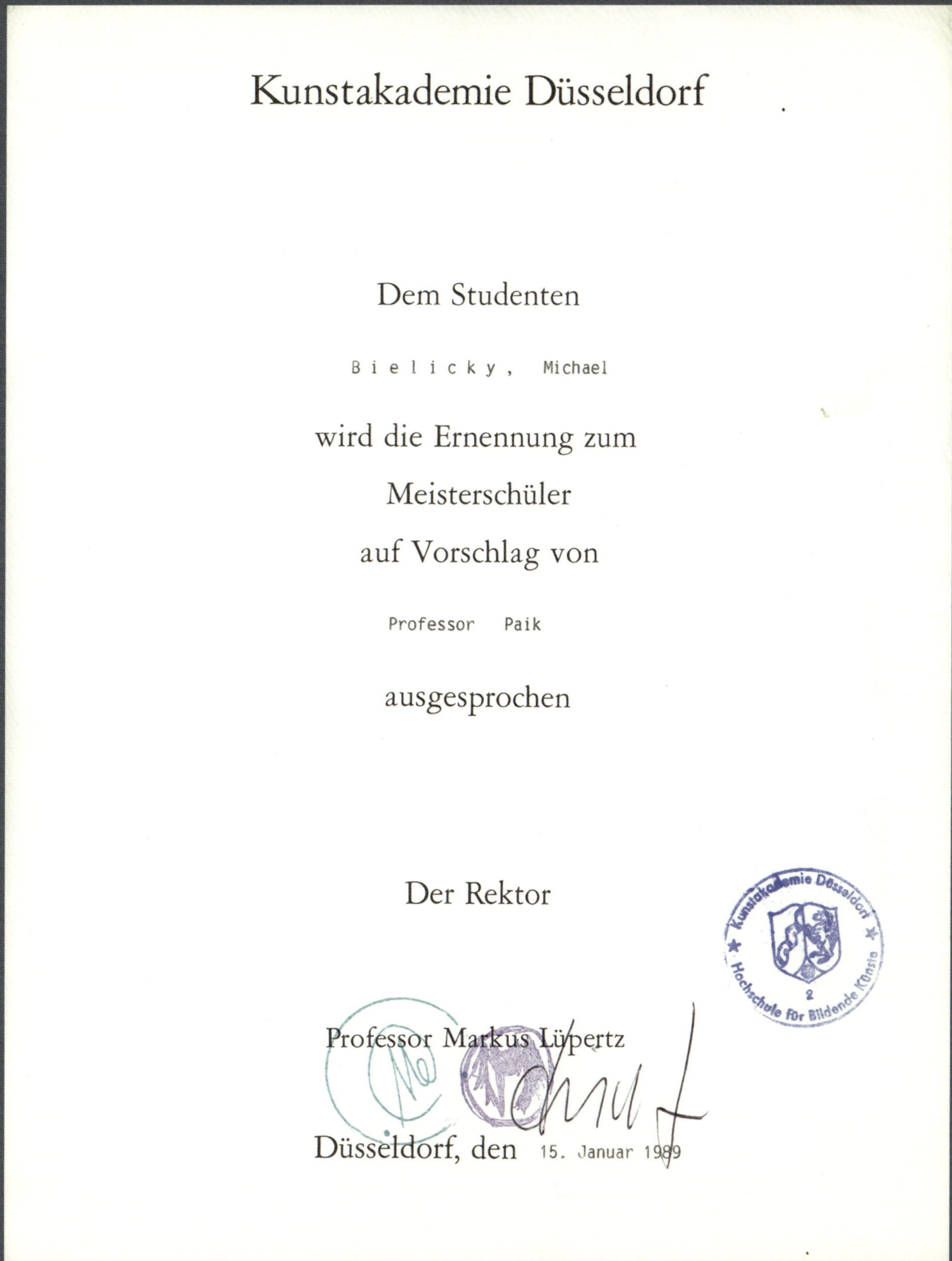

Kunstakademie Düsseldorf

Dem Studenten

B i e l i c k y , Michael

wird die Ernennung zum

Meisterschüler

auf Vorschlag von

Professor Paik

ausgesprochen

Der Rektor

Kunstakademie Düsseldorf
2
Hochschule für Bildende Künste

Professor Markus Lüpertz

Düsseldorf, den 15. Januar 1989

Michael Bielicky, Master class diploma, class of Nam-June Paik, Düsseldorf, 1989.

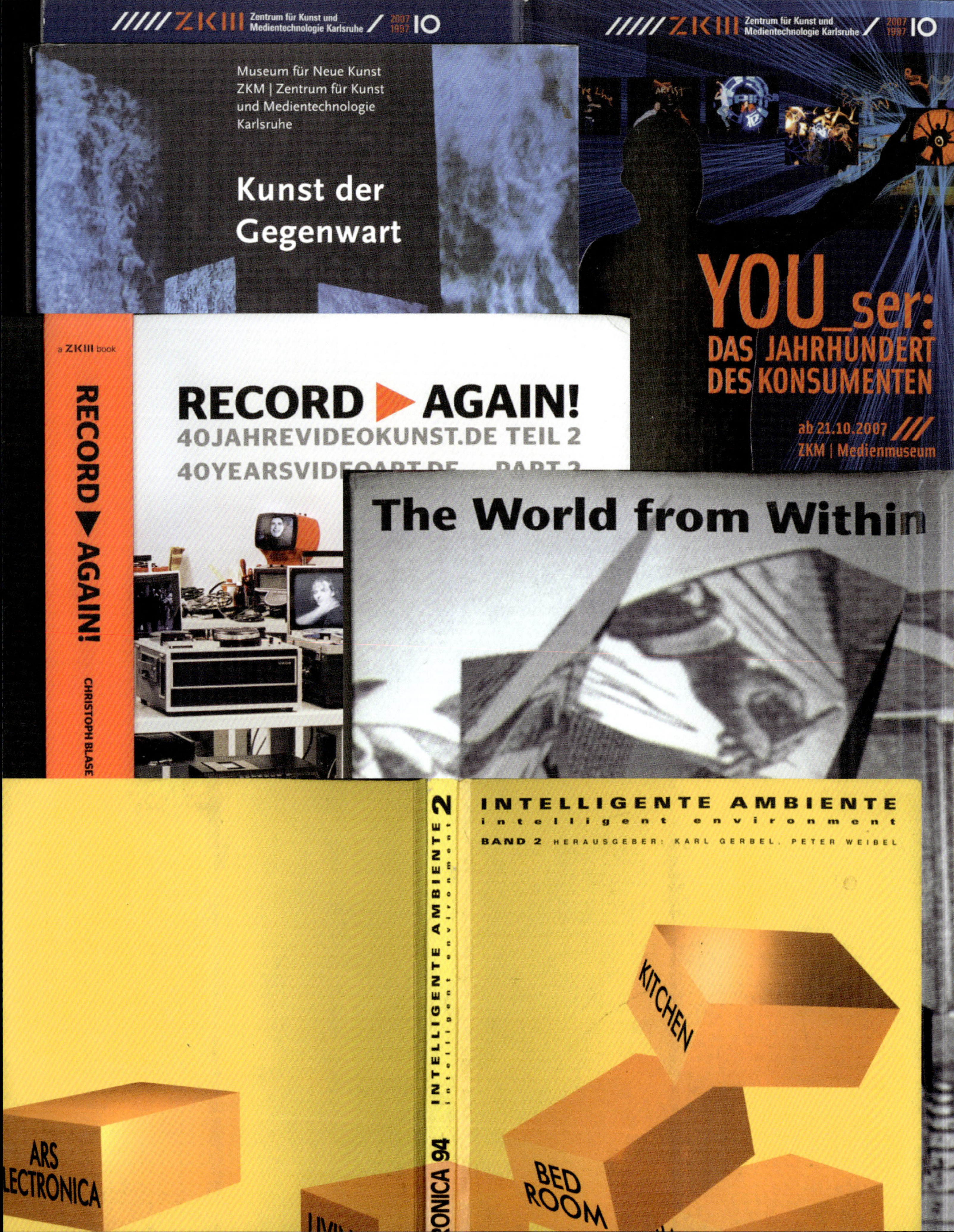
ZKM Zentrum für Kunst und Medientechnologie Karlsruhe 2007 1997 10
Museum für Neue Kunst
ZKM | Zentrum für Kunst und Medientechnologie Karlsruhe
Kunst der Gegenwart
ZKM Zentrum für Kunst und Medientechnologie Karlsruhe 2007 1997 10
YOU_ser:
DAS JAHRHUNDERT DES KONSUMENTEN
ab 21.10.2007
ZKM | Medienmuseum
a ZKM book
RECORD AGAIN!
CHRISTOPH BLASE
RECORD AGAIN!
40JAHREVIDEOKUNST.DE TEIL 2
The World from Within
INTELLIGENTE AMBIENTE 2
intelligent environment
INTELLIGENTE AMBIENTE
intelligent environment
BAND 2 HERAUSGEBER: KARL GERBEL, PETER WEIBEL
KITCHEN
BED ROOM
ARS ELECTRONICA

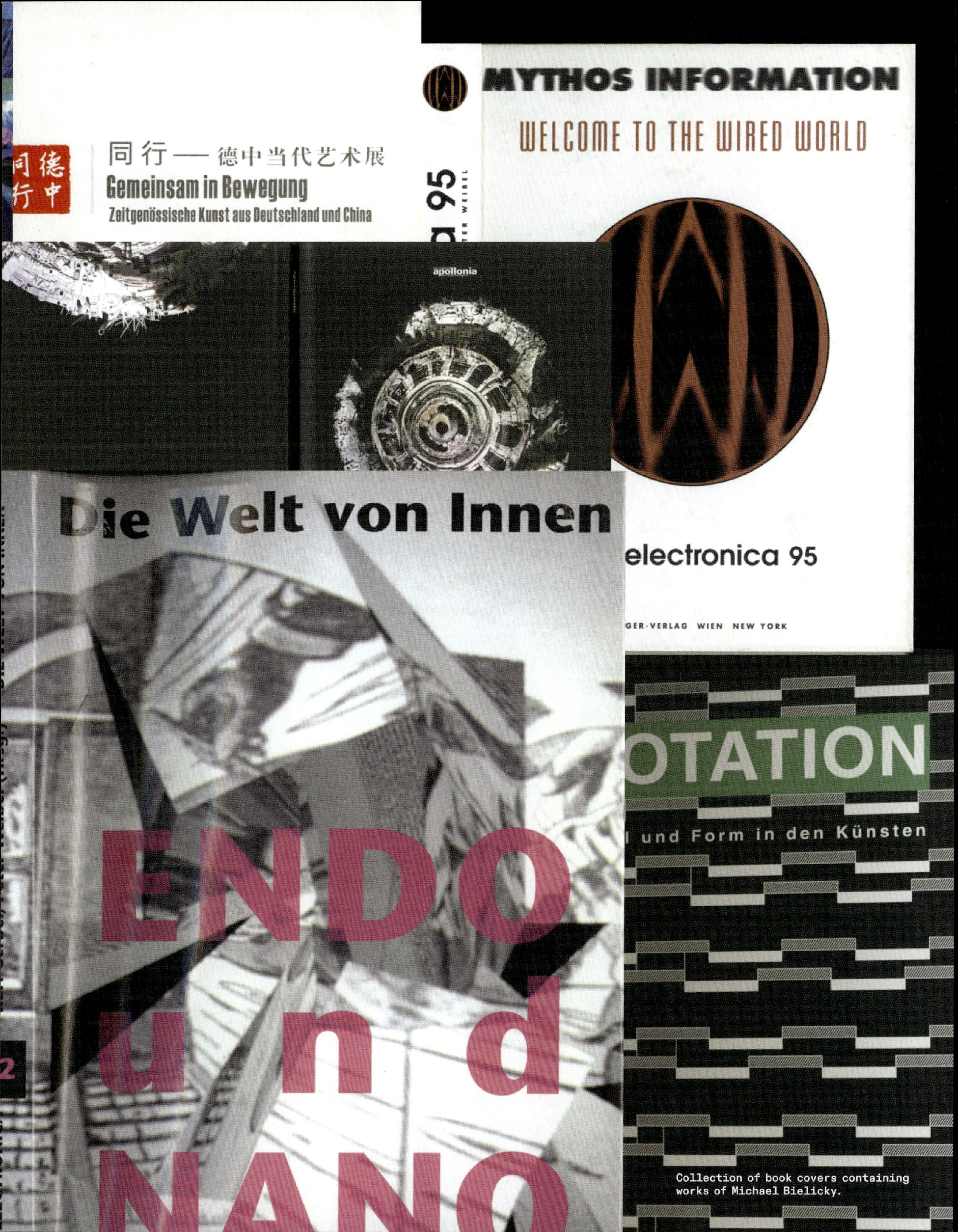

Collection of book covers containing works of Michael Bielicky.

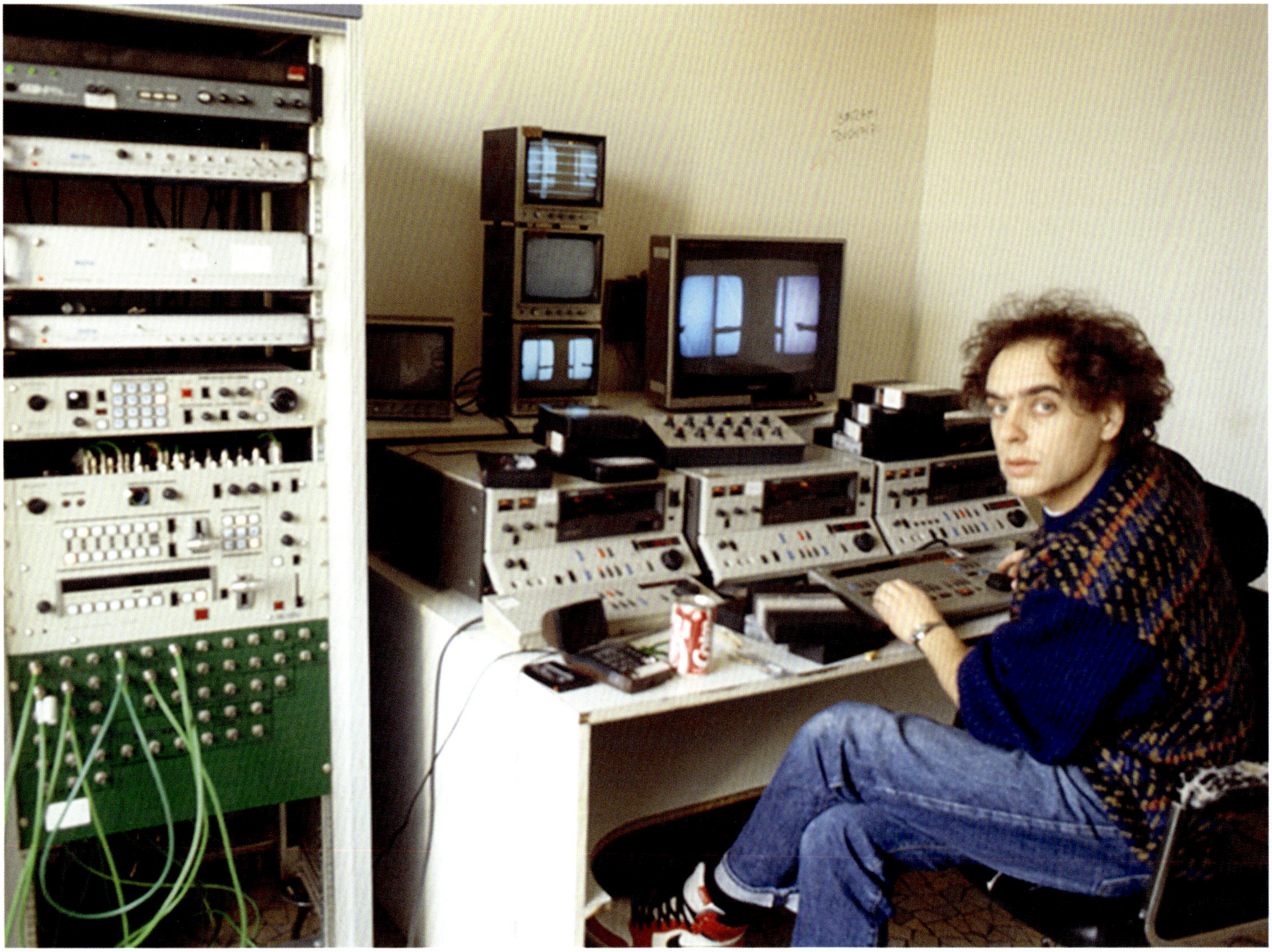

Michael Bielicky at the video studio,
Düsseldorf Art Academy, 1987.

From Videoart to Interactive Art

Alena Kučerová in conversation with Michael Bielicky

Alena Kučerová: The New Media Studio, founded in 1990, owes its origins to a great extent to Professor Michael Bielicky. A Czech by birth who left to go abroad with his parents at the age of fifteen, he returned to Prague after twenty-three years to hold a lecture on the topic of new media at the Academy of Fine Arts. The lecture was so well received that the rector and professors began to wonder whether the study of that new branch should be introduced at their school. And Professor Bielicky accepted this challenge.

Michael Bielicky: The project was very complicated because at first we didn't have any funds at all. First, I managed to get some funds in Germany from my former professor Nam June Paik, who is actually the father of video art. We built a technically modest S-VHS video studio, and in the autumn of 1991 the first students joined us. The German government also contributed money for the entire project, thus supporting the establishment of the first media art department of its kind in Czechoslovakia.

Kučerová: What are your previous experiences with the school and its students?

Bielicky: We were lucky to be able to take part in several international events. For example, last year, OK3, a Czech television channel, featured the *Piazza Virtuale* show, an international interactive television program that people from all over the world could participate in and meet – due to new telecommunications technologies – on screen. It was an experiment that we entered through the documenta IX. The documenta is one of the most important exhibitions of modern art in the world, and within it, a group of Van Gogh TV artists carried out this entire project. International contacts are very important for students. After only half a year of study at our Studio of Video and New Media, they presented their works internationally. I was very surprised by their level, because they could not have more theoretical training to this point. Students reacted smartly, individually, and proactively and already received the first signs of international recognition. One of them attracted attention at the World Festival in Tokyo, another student participated in an international exhibition in the Netherlands, and yet another student was invited to a very prestigious exhibition in Krakow, organized by the Centre Pompidou in Paris. This is definitely satisfying for me, because we achieved interesting results with modest technical equipment and with very limited financial resources. We are currently looking forward to receiving the Silicon Graphic computer, with which the highest quality computer animations can be made. After the documenta, we participated in one of the most prestigious international exhibitions of modern art in the world: the Venice Biennale. Here, too, our students are featured with a very demanding project, which is called *Electronic Cafe* – an entire pavilion equipped with the most diverse audiovisual and communication technologies. We also work closely with the Goethe-Institut, which has already organized two symposia on new media. The latter, dedicated to Vilém Flusser, one of the greatest philosophers from Prague (later living in France), focused on how new technology will change our living conditions and art. Even for this symposium, our students came up with exhibits, which were exhibited then in the National Technical Museum. Personally, I am very encouraged by these outcomes. Some students are really promising.

Kučerová: The first Czech experiments with video art were made in the eighties, when a section for video art was established at the Association of Fine Artists – initiated and led by the recently deceased Radek Pilař. However, it was not until this spring that this group of artists presented themselves for the first time with a comprehensive collection of films abroad, in Spain. Czech video art is presented to the world with a considerable delay, at a time when it may be already in decline.

Bielicky: You are wrong. Today, video art is almost a classic discipline worldwide, as thirty years have passed since its inception. Real contemporary art is all about image digitization, computer graphics, and interactive art.

Kučerová: Could you very briefly characterize the individual development stages and streams of video art?

Bielicky: Two people actually claim to be among the first. Coincidentally, I know both. Professor Nam June Paik, of Korean descent, is officially recognized as the founder of this field. He is a music scientist who began his career in Germany in 1958. He was fortunate to meet personalities such as John Cage and Karlheinz Stockhausen. It was in Germany at that time that the experimental ground for a new kind of music was established, from which Paik drew inspiration for his video art. So, it was not based on fine art. In 1963, he exhibited so-called modified television in a gallery in Wuppertal near Düsseldorf. This entails a magnet manipulating the televisions by distorting the image. In parallel with Paik, German actionist Wolf Vostell from the Fluxus group, which included Paik, [Joseph] Beuys, [Milan] Knížák, as well as Yoko Ono and others, also began to use modified television. This was zero hour. Thus, most of the work was in black-and-white images, sometimes presented on various screens. However, video players were not yet available. It was not until 1965 that a Sony desktop player was released in New York, and Paik was the first to buy it. At that time, the pope visited New York. Paik set out onto the streets to film the people welcoming the pope, then stopped at a coffee shop where artists typically met and showed what he had just shot on a television screen – another historic moment. It points to the straightforwardness of this medium (compared to film), which allows you to show the recording right after shooting, without further technological operations. In fact, many people initially used video mainly for documentation. Land art also belonged to the documentary rather than the artistic branch of video art. Also worth noting is Woody Vasulka, who was born in Brno and set out to America with his wife, Steina Vasulka, a musician; at the turn of the 1960s and 1970s, they founded the first experimental video art center in New York, called The Kitchen, which still exists. As far as I know, Woody Vasulka is coming to Brno to teach video art while we are now speaking. Then came the time when video art began to be used in various ways. In terms of intensity, I think this was greater in America than in Europe. At a time when the hippie movement was en vogue in America, many people realized that interesting effects could be made with video. Various psychedelic images were created, inspired by drug use. That was another branch of video art.

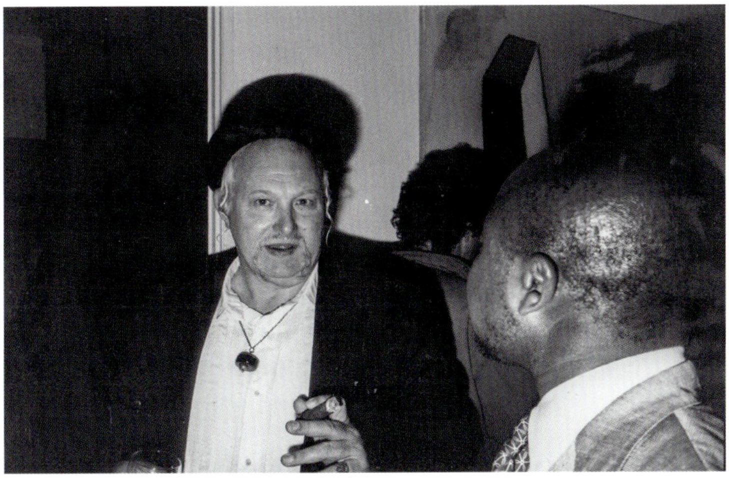

Wolf Vostell at *MultiMediale 2*, ZKM | Karlsruhe, 1991.

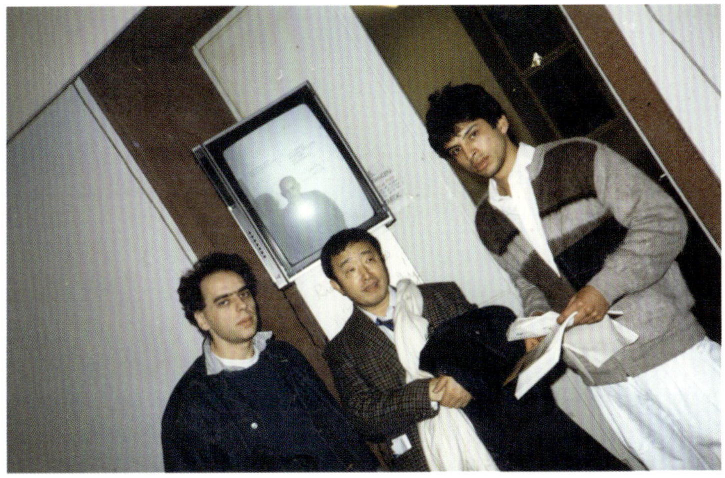

Michael Bielicky, Nam June Paik, Ricardo Peredo (from left), Düsseldorf, 1981.

At the end of the seventies, video art became an independent artistic discipline. Nevertheless, museums and galleries had considerable problems with it: it was mostly exhibited somewhere in the basement or the attic. Gradually, however, some television stations opened up to the new medium and began to broadcast it live; the first closed television circuits also appeared. People created various videos for which a range of festivals were created. Today, galleries and museums have large collections of video art, such as the Museum of Modern Art in New York and the Museum Centre Pompidou in Paris. It is incomprehensible to me that in Czechoslovakia, video art started so late, especially since there is such a long tradition in experimental film from the 1920s and 1930s, which was truly world class. In Hungary, for example, the situation was quite different in this respect. The works of Gábor Bachmann, for example, are well known. In 1980 another artist, Gábor Bódy, initiated the annual release of a videotape called *Infermental*, which contained images from all over the world selected by an international jury. *Infermental* was a meritorious deed and signified undeniable progress in the development of video art.

Kučerová: In Czechoslovakia, this development was strongly hampered not only by the lack of video technology, but mainly by the political climate.

Bielicky: In the 1980s, when video art was just beginning here, video installations and video sculptures were already common in the world; three-dimensional sculptures with built-in television monitors on which something was happening: another dimension, the fourth, is thus added to the third dimension. At present, everything is heading towards the so-called interactive art: the viewer can interfere with the work as an object of perception in some way, and the object somehow reacts to it. This is a very current trend. In this context, I would like to point out that the Goethe-Institut is preparing a symposium in Prague on New Media called "Interactive Media and Philosophy."

Kučerová: Can it be said that abroad, people are already in a better cognitive state to perceive video art? So far, Czech awareness and acceptance for video art is zero.

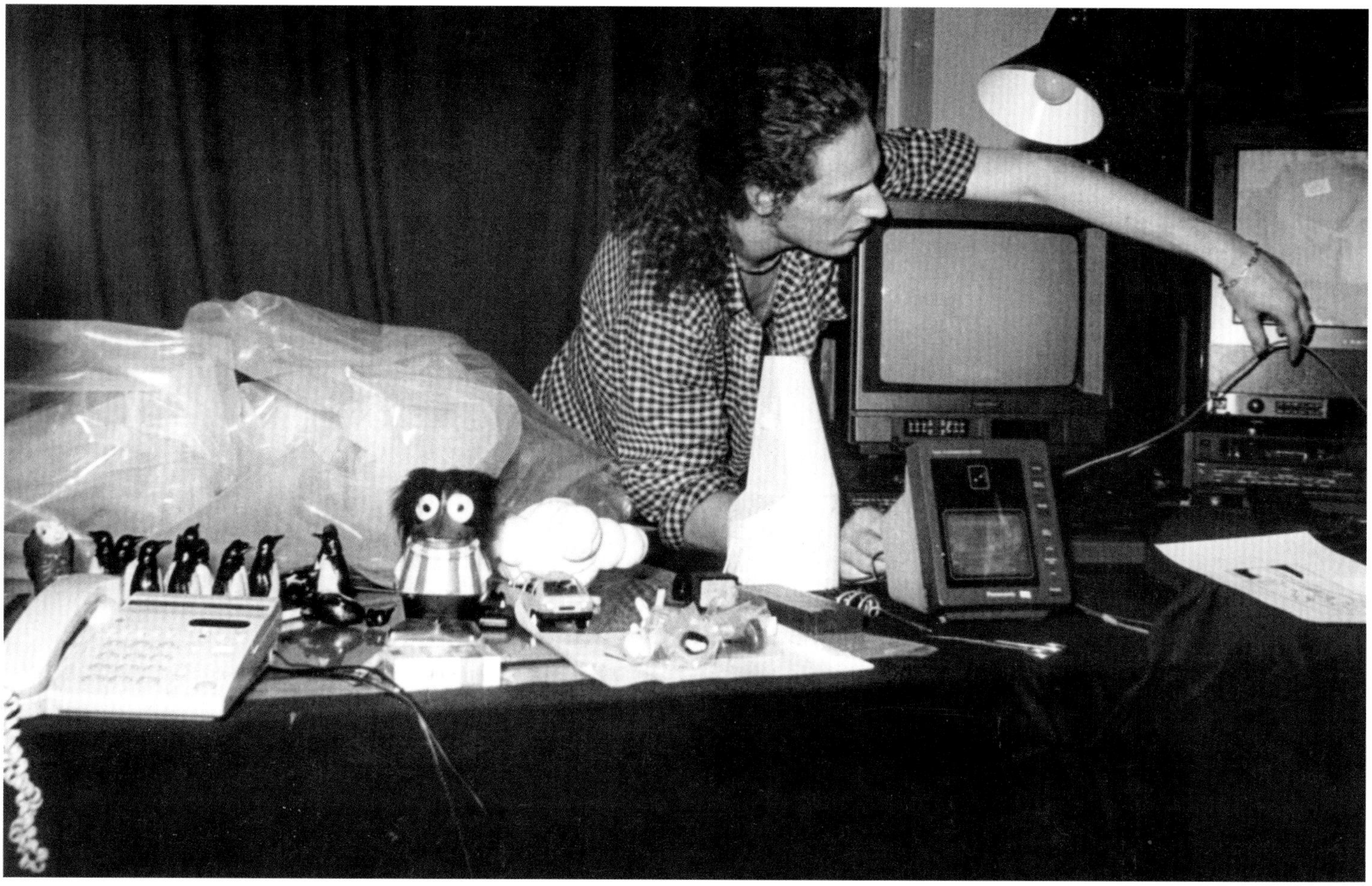

Piazzetta Prague – Piazza Virtuale/Van Gogh TV, Prague Academy of Fine Arts (AVU), 1995. Connecting a picturephone to the installation.

Bielicky: Of course, even in the rest of the world, it took a long time for video art to be recognized as a distinctive creative discipline, and to this day it does not even scratch the seriousness of classical art. Only a relatively small circle of people are interested in video art.

Kučerová: Can you tell our readers what can be imagined by the term *interactive* as well?

Bielicky: I would rather show these communication projects, but unfortunately it is not possible at the moment [...] I will try to describe to you what we installed at the school last year. We had two phone lines in the studio. A telephone was connected to one, and a picture phone was connected to the other; but it was quite primitive, transmitting only static images to the monitor. With this device, we were connected to the headquarters in Kassel, and through it we were able to talk to people from elsewhere over the phone and through [the] picture phone. The whole process of communication was transmitted from Kassel to the satellite, and from the satellite not only to Europe, but also to Japan and America. All people who own a satellite receiver could watch the program on the screen. In Czechoslovakia, it even appeared on television on the channel OK3.

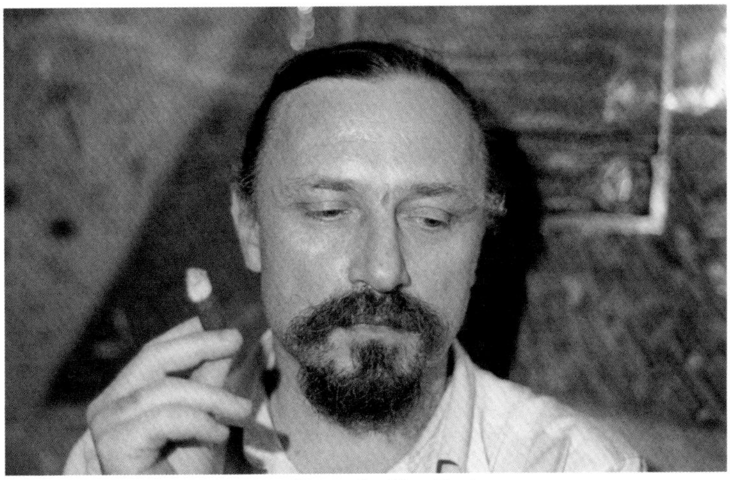

Piazzetta Prague – Piazza Virtuale/Van Gogh TV, Prague Academy of Fine Arts (AVU), 1995. Petr Rezek.

Kučerová: In our country [Czechoslovakia], however, we combine the concept of video art with video images inspired by fine art […]

Bielicky: That is natural. The whole problem is that the development of so-called modern art still corresponds to the spirit of the nineteenth century. Only the use of new technologies in the visual arts will radically change the definition of art. I would even say that video art is actually in the wrong place when it is exhibited in the museum. The "museum" for video art should be television. I mean, of course, magnetic tapes or installations can still remain in the museum. In the future, it will probably fit into a small chip. Of course, they will not wear it as a badge. What they create will need to be sent over the telephone network by email. Their creations, thus, will become literally immaterial. So far, everyone is trying to squeeze video art into the visual arts, but it is clear that this is only a temporary solution. The future will radically change both the definition of art and the focus of academies of fine arts. There will be no *originals*, which are now so valued. There will be no problem at all to not only reproduce video art digitally, but on top of that, no problem to reproduce without any loss of quality – this will fundamentally change our thinking. But this process will take a long time. Let's take another example of a telecommunications project. For one evening, we prepared a so-called philosophical counseling center at school. We invited the Czech philosopher Petr Rezek, who once taught here. He was available to the world on the picture phone screen for half an hour to answer philosophical questions. It did not work very well as communication, because a lot of different people called him, but it was a potential opportunity for communication.

Kučerová: Programs where people call in to have their questions answered are also known from television and radio […]

Bielicky: Another example: students cut out various scenes from old comics and put together a new program. It is then broadcast. People reflected on it and called us. Of course, in this case it was not a matter of creating art and then presenting it. It was really a dialogue. But the whole show was considered one artistic act. Closer to art was another event, which, for technical reasons, did not turn out the best but was very interesting and pioneering in the world. We were invited from Chicago, where one of the largest electronic exhibitions presenting the latest technologies is held every year, to take part in an event called *International Painting Interactive* that was

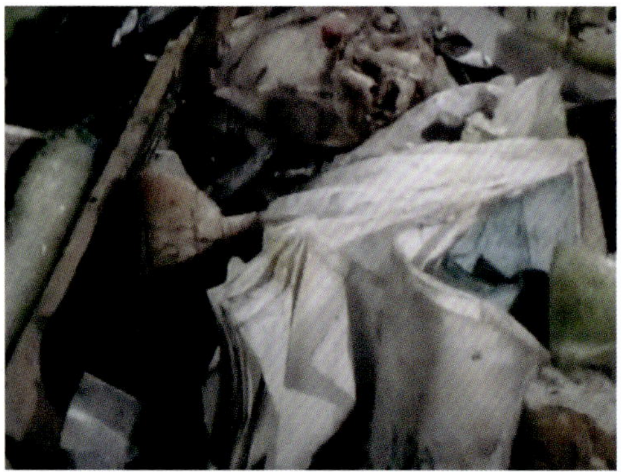
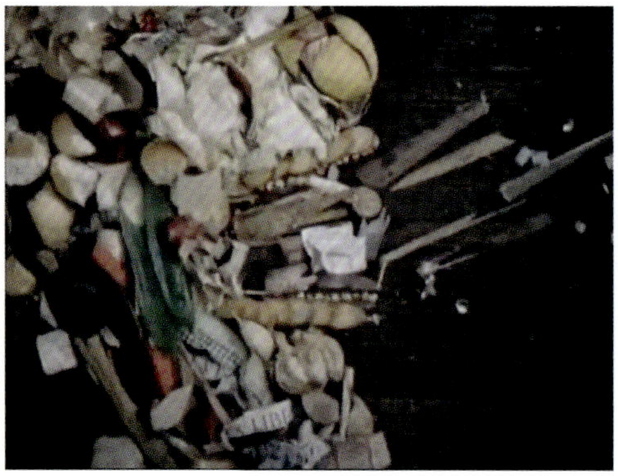
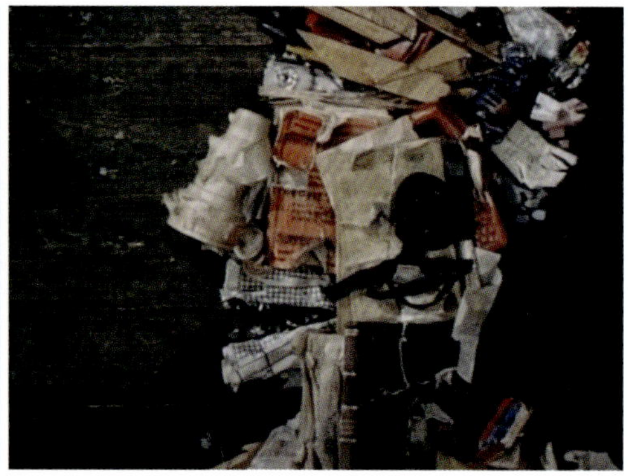

Jan Švankmajer, *Dimensions of Dialogue: Dialog Vecny*, 1983, single-channel video. Video stills.

organized amongst thirty-five countries. On a wall with thirty-five HDTVs, we were able to paint one large picture together using a high-quality Silicon Graphic computer.

Kučerová: These are very interesting projects, but our artists still gravitate towards the artistic line of video art. [...]

Bielicky: The examples described are, of course, very experimental in nature, with global-scale attention and sponsored by large companies fueled by a scientific interest in media.

Kučerová: What do you say to our video art? I think Radek Pilař went the furthest. The poetry of his films, which are also broadcast on television, is very close to the Czech audience, and they are also works "about something." People understand them because they capture the atmosphere of our time.

Bielicky: I really appreciate many artistic disciplines in Czechoslovakia. When we talk about experimental film, Jan Švankmajer is a real master of his field. However, if I compare Czech video art with what is produced in the world today, it is not very famous. I say it openly. This does not mean that there is no talent, that something interesting cannot arise here soon. I knew Radek Pilař personally. His works are based on animation and have their charm, their quality. But all his work is fueled by an artistic drive. It is very artistic, if you will. That is why, from an international point of view, it cannot play such a large role. The idea is important in art, but also what you "transfer" it to. There are no rules for that. After all, it would be terrible if such rules in art existed. The fact that everything is open in art is the most beautiful thing about it. [...]

First published in *Video+Film*, no. 7 (1993): 148-49. Translated from the Czech by Paul Kenig.

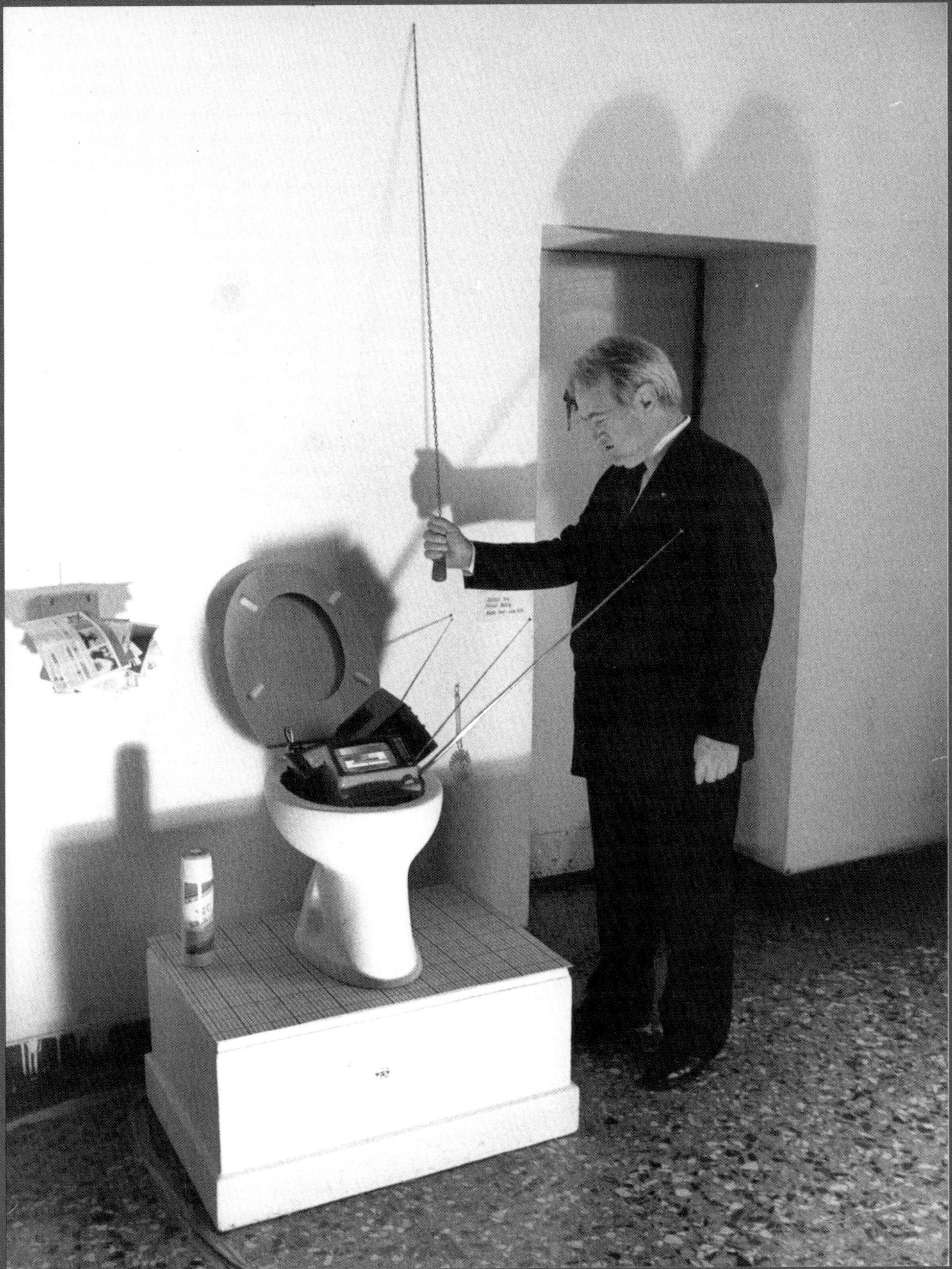

Johannes Rau, Düsseldorf Art Academy, 1988.

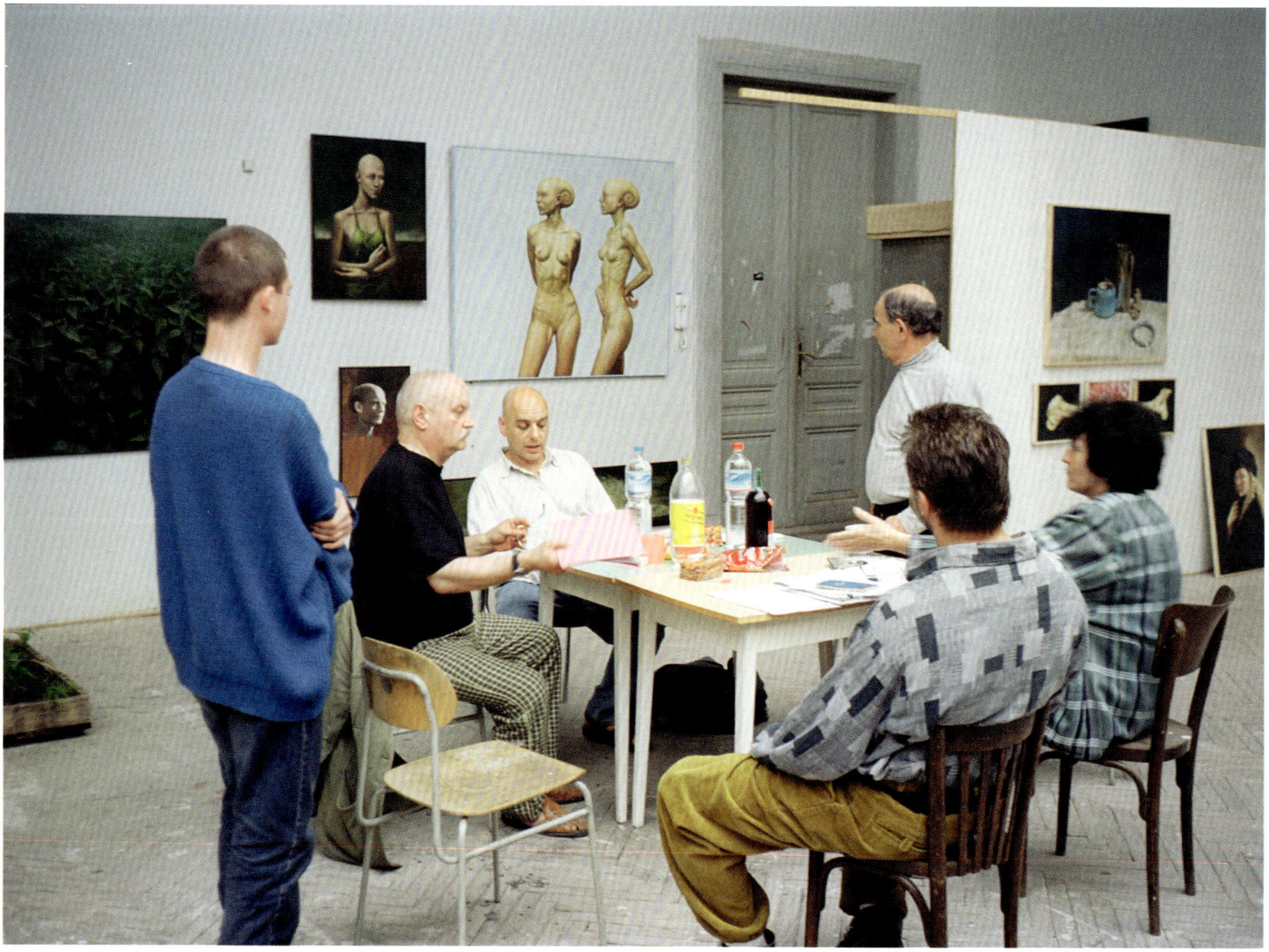

Exams at the Prague Academy of Fine Arts (AVU), 1992.

In Between Botticelli and Tesla

Živel magazine in conversation with Michael Bielicky

Michael Bielicky is a personality who since 1991 has been inextricably linked with the controversial New Media Studio within the Prague Academy of Fine Arts (AVU). He is responsible for filling this open space with a cultural context, which was neglected in Czechoslovakia until the 1990s. With the advent of the internet, the boom of cyber culture, and a redefining legacy of conceptual tendencies in the art of the 1960s and 1970s, his personal task is to infect young Czech culture with issues that have existed continuously in the Western world for several decades. He bases his projects on the search for contemporary spaces of artistic expression with the help of new technologies. His vision is to free the modern artist from the enduring tendency to understand art from the perspective of the twentieth century. Bielicky lives in Prague under the Žižkov Tower, as well as in Düsseldorf and in the network. He doesn't like Leni Riefenstahl, but for him she cooks great spaghetti à la Naples.

Živel: What was the reason for your statement that it would be best to close AVU?

Michael Bielicky: A very simple and very clear reason. The Academy of Fine Arts in Prague was established on the basis of philosophy and with the intention to understand nineteenth-century art. We are now two years before entry into the third millennium, and we are faced with the question of whether this institution still has any relevance in relation to society. Whether its persistence on the model of tradition does not mean stagnation and isolation in the social context, it is on its way to becoming an absolutely irrelevant institute.

Živel: Is your proposal to establish modernism in place of academism?

Bielicky: I would confirm that. But to be precise: it is very positive that there are classical disciplines at the AVU, traditional studios of painting, sculpture, architecture, et cetera. I do not question them, only question the condition that radically new views are not allowed there. I can imagine a studio, albeit very far from the current spirit of the academy, that would deal with musical performances in real and virtual space. In my opinion, this would give a great impulse to other studios as well. At the same time, I would invite many more people from outside. In this sense, the academy is still very closed. There is great xenophobia, great skepticism about everything that is not *ours*. I would not employ anyone at the academy for more than two years, and on the contrary, I would base it on the names of people from outside, and not only artists, but also philosophers and scientists. I would make it much more multidisciplinary. Then there would be some guarantee that it would give an impulse to the people studying there, that it would give them a slightly different shift in perspective on today's reality.

Živel: In your proposed scenario, completely different spiritual conditions would exist. The status of it as art would be questioned.

Bielicky: Without a doubt. We still define art as art, as fine art; that is a problem. I know that schools like the academy are experiencing a similar dilemma elsewhere in the world. Their problem is how to get out of this situation, how to break out of the cage of a nineteenth-century understanding of art. This is not just our Czech problem. For example, the academy in Düsseldorf, which was one of the most influential, innovative in the 1970s, lost relevance similar to the Prague Academy. For a while it couldn't quite incorporate the zeitgeist somehow. It is certainly not entirely easy to break free from those old views. That is why the so-called media academies are being established. But they again have a problem: they are just media academies, they lack something related to tradition, they lack a link to the past. It can't be cut or questioned within the artworks.

Živel: Is this caused by a lack of information?

Bielicky: I think the information exists here. The problem is the very idea of high culture, not only in central Europe. There is a strong line between high art and pop culture. There is far more going on in music today than in fine arts. I would venture to say that this is ignorance in our country, because access to this information is already here today. We are not behind any iron curtain, and even at our school, everyone has the opportunity to sit down and look at the network. Maybe it's the fear of rethinking the inertia of twentieth-century ideas, why people stick to it so incredibly. In fact, I understand when someone has believed in a certain life concept and suddenly this concept breaks down, so I do not mean to say it is an easy task.

Virtual reality apparatus at the Ars Electronica Center, Linz, 1996.

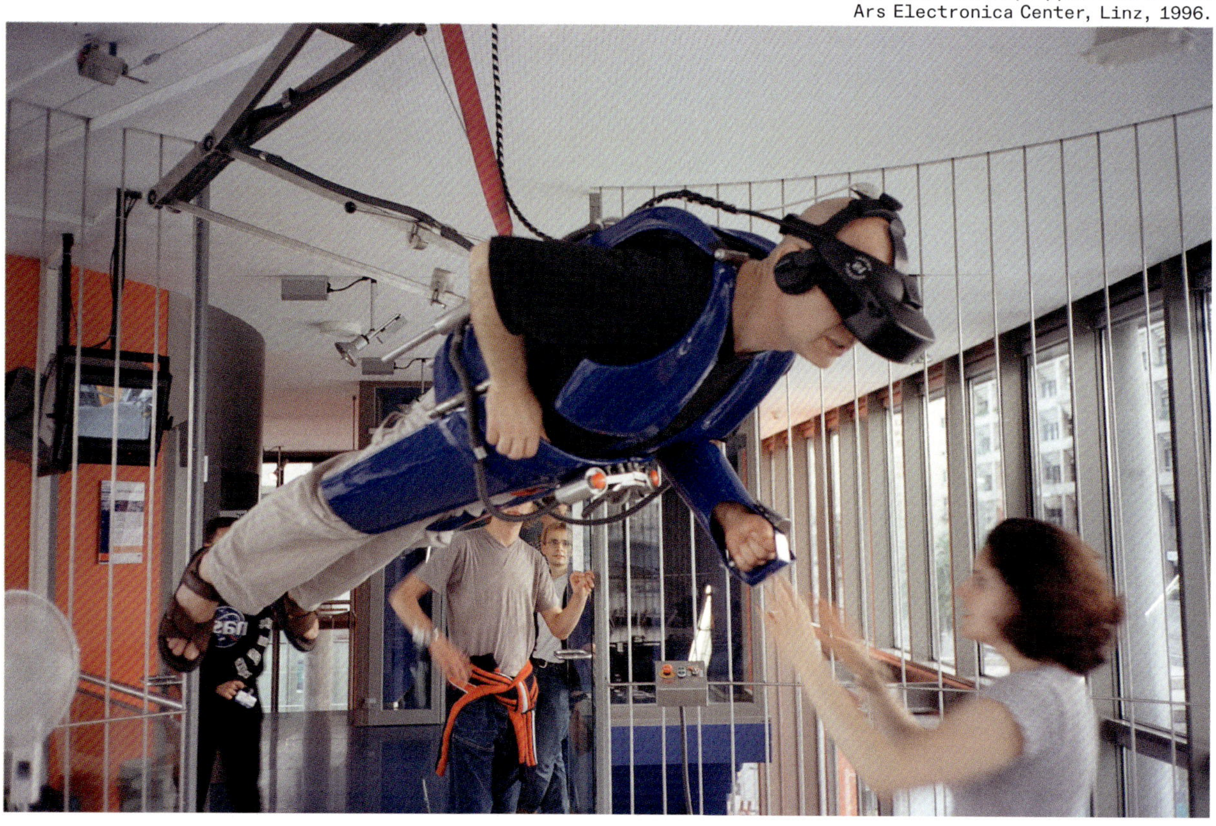

Živel: Isn't it because, in the European context of art, there is a firm distrust in technology?

Bielicky: I have a theory. On the one hand, it [technology] is terribly foreign; on the other hand, I would go so far as to claim that a place like Prague has a tradition of using innovative technologies in an artistic context that go back to the sixteenth century. There are historical examples. This attitude here derives from the Renaissance and mannerism: golem, robots, artificial intelligence, the very first interactive Czech cinema, *Kinoautomat* [presented at the Montreal Expo '67 in 1967], and many more are Czech inventions. For example, Rabbi Loew invited Emperor Rudolf to his house, and that night he turned his simple house into a chateau. And how did he do that? Using the camera obscura, he projected the interiors of Hradčany on the wall of his house. So he created an example of virtual reality. I think that Prague has a cultural constellation and historical consciousness to be open to these meta-realities, which one just needs technology to visualize.

Živel: Does the Czech cultural avant-garde react to contemporary artistic trends? Are there scientists, artists, and philosophers who infiltrate these ideas into the young generation?

Bielicky: These are rather big exceptions. I'd say no. The problem is the big gap between the so-called art scene, which I don't want to declassify here, and the environment in which it exists. I see a big crisis of cultural identity in the Czech avant-garde.

Živel: Do you think that it would be possible to organize an event of the proportions of Ars Electronica in the Czech Republic?

Bielicky: Without a doubt. But it would be necessary to adapt it to this cultural and historical environment. Transferring some *Electronic Ars* here in a one-to-one ratio is nonsense. It would have to be something that is specifically related to the environment. There is some continuity here; it would just be a matter of connecting and making it adequate today. Last but not least, it would also be a matter of connecting certain groups of people who still have little communication with each other: break the artistic circles, create a wide space of different ideas, dialogues, creativities, visions. I think that although there are people here from these seemingly noncommunicating groups, in principle they are interested in very similar problems. I suffer from similar concerns, and in this sense it makes sense to break the restrictive boxes. The cultural and historical environment, the historical burden, from which everyone in Prague draws and lives – to which I still relate – even this could be used and misused for an event of this type. Perhaps a conservative and intolerant environment would even benefit from it in a broader context.

Živel: Has digital culture changed our perception of the world in any way?

Bielicky: Yes. Radically. Because with the help of these digital technologies, we are able to produce artifacts, not only on the spot, but also in a fictional, virtual space. Today we can create an artifact, which can be found, for example, on the internet. And this knowledge, this experience that the product we create is in a context that is beyond space and time, such as in the space-time of the network, in itself changes the diametric perception of our creative environment. There is a radical break, a new issue arises, what the threshold of creation and presentation might be. However, this cannot be assessed from our point of view. The judgment is up to a new generation.

Živel: What could be the turning point?

Bielicky: The liberation from the very concept of art. Maybe there's something for which we don't have a terminology yet. A creative activity, and I might not dare say it's artistic. The artist gets rid of this boundary. It's somewhere else. It is out of an artistic context. There are people who are on the verge, for example, Ingo Günther, an artist who lives in New York and Germany. His work is based on art; he works on projects that are in the network, have a strong political and sociological dimension. He is currently doing a project called *Refugee Republic*. This is completely beyond art. And for me he is the real artist; he is the avant-garde of today. They are people who move outside of art, and yet they probably do the most interesting art. The problem is not that the artist loses relevance. What is losing relevance is the framework: the public cultural space, which are museums, critics, magazines, TV. This framework is no longer compatible with the new artist. This is the tragedy.

Živel: Why tragedy?

Bielicky: If art is to have any weight, there are two possibilities: either the framework opens completely new spheres, disciplines, contexts, or art will take place outside the artistic context.

Živel: How do you view the claims of Marvin Minsky and others about the end of humanity?

Bielicky: If we achieve a certain connection with technology, there is no way back. It is a question of willingness to define what humanity is and what it is not. If we are willing to commit to a project with the goal that in fifty or one thousand years, our human selves will live only in the network, they *will be* our true copies with all consequences, and our physical selves will disappear. The question is whether we will understand this as human or not. The whole evolution of humanity is entering a completely new phase with the help of technology, where the essence of our physical self will certainly change in some way, and at the very end, for example, we will already exist on the basis of information.
Perhaps this is what many people will devote to, to protect the value of the physical body and work systematically to ensure that its functionality is not lost. I can give an example of my friends working on something similar: it is a project called *Universal Companionship* (*UCO*). Their goal is to create a secondary consciousness in the network, a second consciousness, albeit in a very complex form, not only with intellectual but also with emotional abilities. The goal would also be that one could leave this world and continue to exist on the network only in the form of a digital cluster of codes and continue to evolve. The question is whether a person's personality will still be preserved. It is more a question of definition. That there is a breakthrough and a tendency to reach an absolutely new type of human being is a common truth. I already feel these changes myself, although the changes are still relatively minimal and invisible.

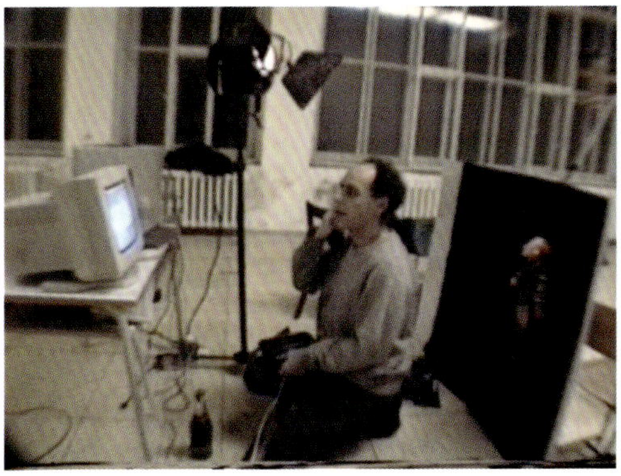

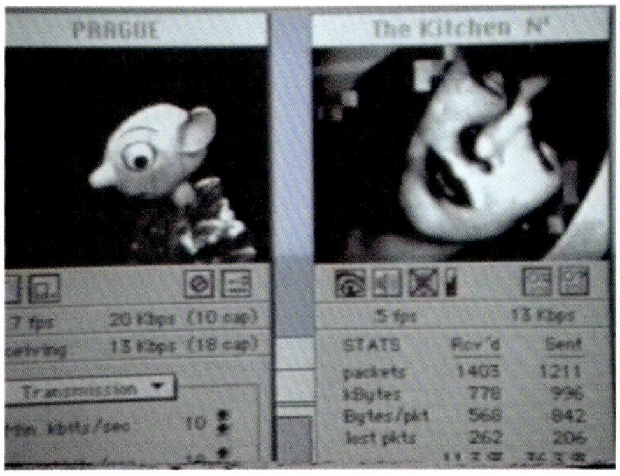

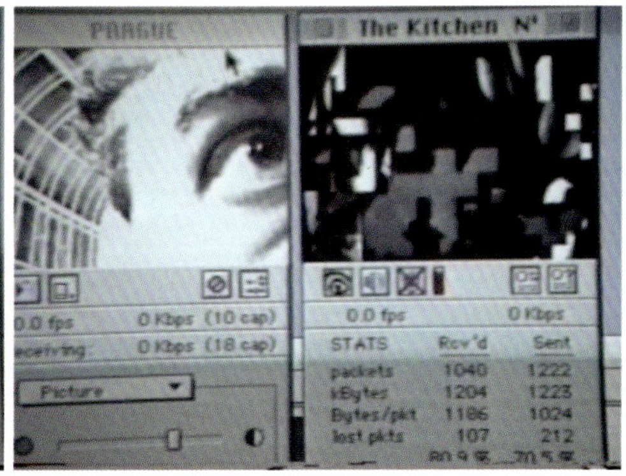

Cathy Weis, Michael Bielicky, *Unitled,* 1995, CU-SeeMe telematic performance, simultaneously at The Kitchen, New York and Prague Academy of Fine Arts (AVU). Screenshots. The telematic performance was part of an evening called *Cathy Weis & Friends* at The Kitchen, New York, December 3 and 10, 1995.

Živel: Is technology a new stage in human evolution? What actually entitles us to state that? What entitles us to establish man as the constant of the highest degree of life?

Bielicky: I don't think we have any right to do that. For example, John Cunningham Lilly is still exploring communication with dolphins and other cetaceans. In this respect, we are still in the Stone Age, and the communication systems of these creatures are so complex that we probably still don't understand them fully. Maybe one day we'll see how and what kind of information these beings pass on to each other. It's an exciting opportunity to discover phenomena here on Earth that we think we know everything about.

Živel: In *Blade Runner*, they had the Voight-Kampff test to determine humanity.

Bielicky: If we agree that all psychological processes are based on some biochemical programs and codes, then it is very difficult to say how much a being is a machine or a being. After all, man makes art, believes in God, loves – these are all qualities which cannot be measured in any way. Maybe that quality is the guarantee that it's a human being. I would like to return to one personal experience. There is the CU-SeeMe program, where one can meet different people on the network using a camera. I myself use this system for various art projects. About two weeks ago, I received an email: "The CU-SeeMe art project, from next Friday. You can look there." So I looked there. Several human heads appear there, and you can communicate with them through a window. The interesting philosophical statements concerning media stated there fascinated me. So I talked to those people. It took me about half an hour to realize that one of those people didn't seem like much to me. He didn't react right away, even though he said quite interesting things. I accused him of being a robot. He didn't respond. But in about half an hour, I found out that I was the only person there; the others were human beings who were videotaped, but the texts were written by a robot, a program. Eventually I found out it was an art project. And I sat with the gentlemen for about an hour and talked to them for an hour. I got angry because I felt cheated. They cheated on me. Maybe I just wasn't in a perfectly awake state; it was late at night. But it was the first time I had such an experience, and I was upset and even shocked. So sometimes the interface is debatable.

Živel: Can the clone sheep Dolly be understood as art?

Bielicky: In the broadest context, it is art, but it depends on what awareness you perceive it with. It is possible to be understood as a creative act that has a much stronger effect than a painting in a museum.

Živel: Can you imagine art based on biotechnology?

Bielicky: Without a doubt. And it's nothing new, too. In 1994, Ars Electronica focused on this topic in Linz. Various artists have presented and performed various projects here. For example, various genetically engineered plants. There was an Austrian woman living in Japan today who showed off cacti whose roots were connected to sensors capable of registering plant reactions to the outside world. When you approached and touched them, digital plants developed adequately to your touch at the adjacent projection.

Živel: What about genetic manipulation of humans?

Bielicky: I myself am in two minds about this matter. On the one hand, I see it as why not, and at the same time, I'm feeling shivers down my spine. After all, my predominant knowledge is that the moment of chance in all aspects of life is something so magical, something so unpredictable and that I marvel at every day on multiple occasions, that I would rather leave these things to nature or God. I like coincidence more than deliberate manipulation. Here I move on the border of fascination and horror. I don't think the problem is that there will be the possibility of some fascist tendencies to create soldiers or superhumans. By interfering with genetics, a person will be more deprived of something in my books.

Živel: Do you feel closer to Botticelli or Tesla?

Bielicky: Not exclusively to one. Both are classics. The moment I started identifying with Tesla or Botticelli, I would be limiting myself. Today's context is different than it was during the time Botticelli or Tesla lived and worked. They are parallels in a specific historical and cultural environment. But it is just fascinating that today we can completely redefine these things, these relationships.

Živel: So how would you define a twenty-first-century artist?

Bielicky: I would say that she or he is someone who must have a very broad knowledge of science, culture, linguistics, et cetera. Of course, it is a bit of a parallel to the Renaissance, where there was also a universal crossover, the application of science to art and vice versa. Because there is also relatively easy access to information resources today, there is a danger that we will get lost in a sea of information. We will need restrictions. It's a matter of dynamism. What I would define today as an artist of the twenty-first century in five years will not apply at all. And I really like that.

Živel: The artist will still be a certain type of person who is somehow excluded from society. Does he live outside of her? It is a question of autonomy, a question of having another point of view?

Bielicky: Without a doubt. Take, for example, the model of a terrorist – he has a certain sensitive perception that the average person does not have. He has his own worldview. For example, Zapatistas: for me, these are people who have a high social consciousness, feel a certain social injustice, and react to it in their own way. And whether we call them terrorists, saviors, or otherwise [...] you can say it's a creative activity.

Živel: So Unabomber was an artist, who tried to break the pressure of the system?

Bielicky: He was certainly a strong personality, an individual who has a strong awareness of the reflection of society and the laws of society. That is the reality. How he finally reacted to it, how he tried to solve it – is debatable. However, is he someone who has an above-average ability to reflect certain social phenomena (in his case, technical progress)? There is no doubt about that.

Živel: In fact, he is a mad mathematics professor who did not associate his activities with art. You can even extend your argument and go so far as to call Hitler an artist. Can art have any morality in your view?

Bielicky: This is very difficult. It is about responsibility. If the artist has an above-average sensitivity, greater than a normal citizen, if he has worked his whole life trumping state mechanisms, he must also have higher moral responsibility sensitivity. He must be a seismograph of society. I'm not saying this from any pathetic point of view. I will give an example: people often argue about the role that Leni Riefenstahl played in art. I am a great opponent of dealing with her work, dealing with her person, giving her any attention [...]

Živel: Why? Have you seen the movie *Blue Light*?

Bielicky: I didn't. I don't even care. I don't want to see anything from her. [...]

Živel: This shows the blinkers 'round your eyes!

Bielicky: There are, and I'll say why. What she did is unique, absolute. Her films have a unique aesthetic, visual form. No doubt about it. But that doesn't matter. It's about what purpose it was done for, what purpose. [...] The purpose was to support the most unreal and most inhuman system that was ever established. If I feel like someone has a certain sensitivity, she also has a certain responsibility. And that's why one cannot blindly serve anything – which were the arguments Riefenstahl made in connection with her films – that she was unaware of what system she was serving. I do not believe this. Let's not forget one thing. All of her colleagues, who were also creating at the time, were on the run, people of greater Jewish descent, ending up in Hollywood or in a concentration camp. Her competition was eliminated. And from this point of view, if there was only a bit of moral responsibility in her, she should have stopped producing anything at that moment. I have no doubt about her abilities. But if she created a unique work that serves something like fascism, it is completely destructive. It is against life, against freedom. It is an advertisement for the extinction of man. She served this ideology. He must have known everything about her. How could she do that from this point of view? I am not able to draw a line here and say: it has quality; it has rare vision. I see a lack of moral responsibility in this.

Živel: David Cronenberg said that an artist must not be held accountable, must be able to exceed [...]

Bielicky: He is not able; he must cross. But she served; she did not exceed. I would appreciate her far more if she had worked against regime movies, if she went beyond.

Živel: And you are not interested in both extremes of man. That which will yield something and that which will not?

Bielicky: Yes, but as a phenomenon. But how can something that is against human life have artistic value?

Živel: But in *Blue Light* there is an archetypal value: the rebellion against the old world.

Bielicky: But that brings us back to the question of what an artist will be in the twenty-first century. I think they will be hackers. These will be the real artists. These will be the first guarantees that we will not find ourselves in any fascist world of the future. Maybe when humanity gets completely into the dimensions of a system that will control us with those beautiful new technologies, hackers will be the last to show us reality and truth in some way. Maybe they will be the only guarantors of any self-preservation.

First published in *Živel*, no. 9 (1998): 34-37.
Translated from the Czech by Paul Kenig.

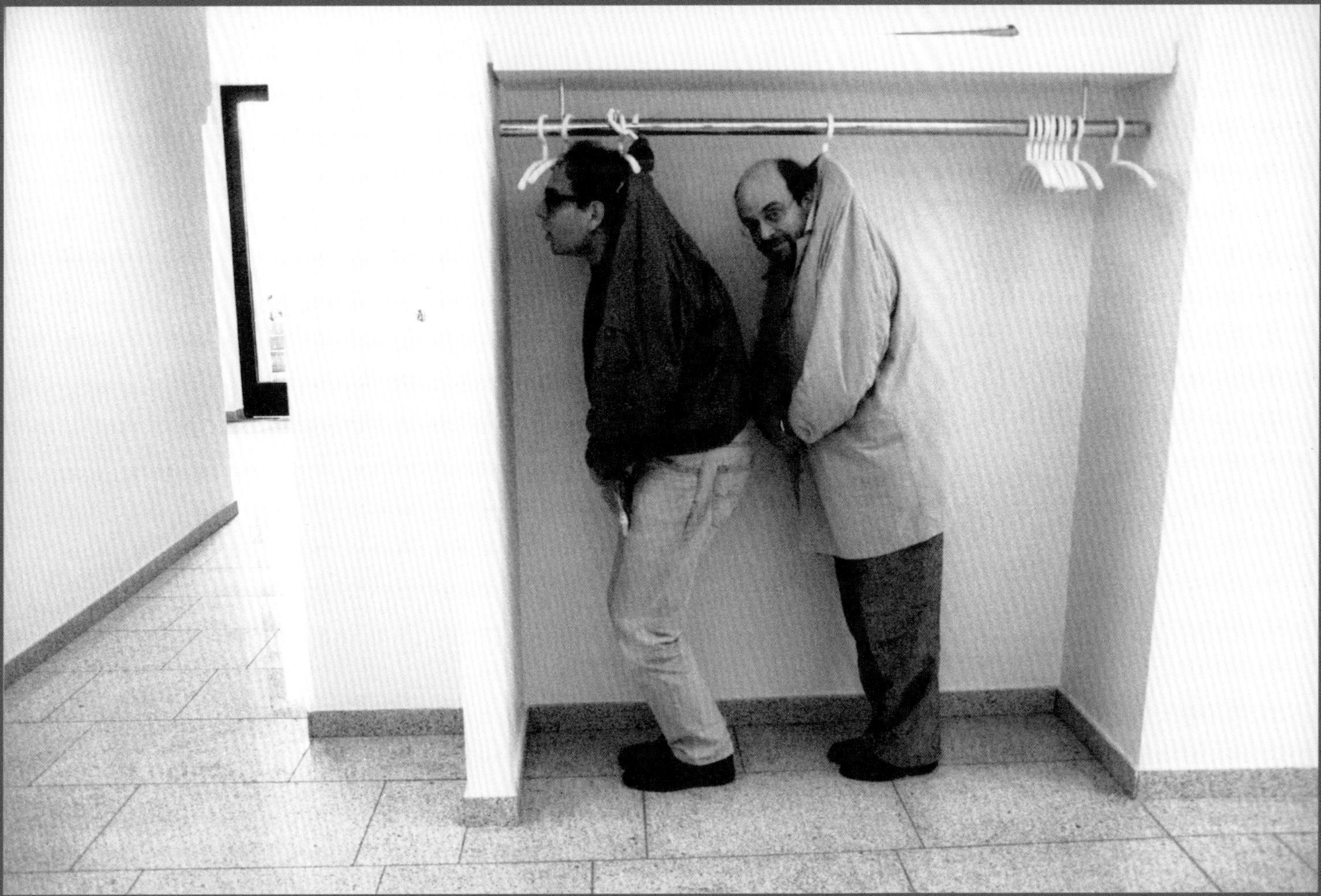

Fredrich Cantor (photographer), Bielicky brothers at Peter Bielicky's doctor's office, Düsseldorf, 1992.

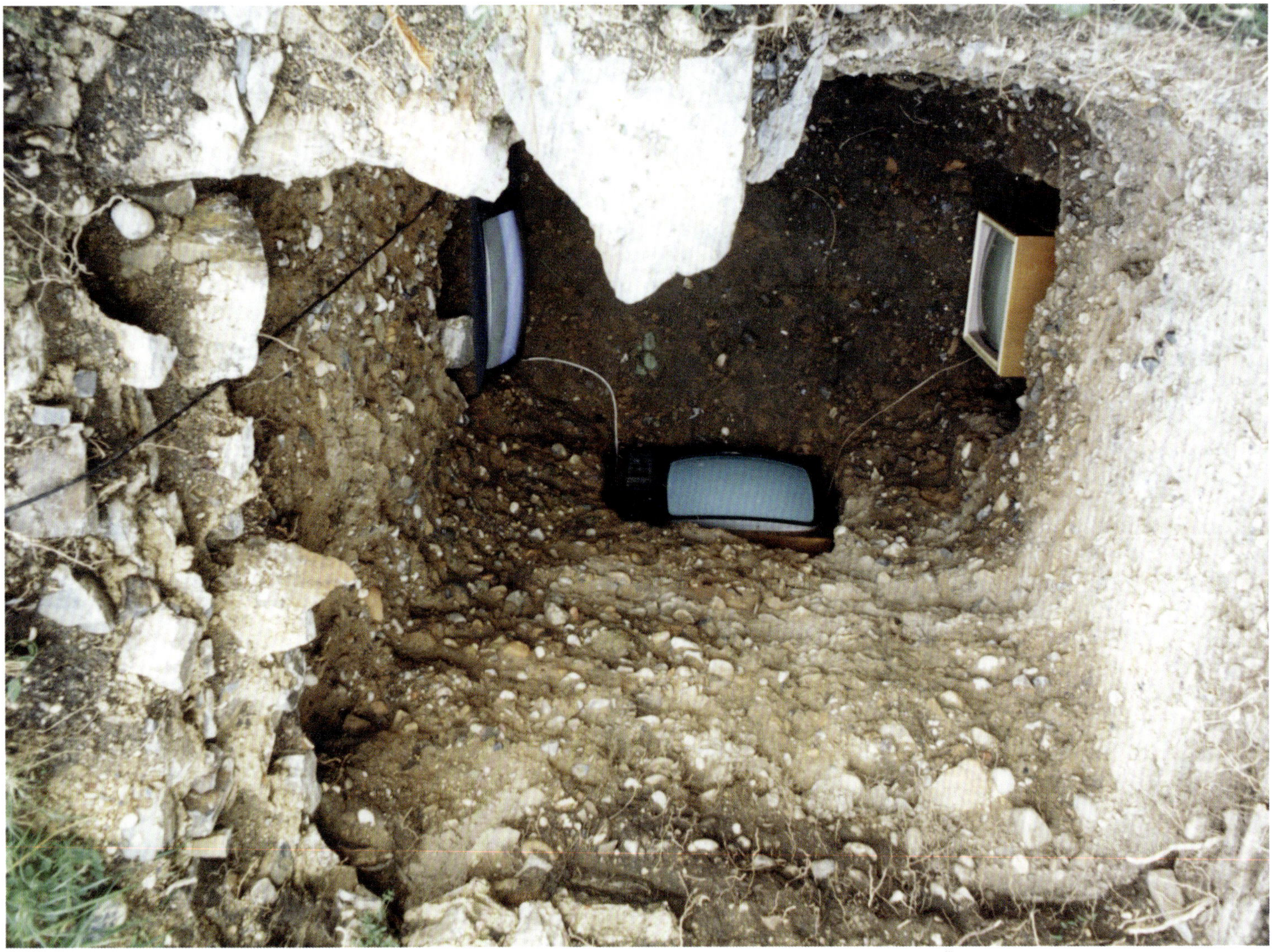

Lubomír Čermák, *Untitled*, 1993, monitor installation. Prague Academy of Fine Arts (AVU).

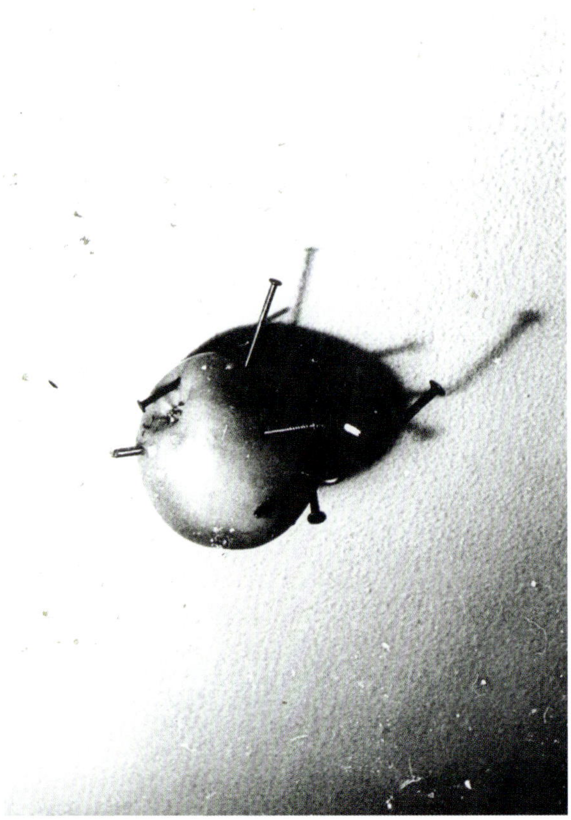

Untitled, 1973, photograph. Michael Bielicky's first artwork.

Relevant Artists Will Operate Completely Outside of the Art System

Michal Murin in conversation with Michael Bielicky

Michal Murin: You are one of the artists who often presented themselves at Ars Electronica (AE) at the turn of the 1980s and 1990s, whereas since the middle of the 1990s, you have been absent from this event. How do you perceive the change of AE after the change of the director?

Michael Bielicky: I would like to correct this information. In 2000, I reappeared at AE – we even got an award for *Room with a View* – but admittedly only on the sidelines. This is a question that can probably be answered on various levels. Of course, with the departure of Peter Weibel, who became the director of ZKM about two or three years later, an era ended concerning quality and even concerning the courage and willingness to take risks. Weibel was bold enough to accept projects to AE with unclear reach and was willing to risk potential *failures* within the AE topic, and not only on the project level: he also took risks with his participants' selection, which certainly cannot be said of the new directorate.
Of course, the change of AE leadership was largely influenced by various political forces and was primarily a struggle for influence. But this fact alone does not suffice for an explanation, because time has also shifted: this does not only concern AE; we are really in a different time than we were in the early 1990s. This can be clearly seen, for example, in the program, when for the third time in a row the same theme of *Life and Science* is repeated, which as a title does not address electronic art so much, but rather the connection between art and science in general, for example, toward biology and genetic manipulation. This topic was proclaimed last year, is proclaimed this year, and will be next year [2001] at AE. The time has shifted, and the management dictating the form of the festival has their priorities. What I criticize the most about the selection are the various strong production companies, ultimately based in Hollywood, which receive recognition at AE. I'm not even sure if these still really belong there, but that's my personal opinion.

Murin: You teach at the Prague Academy of Fine Arts (AVU); you have experience with the ZKM | Center for Art and Media Karlsruhe – how would you characterize the European educational system, specifically concerning new media? And with regard to activities around the Center for Culture & Communication Foundation (C3) in Budapest, what are the differences between East and West?

Bielicky: This again is a more complex topic, because, on one hand, in the West, they are, of course, at an advantage in terms of material equipment. But since, on the other hand, a certain environment is also necessary for creation, I would like to say that the need to use rubbish (technology) in the East, such as in Hungary, but also in the Czech Republic, leads to an advantage in the *approach* to art. I perceive this environment as more inspiring. I visited the Art Cologne Trade Fair, where the Kunsthochschule für Medien from Cologne was presented. It is the only academy for media to this date and was founded about eight or nine years ago. Those students have a big budget – they can buy new machines if they need to – but the things that were exhibited there didn't look like what one would think they should look like. This means that the potential for art is not only in the material equipment of the school, but that it is still the legal factor that determines the quality. It is from this point of view that I would say that we are not at a complete disadvantage, although it is very true that in the West there is an interconnection of institutions, which creates networks. Next week I will go to Paris for the International Symposium on Electronic Arts (SEA), where the scene is comparable to the scene at AE but nevertheless is still a relatively small international scene. I like to say this network in particular is almost incestuous. Then again there are many artists today who produce interesting things that are not exhibited in the context of AE, SEA, or ZKM at all. I wonder if only what these institutions present is relevant today? Doesn't this situation create an art ghetto environment, and is it really the only frame of reference for us?

Murin: I detect a certain opposition to academicism in your statement, as well evidenced by the widening gap between contemporary artists and theorists, who are unable to follow current trends because they are overwhelmed by institutional problems. What do you think, how will the artist work in the future?

Bielicky: This is a very interesting question. Again, I could give a long answer, if I had to be honest, but I guess I do not have to be. I like your statement, and it seems to me that the systems we are used to, that is, museums, galleries, critics as spokesmen of art and other institutions that revolve around the visual arts, should and could open up if they wanted to; they could achieve wholesome societal value again by providing the public with current events, events that address a broader societal context. This would mean that art intermediaries could learn from their own practice, could open up to new disciplines that intervene in completely different directions, such as sociology, philosophy, or even genetic technology. I think that in these fields, they will learn the most, also about themselves, so that they will have the opportunity to catch up on what is happening outside the institutional walls.

Murin: This is a consequence of new technologies.

Bielicky: It is partly a consequence of new technologies, but it is also a consequence of the changed environment and the time in which we find ourselves. You will also know this is related to globalization, which is also partly a consequence of technology. The philosopher Vilém Flusser says that every revolution that took place in the history was, in fact, a technical revolution. So, if we agree with that, then it would really only be up to those technologies. But again, technology is a dialogue between technology and humanity, and vice versa, and it gets so dynamic that even society begins to change. Certainly, for example, the phenomenon of the internet will change the sociological, political, but also economic context.

Murin: Just as technologies bring globalization, do they thereby bring individualization? As we have said – the camera and the internet enable everyone to create their own identity, which is a counterbalancing part to globalization.

Bielicky: I have to disagree. Really, on the one hand, there will be completely different types of artists. There will not only be video artists, but the video artists are simultaneously also film directors, because with digital video technology, it will be possible to make films without going to film school. New individuals will be born that will use, as you just said, up-to-date technology individually, and completely new creative strategies will emerge. That's one accelerator. The second accelerator is, of course, the internet as a ubiquitous medium in which our high- and low-quality products will develop with incredible speed through network cooperation. Bad things will grow out of these developments, too; according to statistics, this is a natural side effect and will have to occur in this area as well. However, and this is the point, there is a major shift for the artist – and it might even be a cliché for future artists to be called artists of some new kind, and it is an open question whether we should not begin to look for a new terminology on her or his labeling. To get back on track: in this context I see the big problem of education, the great shortcomings of educational institutes, such as the academies, that will be left behind over time. It is also related to the critics, the spokesmen of institutions and their warnings about new trends, although it may not even be their fault: even catching up with current trends is not enough today, and even I would be very careful to recommend following the current trends.

Murin: Maybe recommend a new concept?

Bielicky: I almost feel that there are two possibilities: either the real artists, the interesting ones, *the really relevant artists will operate completely outside of the art system*, the art system represented by the museum, critics, galleries, magazines, and so on, and they will be absolutely independent, but they will not be taken into account, and yet they will exist as such. Perhaps the more interesting art will really take place outside the artistic context. I will not rule out or determine the properties here or even give examples. The second possibility is that the system as such will finally open up to other disciplines, different contexts, and will be more interdisciplinary. This would be a completely different context for understanding art, too. Last but not least (and last but not last): Who says that in the future art will exist as such? Maybe there'll be the arts, the plural. Who says that there is such a thing as art history as such, which has a singular character? I'm not sure if there is such a thing as art histories in plural, and I have some clues to offer: I met with a gallerist in Barcelona who came to the Walter Benjamin symposium and who described himself as a cultural terrorist, claiming to have discovered that the famous, historically inspired art project *Guernica*, by Picasso (a famous painting that every art historian knows, and even children start to recognize), might not actually be inspired by Guernica, and that it was titled incorrectly. He has evidence that a comparable massacre, such as Guernica, had happened a few months earlier in Malaga, Spain, and that *this* was the impetus for Picasso to paint the picture. Through this example, I just want to show that the history of art and mythology go hand in hand; that man has a certain tendency to make mythology a history, not only in the artistic context, but in general, in the general history of man.
The further back I go in history, the more I personally question what is stated in art history books. Of course, certain moments have happened, but I do question the fairy tale of a linear development, which we were taught. From this point of view, it is possible that the whole or the unity of fine arts will cease to exist, and we will begin to get used to the fact that there will simply be those fine *arts*, and that they will not be related to each other at all, and that it will no longer be possible to include them in one concept of fine arts –

perhaps the concept of fine arts is very unfortunate today. Today, there are artists who come from the visual arts and are DJs. The very talented Elen Řádová, who is today's most important female DJ in the Czech Republic, and not only in the Czech Republic, but also in the international context (Vienna, Berlin, et cetera), studies in my studio and is a visual artist as well. This means that the concept of fine arts is a very restrictive one and that the field itself is limited.

Murin: There are many artistic activities, trends, and concepts, and we don't have to only talk about new technologies, which some theorists cannot accept, or even name.

Bielicky: I know, but I'm not worried about them. They should worry about themselves, and the most important point is: I think artists can handle it. After all, there are artists who do curatorial work, for example, on the internet, or even one of my students does exhibitions for other students, and in the end they may not need those curators at all, and there certainly are curators who will not change and do not want to change. Actually, curators *have* the duty to educate; they have the duty to expand their knowledge, although I know that this is difficult at a time of information inflation, just as it is difficult to orient oneself today. I myself am sometimes confused, and I don't say that I'm quite clear, but I know one thing: one has to be open and maybe even has to train and learn how to filter information. On the other hand, I think that our whole generation is experiencing a turning point, and that it is a societal guinea pig: it is a very interesting time, and I even think we live in very exciting times, and it is this uncertainty, ambiguity, and fogging that holds great potential for something incredible to arise. Perhaps there is something radical in the making, something we would not dare to call art today, and yet it has to do with art.

Murin: You say that every project is new to you. What is your project in New York all about?

Bielicky: I will probably disappoint you. I will only go to New York, where I lived in the 1980s and where the environment is highly inspiring, for personal meetings with friends and partners with whom I did various projects. For example, at the beginning of the internet age, we performed internet performances together in the years 1995–96 using simple conference programs, where students could see and meet in one virtual space. But since you have asked about the future, I really have an unpretentious project that should have been implemented a long time ago. The topic is communication, and it is about speech that dies out, disappears. There is one nonverbal language, called El Silbo, or Silbo Gomero, and it comes from the Canary Island of Gomer next to Tenerife, where I have been four times in the last ten years. The landscape of this island is very diverse; there are very deep canyons, which led to the formation of whistling speech. Here, they talked in this way over long distances, and I mean a few kilometers – at a time when there was no communication media yet, when there was no telephone or other communication system. This speech dies out or, to be precise, is almost extinct. I had the opportunity to meet people who still speak this language; they try to teach it in schools, but it doesn't look promising. On the other hand, in the internet network, we again encounter a certain colonization of the network through the English language. I decided that I will try to transfer this

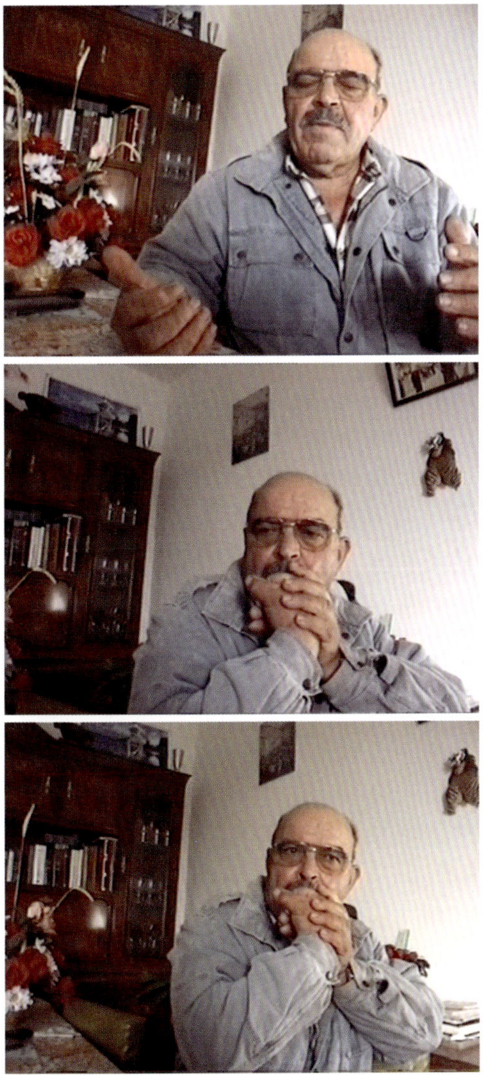

Isidro Ortiz Mendoza performing El Silbo, 1999. Video stills.

language at least partially to the internet. I would like to create a universal lexicon of words that translate into our language. It would include certain statements about human communication, and when a visitor on the website clicks on these statements, he gets link in the form of the respective whistle. So, I would create a single database or lexicon that would translate the written language into whistle language. In fact, the project was originally supposed to look like an internet sculpture with two material mythical heads and a sound device connected to a network. The spectator who comes to the gallery – you see for yourself, at first I wanted to compromise, again I wanted to place it in the gallery – could approach the object with two keyboards and write or select a sentence from the menu and the object would translate the written text into acoustic whistled speech. At the same time, the entire sculpture would be connected to the internet, so that people from the outside could also control the whistling sculpture.

Murin: Or the sculpture could decode the registered notation of the spectator and at least approximate the significance of the whistle, respectively the absence of meaning.

Bielicky: This is another idea that I have to think about. So far, it is just something that is in my drawer that I'd like to do with sentences, because I need a sponsor and infrastructure for the project. With this project, I want to pay tribute or recognition not only to this particular dying speech, but also to all the new speeches that are emerging on the internet. People in it say "k" instead of "OK"; they use different smiles and different characters. I mean, last time I got into a chat [discussion group] where I didn't even understand a single word. This means that even in the network, languages are created and disappear; the network is the societal organization form, which is subject to the greatest dynamics and transformation forces in the history of mankind.

First published in *Profil*, no. 4 (2000): 44–51.
Translated from the Slovak by Paul Kenig.

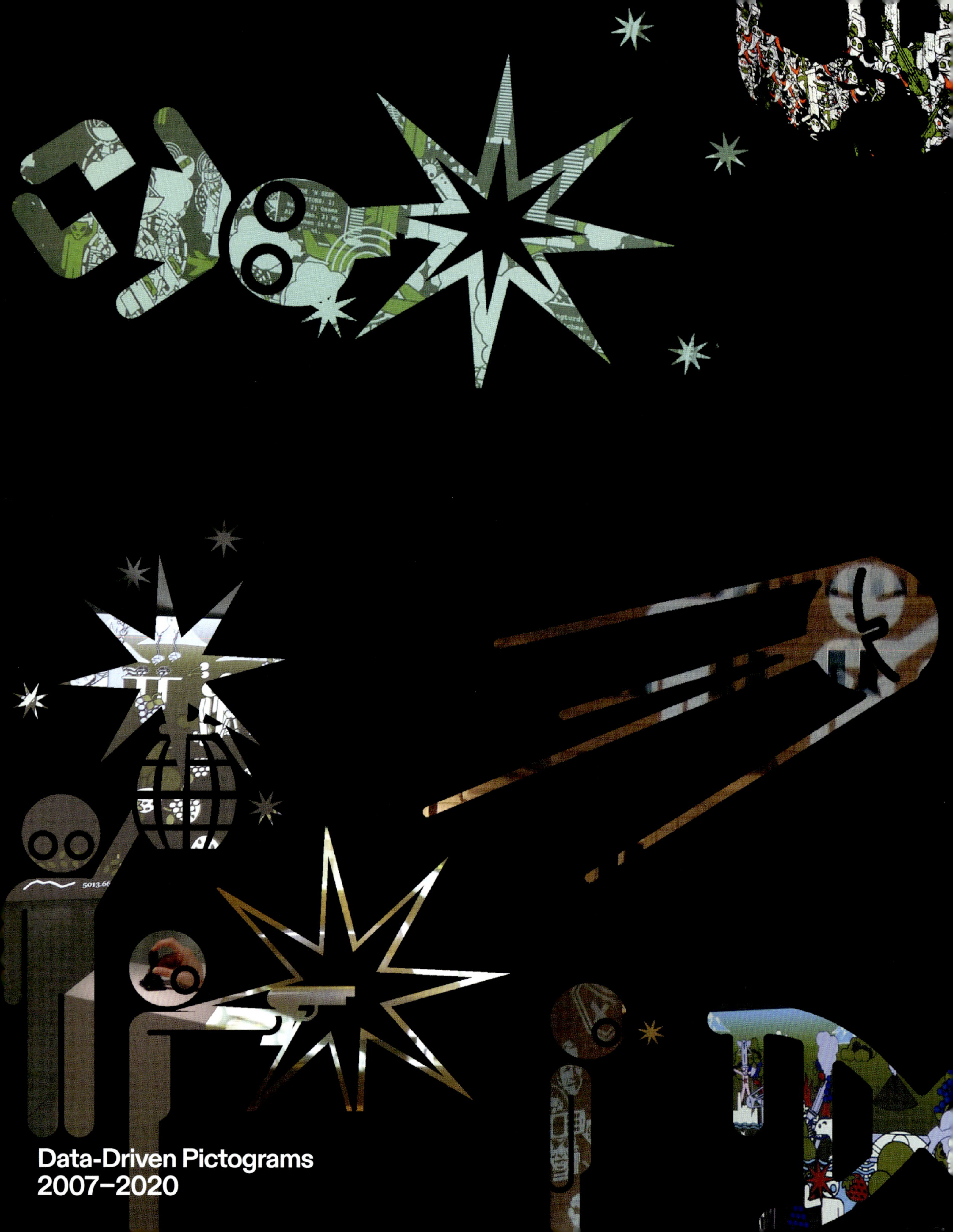

Data-Driven Pictograms
2007–2020

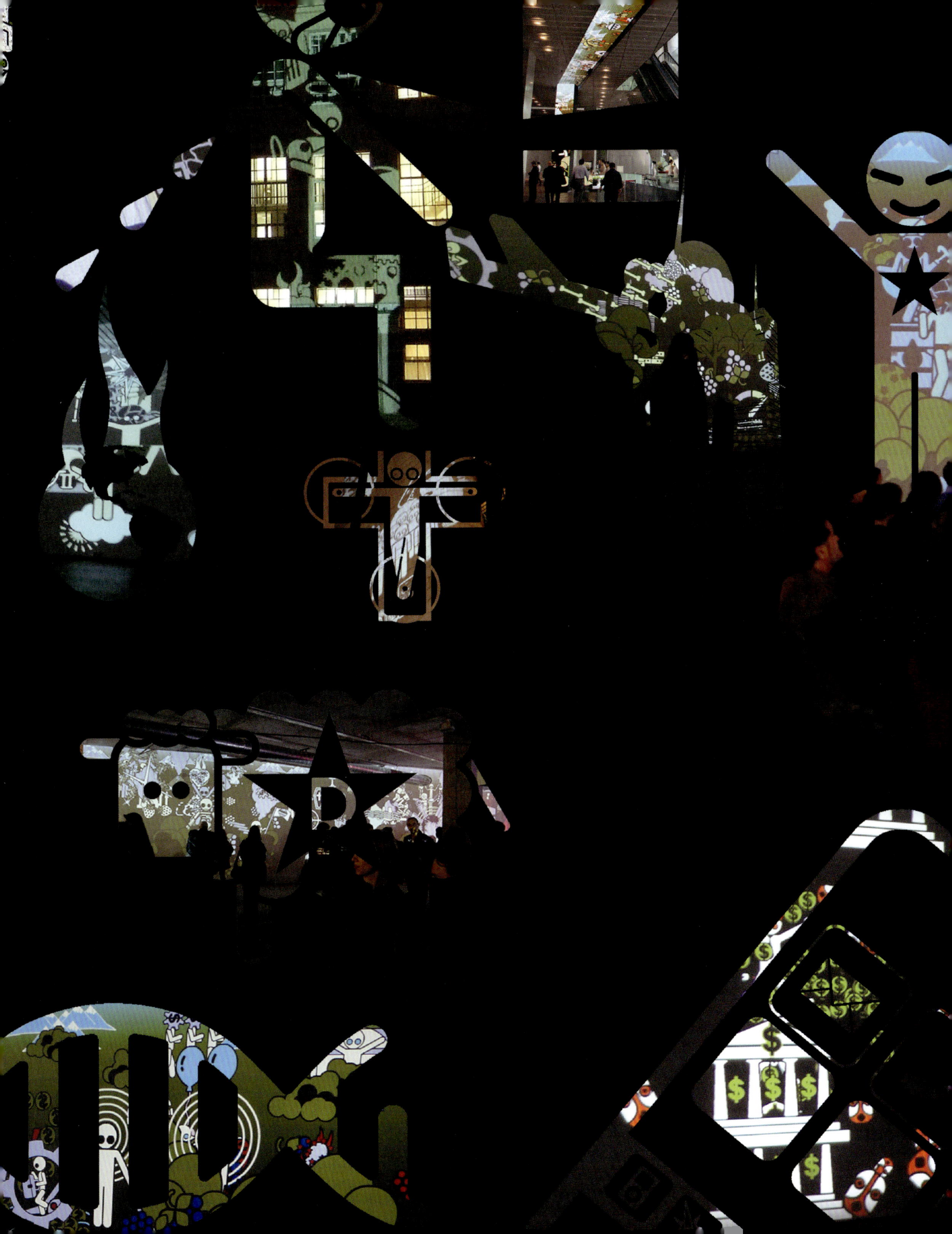

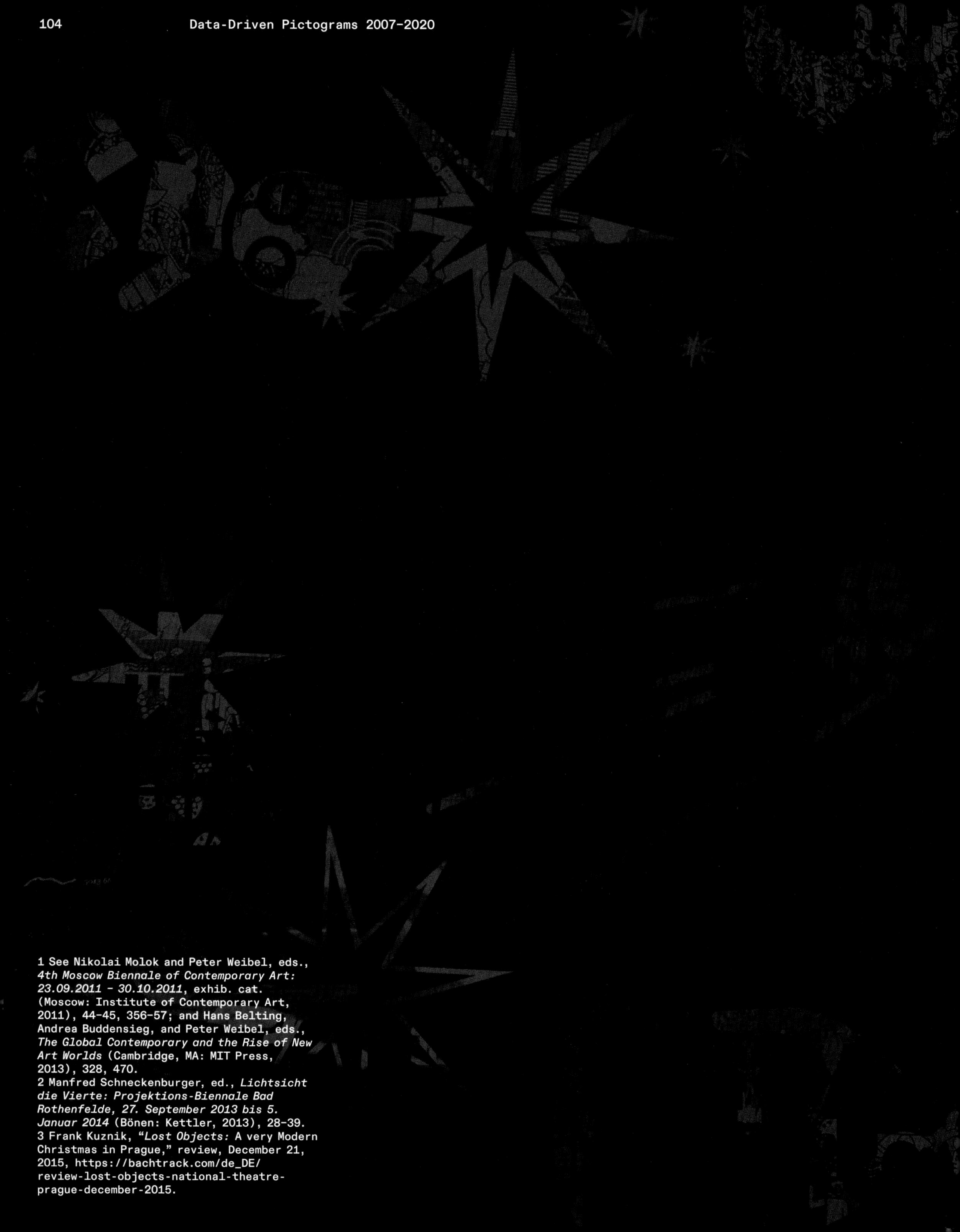

1 See Nikolai Molok and Peter Weibel, eds., *4th Moscow Biennale of Contemporary Art: 23.09.2011 - 30.10.2011*, exhib. cat. (Moscow: Institute of Contemporary Art, 2011), 44–45, 356–57; and Hans Belting, Andrea Buddensieg, and Peter Weibel, eds., *The Global Contemporary and the Rise of New Art Worlds* (Cambridge, MA: MIT Press, 2013), 328, 470.

2 Manfred Schneckenburger, ed., *Lichtsicht die Vierte: Projektions-Biennale Bad Rothenfelde, 27. September 2013 bis 5. Januar 2014* (Bönen: Kettler, 2013), 28–39.

3 Frank Kuznik, "*Lost Objects:* A very Modern Christmas in Prague," review, December 21, 2015, https://bachtrack.com/de_DE/review-lost-objects-national-theatre-prague-december-2015.

Data-Driven Pictograms 2007–2020

The follow-up project to *Columbus 2.0* (2007–19) is the earliest data-driven pictogram-based work by Kamila B. Richter and Michael Bielicky, called *Falling Life* (2005–07) and *Falling Times* (2006–09; with a predecessor, *Falling Stars*, 2004). The more complex, later two web-based projects with Richter are *Garden of Error and Decay* (2010–19) and the *Why Don't We* series (2013–17). *Garden of Error and Decay* operates on the text-to-pictogram converter algorithms of *Falling Times* and accompanies its generated pictograms with the texts that generated them on screen, against a kind of Garden of Eden backdrop. Adding the wave animations of *Columbus 2.0* and its interactive approach, *Garden of Error and Decay* engulfs the exhibition visitor in an information environment occupied by skeletons, warlords, and explosions, with the option to stop ("shoot") a pictogram with a joystick mounted in front of the projection: a desperate attempt to lessen its impact on the world of information – it is displayed smaller or even vanishes if successfully hit. Yet there is a meta-information feed overriding all human interaction with the visual data flow on screen. This meta-information feed is that of the New York stock exchange, and it influences the dimensions in which the messages and pictograms are displayed in a far greater way, to a point where the interaction of the visitor does not count at all.[1] *Garden of Error and Decay* was displayed among others in Wuhan (2010), Moscow (2011), Karlsruhe (2011), Vienna (2012), and Seoul (2013).

The *Why Don't We* series takes a slightly different approach to data-driven narratives. The narrative is not endless and pluralistic, displaying many social media messages in parallel, but randomly picks one message, displays it for the visitor to see, and tells a short story in automatically generated pictograms until the next digital (news) text is displayed and the next narrative is visualized.[2] *Why Don't We* was displayed among others in Vienna (2013), Berlin (2013), and Bad Rothenfelde (2013, 2017).
There is potential for cultural criticism in those works, which could even be misinterpreted as cultural pessimism. Intertwining gaming, finances, wars, and international political unrest in an interactive artwork, with the intent to question each individual's freedom to influence those cultural forces, surely has all the potential in the world to be classified as culturally critical and pessimistic. The whole point to the *Garden of Error and Decay* and the *Why Don't We* series lies not in the technical prowess or socially critical content it encapsulates, but, once more, in the reception history: the fact that time and time again, both curators and visitors tend to be blinded by a pictogram aesthetic to judge those works as the exact opposite – as funny or even cute, completely overlooking the cultural absurdity the piece conveys. The technically advanced work is again a container for human behavioral patterns, which were established over time and which have long since slipped out of the realm of cultural consciousness, withdrawn from reconsideration.

In 2015, Bielicky and Richter used their narration algorithms to project a self-similar, or fractal, compartmentalized, endless, dense, and orchestrally controlled narrative of pictograms. Not only did they feel uncannily at home on the scanae frons behind the theater stage, but they were even the sole protagonists and the pivotal part of the piece. Appropriately called *Lost Objects* (2015)[3], the opera was displayed at Prague's National Theatre.

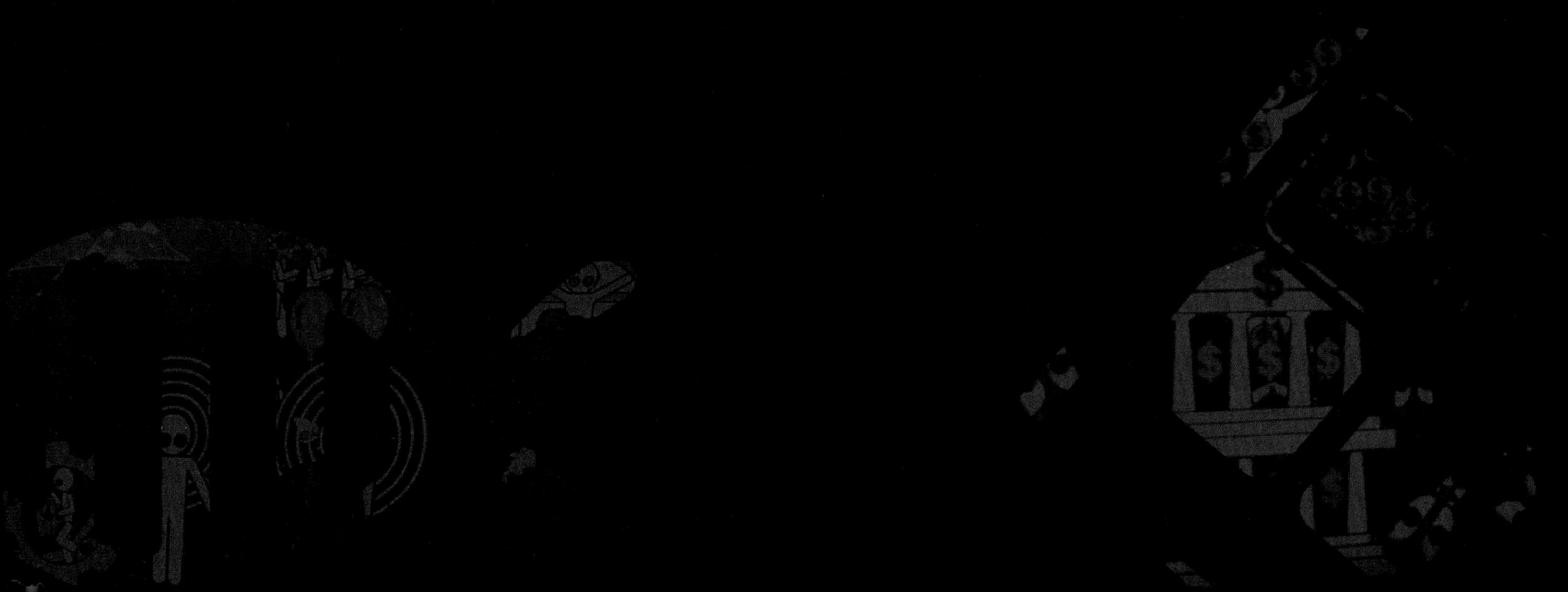

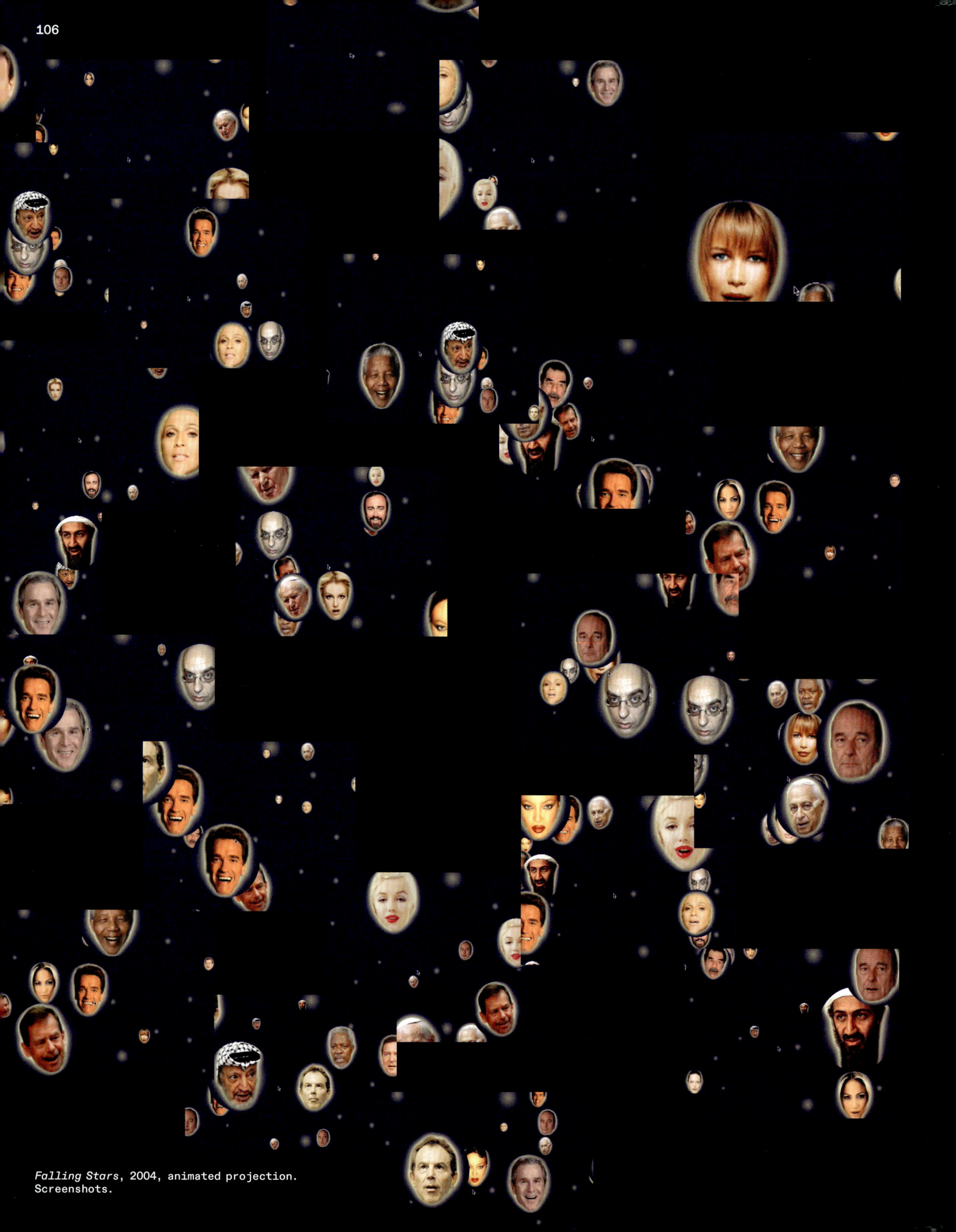

Falling Stars, 2004, animated projection.
Screenshots.

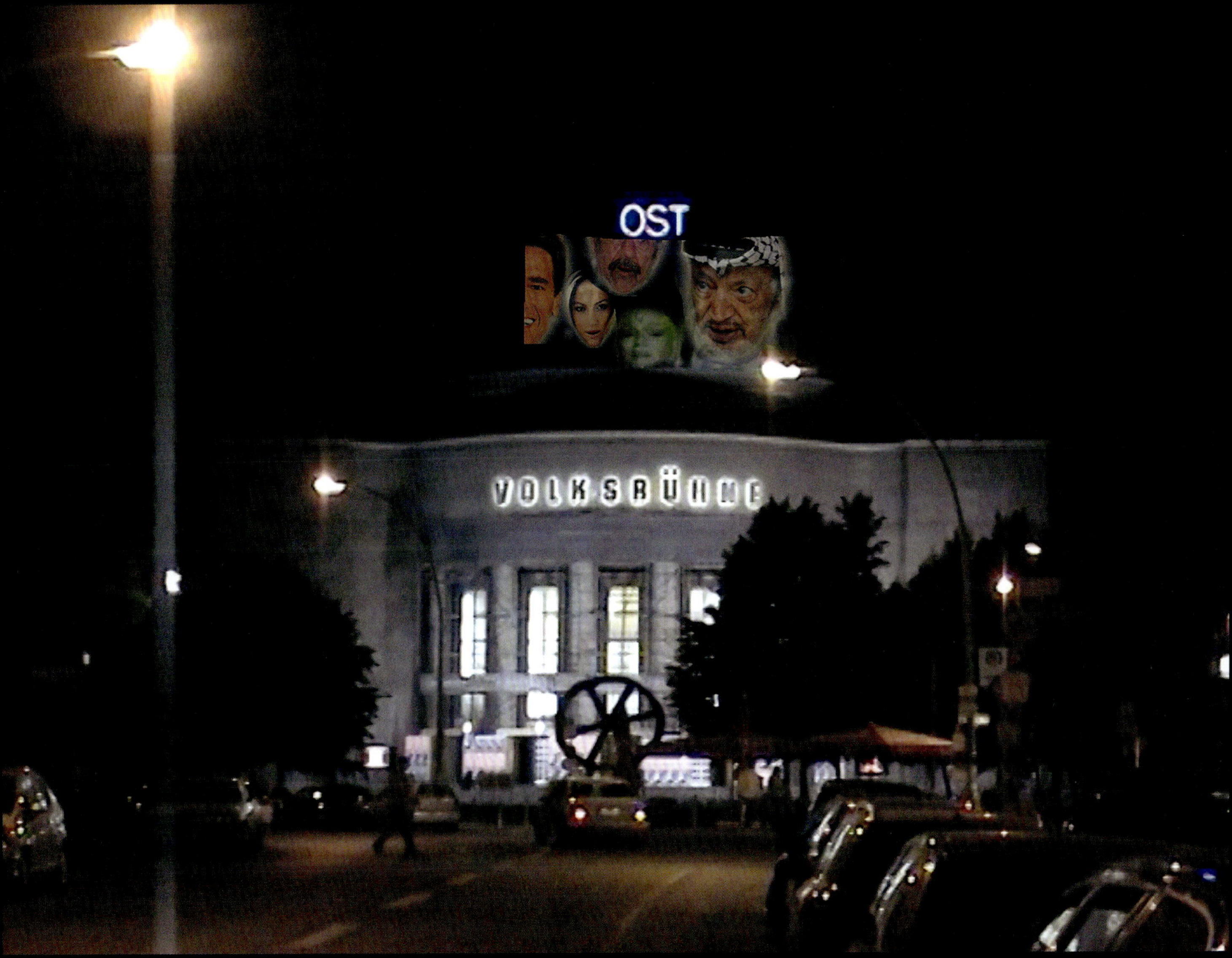

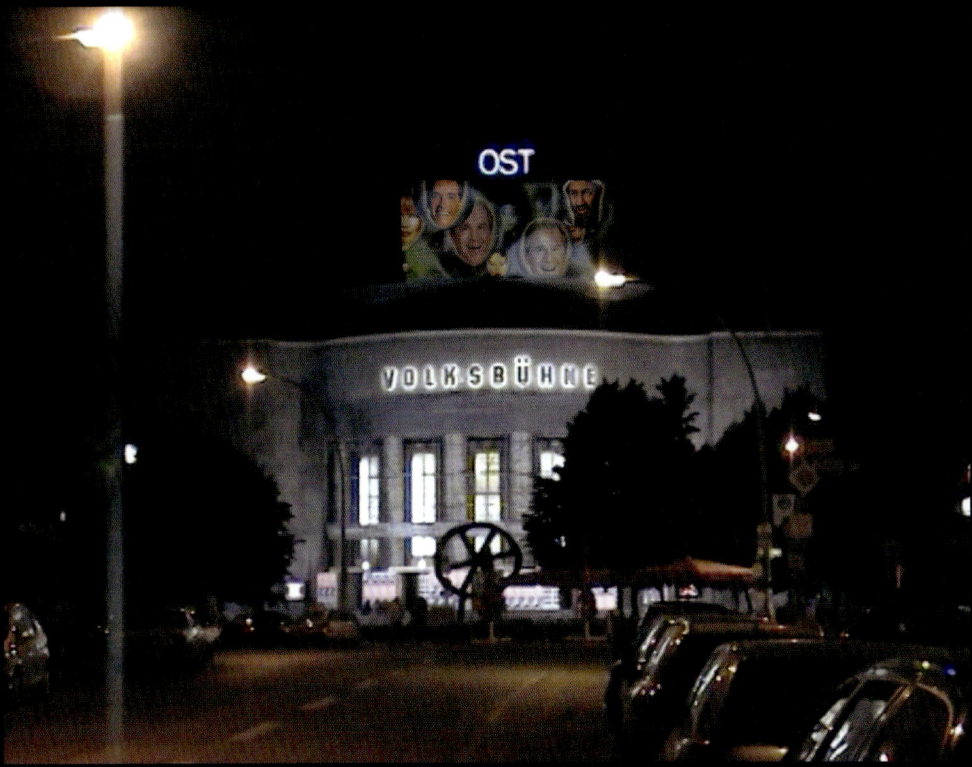

Falling Stars, 2004, animated projection. Installation view, Volksbühne, Berlin, 2004.

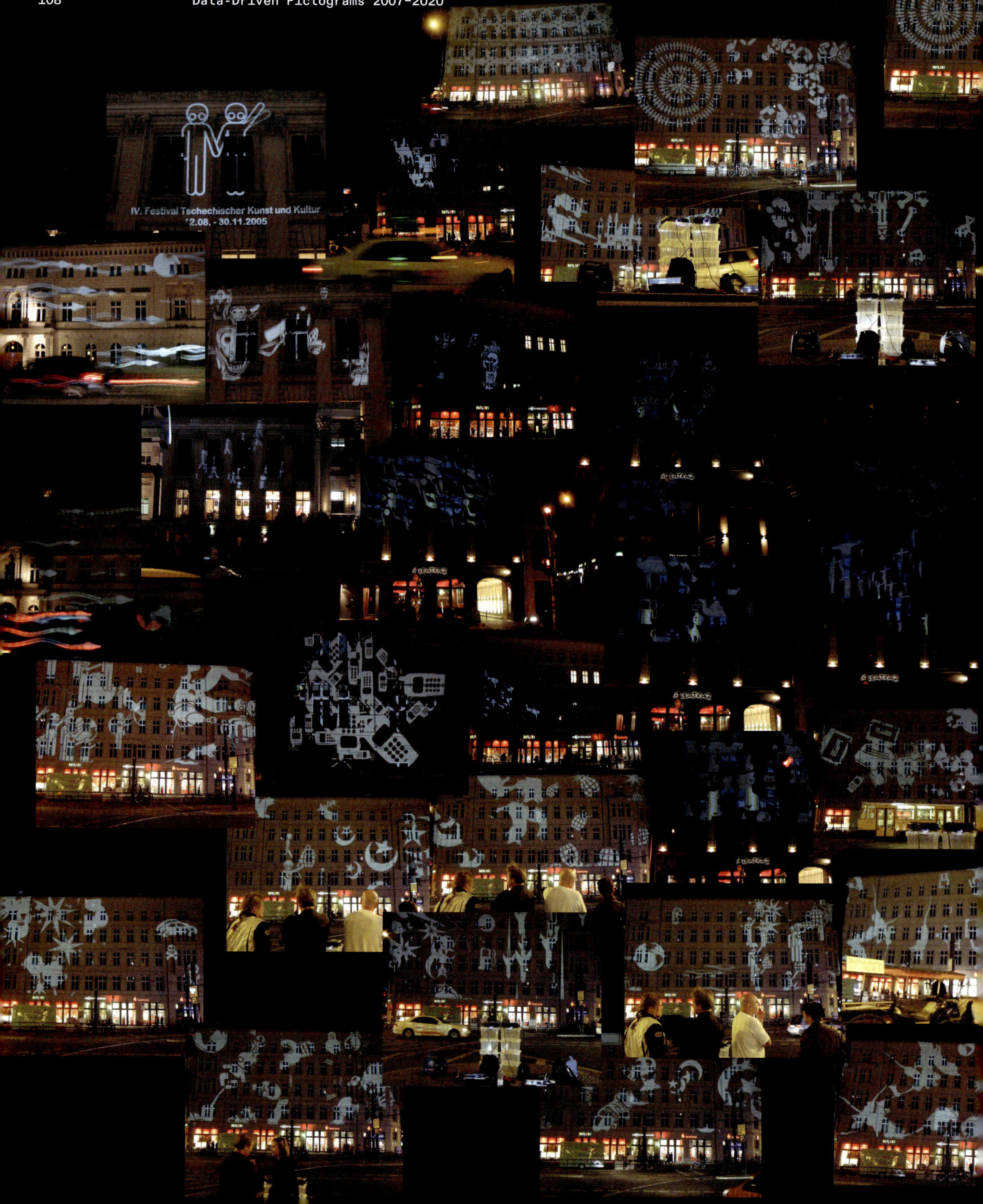
IV. Festival Tschechischer Kunst und Kultur
2.08. - 30.11.2005
ALCATRAZ

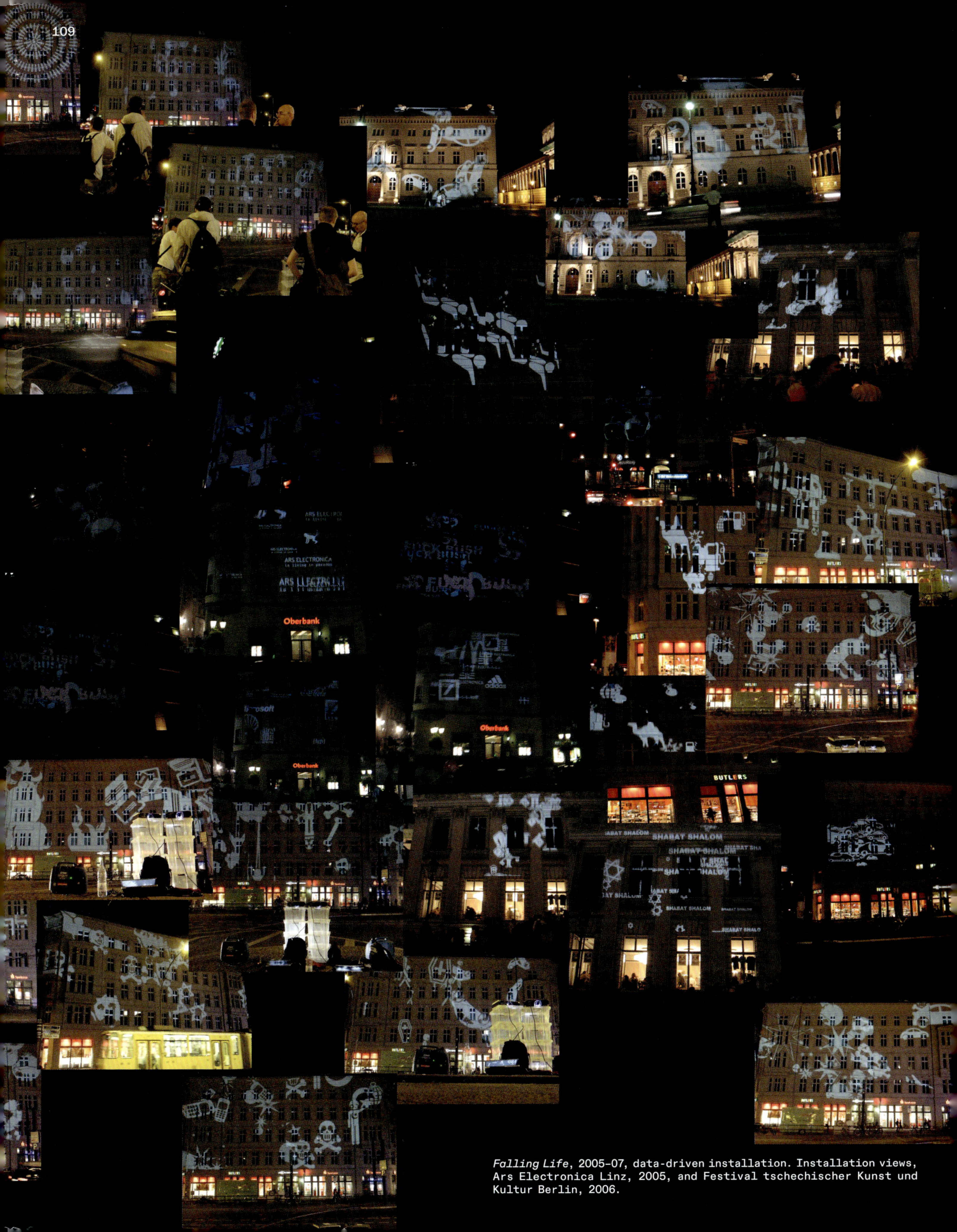

Falling Life, 2005–07, data-driven installation. Installation views, Ars Electronica Linz, 2005, and Festival tschechischer Kunst und Kultur Berlin, 2006.

Bielicky

Georg Diez

We stood in front of Number 24 and looked down the street at the broad facade of the Volksbühne, where the heads of Claudia Schiffer, Kofi Annan, and Saddam Hussein were just sailing down. Only the art connoisseur next to me looked not at the artwork, but at the legs of the young girl in front of him. She was wearing pink stockings and a skirt that reached to her knees. The man next to me had a face that was pale and a little meager. Before that, he had scribbled a few words on his pad and leafed through his portfolio. Now he looked at the falling heads – which could be meant as a kind of criticism of time or could be just beautiful – and sometimes he looked at the girl's legs, which were very uncritical and really beautiful. He smiled a smile as someone who observes himself from the outside. At that moment he looked like someone who wants to be happy against all the odds.

In front of the house with the number 24 on it, there were now ten people around the artist Michael Bielicky, who had invented this video projection. He was wearing a black jacket that only video artists would wear, a kind of Asian jacket variant, and black trousers, his head bald. His slim, likeable girlfriend was standing next to him. Bielicky's brother was also there, a dermatologist from Düsseldorf, who used his digital camera to show the pictures of his impressive collection of Czech paintings. A man said a few words as greeting. We were the tiniest vernissage on this big Art Berlin weekend.

There was the Art Forum, where the people in well-tailored suits pushed themselves knowledgeably through the aisles. There were the bright windows of the galleries that shone into the night like a promise that no one believes in. There was the Art Forum party inside the Volksbühne, where a lot of English and a little French was spoken. And on Tuesday the big flick buoyancy would follow, where mainly German would be spoken. It was a moment of silence, the ten of us before number 24, while culture was raging around us.

The man next to me was beaming with joy. He congratulated the artist Bielicky; he talked to the head of the German-Czech culture weeks; he looked at the falling faces again and said loudly, "Great." Then he said, "I have to get out of here."

I then drove to the art works, where the party had unfortunately taken place one evening before; I went to the Volksbühne and served myself at the Thai buffet – I sat briefly on the stairs and then went to the gallery next door, which was still open and from where a young man drove me away, a man who had looked at the geometric pictures and chased me with the call: "The square, did you see, the square is back?!"

I met Michael Bielicky with his girlfriend in front of the gallery. The projector was broken, he said; they had to go up to the roof and look. Then they disappeared into the dark. I stopped briefly in front of the house with the number 24 on it and turned around. The night had just swallowed up the art.

First published in *Frankfurter Allgemeine Sonntagszeitung*, no. 39 (September 26, 2004). Translated from the German by Paul Kenig.

Bielicky's Way to Hell

Maxim Biller

Together with his wife, Kamila, Michael Bielicky makes great media art. Why doesn't anyone understand it?

Whenever I want to annoy my friend Bielicky, I always say to him, "Bielicky, I really feel sorry for you. Why didn't you stay in Bernd Becher's photo class in Düsseldorf back then? Then you'd be a millionaire today!" And that's exactly what I said to him now, and he replied, "You mean like Struth, Gursky, and Ruff? Do you know how I find their big, cold, boring photos?"

"Yes," I said, "I know."

We walked through the snow-covered, quiet Tiergarten and froze and talked more about Bielicky's missed opportunity to be a world-famous artist – just like his fellow students. Poor, consistent Bielicky! At that time, in the troubled seventies, the holy Prussian seriousness of the Becher students was bugging him at the Düsseldorf Art Academy, so after six months, he switched to the clever and chaotic video artist Nam June Paik, who didn't care whether his students worked or not. They should be independent – and trust no one except themselves.

"Will a lot of people come to your installation in the Czech center tomorrow?" I asked.

"Hopefully enough not to put me in a bad mood," he said.

"And what would improve your mood?"

"A world without curators and gallery owners."

Bielicky has been a professor of media art at the Karlsruhe University of Arts and Design (HfG) for seven years. At his inaugural lecture, he said that the art world was one huge brothel, and then he said who the pimps, hookers, and clients were. Still, nobody was angry with him. Probably because he was right. And because he – huge head, huge bald head, huge smile – looks just as sympathetic and funny as a Jewish Schwejk. We stopped for a moment while it started snowing lightly again, and the last rays of sun were swallowed up by the ice-white sky above us, and I took a picture of Bielicky and myself on my phone. Behind us you could see the statue of a half-naked woman on a horse. She had snow on her head, on her bare arms and breasts, and when I saw that, I realized how cold I was now. I showed the photo to Bielicky, and he said, "You used to look younger, somehow." I laughed. "And you used to look much better," I said. Now he was laughing.

The installations that Bielicky makes with his wife, Kamila, are like nightmares that you would like to have yourself. Hundreds of glowing pictograms fly over the wall in a dark room; you see an evil clown juggling with rotating dollar signs, you can see Osama bin Laden's burning heart and praying human dolls, and again and again staring at an alien made of black cat's eyes, and skeletons that wave with bombs. It is like looking into the head of someone who is so afraid of the world as it is today and imagines it even more terribly, day and night. But that's not all. Bielicky's imaginary paranoia doesn't just see pictures. He at the same time listens – a new, crazy algorithm is responsible for that – to all ghostly, global Twitter mumbles that are fed into the algorithm, which creates ever new and beguiling picture sequences from those mumbles. This really has nothing to do with the pretty, frozen nothingness of the Becher school.

"Are you so cold too?" I asked.

"No," said Bielicky. He was wearing only a shirt and his thick green down jacket, which was half open, and on his bare bald head, large shiny snowflakes landed and thawed. "I have to go home now," I said. "All right," he said. "And I'll go back to the hotel and calm down." He paused. "Do you know how to get back to Potsdamer Platz from here?"

"The Big Star is over there," I said. "That is everything I know. I have to go there now. Are you nervous about tomorrow?"

"No," he said, "I'm never nervous. I just get insanely charged up sometimes." He grinned, turned, and walked away slowly.

I smiled too, but he didn't see that, and as he got smaller and smaller on the wide, white, shiny park path, I thought that he often said to me on the phone that people like us should be happy when they are happy. He himself was happy that he could work with Kamila in peace and that he could show off his happy digital nightmares every now and then in a museum or at a big show in Beijing, Havana, or Vienna. And that until now no collector had bought one of his projections only meant that he was not an art whore – in other words, Nam June Paik would be really proud of him. I watched him for a while, and then I started walking towards 17th of June Street, and I thought: I'm glad that an adventurer like Bielicky is my friend.

When I came to the Czech center on Wilhelm Street the next evening, there were only a few people in the huge, dark room. None of them were talking. They looked in silence and as if enchanted at a high, large, long wall on which, to the sounds of cheerful space music, Bielicky's and Kamila's digital hell panorama slowly passed over. The green-yellow flickering light of the projection was reflected in the happy faces of the viewers, and so they gradually became part of a show that people might never understand.

First published in *Die Zeit*, no. 15 (April 4, 2013). Translated from the German by Paul Kenig.

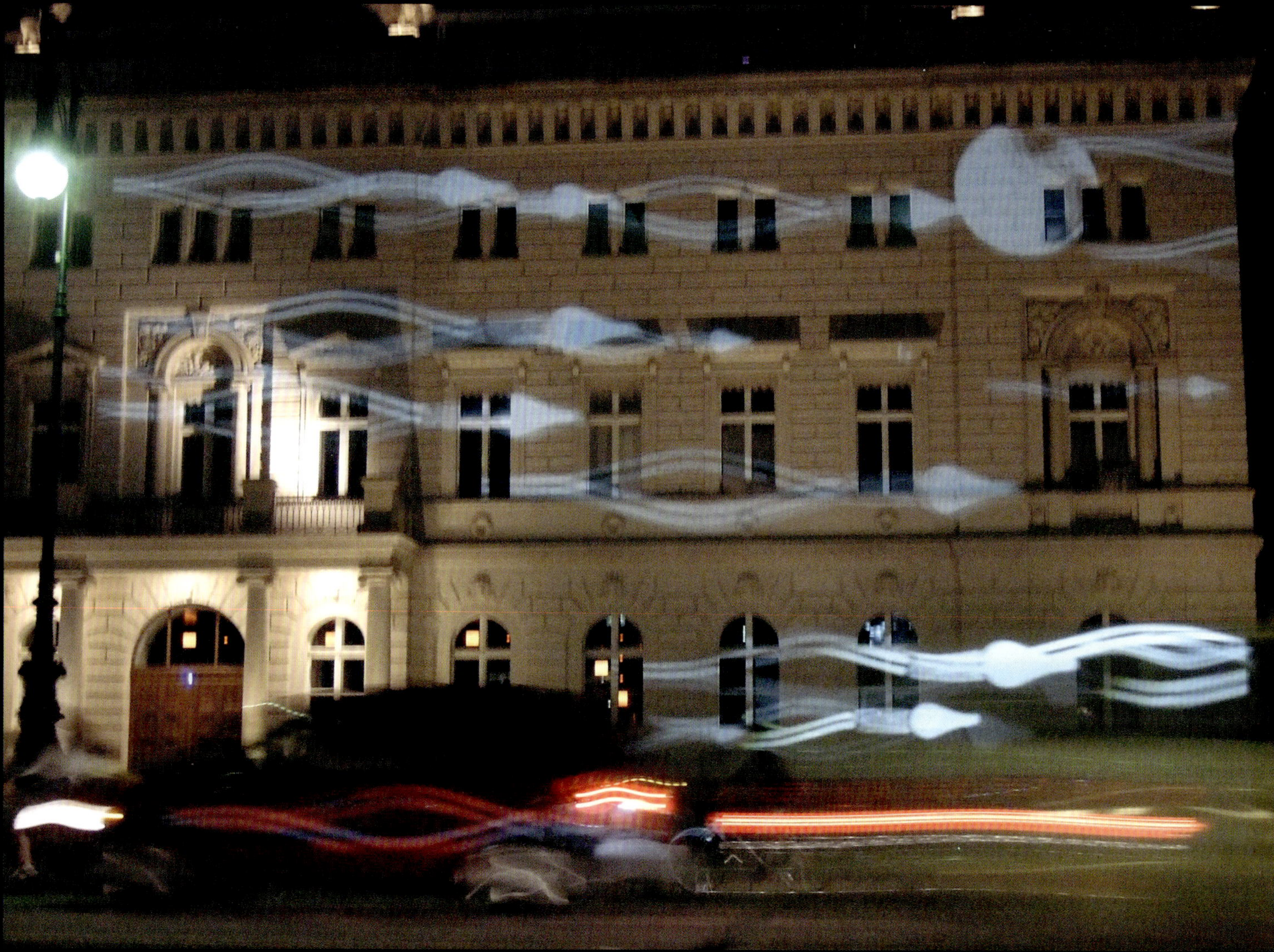

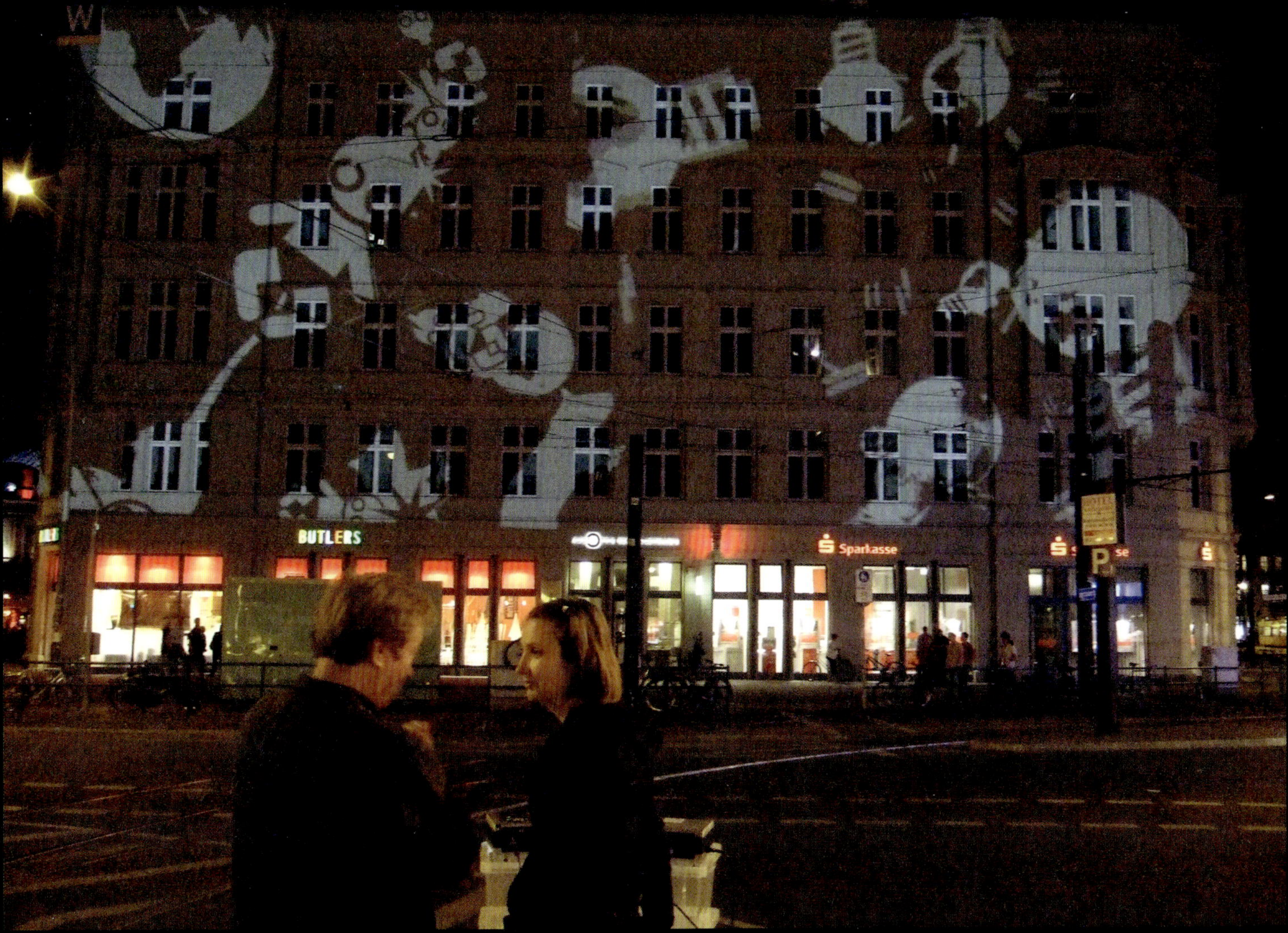

Falling Life, 2005–07, data-driven installation. Installation views, Ars Electronica Linz (left), 2005, and Festival tschechischer Kunst und Kultur Berlin (right), 2006.

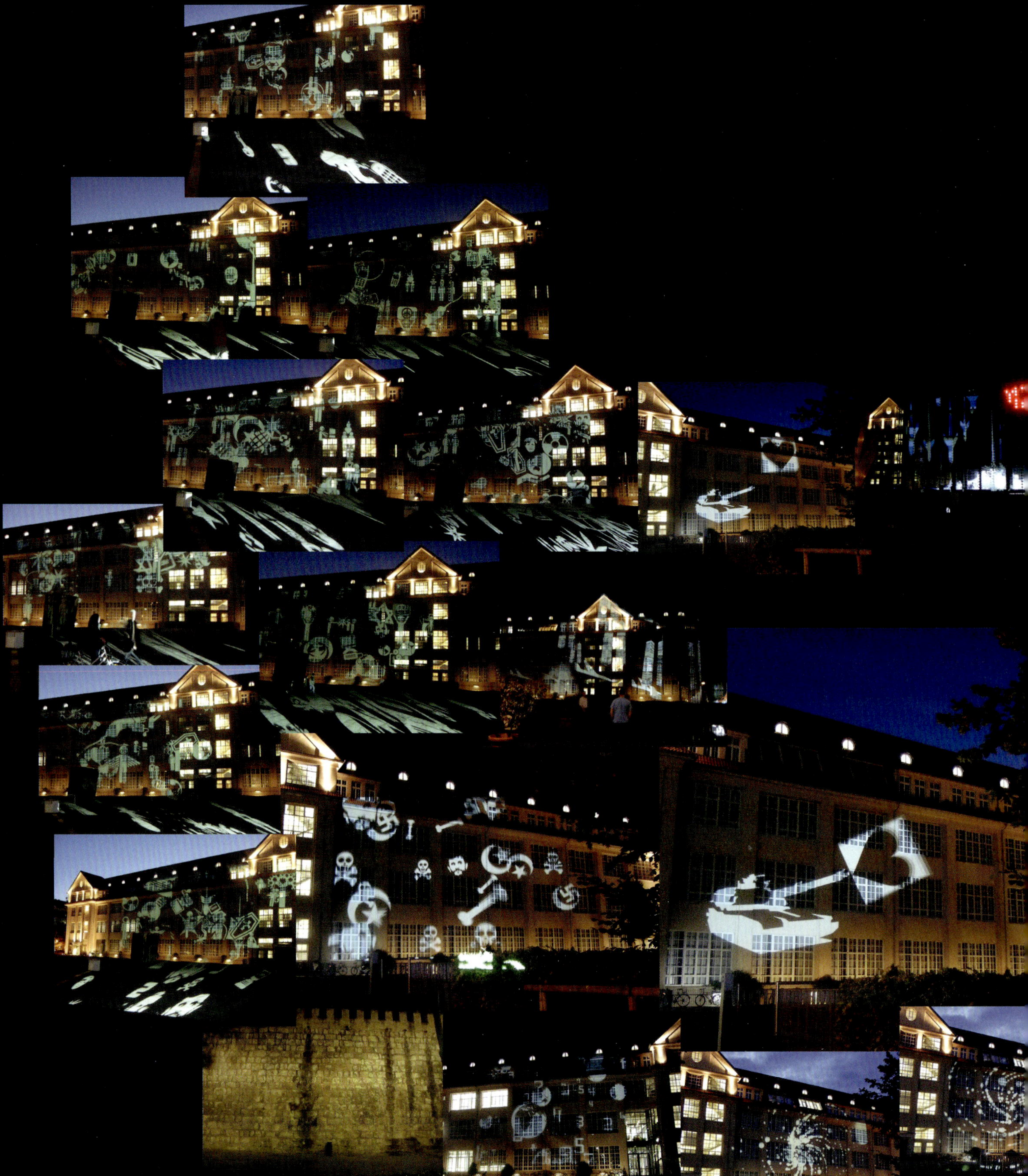

Falling Times, 2006–09, data-driven installation. Installation views, ZKM | Karlsruhe, 2007.